STAR
SPANGLED
SECURITY

STAR SPANGLED SECURITY

APPLYING LESSONS LEARNED OVER SIX DECADES SAFEGUARDING AMERICA

HAROLD BROWN

with

JOYCE WINSLOW

BROOKINGS INSTITUTION PRESS
Washington, D.C.

Copyright © 2012 by Harold Brown

THE BROOKINGS INSTITUTION
1775 Massachusetts Avenue, N.W., Washington, D.C. 20036
www.brookings.edu

Library of Congress Cataloging-in-Publication data are available
ISBN: 978-0-8157-2382-0

06-11-13

9 8 7 6 5 4 3 2 1

Printed on acid-free paper

Typeset in Sabon and Poetica Chancery

Composition by Cynthia Stock
Silver Spring, Maryland

Printed by R. R. Donnelley
Harrisonburg, Virginia

For Gene and Zoë

CONTENTS

ACKNOWLEDGMENTS   xi

PROLOGUE   xiii

1 Oh, Say Can You See
THE VIEW FROM THE TOP   1

2 What So Proudly We Hailed
ENSURING NATIONAL DEFENSE THROUGH ITS BUDGET   6

3 Stripes and Bright Stars
HOW THE TEAM AT THE TOP AFFECTS SECURITY POLICY   38

4 The Perilous Fight
IRANIAN REVOLUTION AND THE HOSTAGE CRISIS   74

5 Rockets' Red Glare and Bombs
PLANS, PROGRAMS, AND AGREEMENTS   86

6 The Ramparts We Watched
DEALING WITH THE OUTSIDE WORLD   135

7 That Banner Yet Waves
PREPARING FOR WHAT LIES AHEAD   183

8 *Land of the Free*
   STIMULATING THE NATIONAL ECONOMY FOR
      INTERNATIONAL SECURITY   214

9 *Home of the Brave*
   AMERICA AT A TIPPING POINT   233

   AFTERWORD   243

   NOTES   251

   INDEX   261

   ENDNOTE   277

ACKNOWLEDGMENTS

Turning recollections, thoughts, and judgments into a more or less coherent book is no easy task. I was therefore very fortunate to have Joyce Winslow as my collaborator on this one. We worked hard during our interviews and subsequently on the text to ensure that the book represents my views in my voice. Her efforts were even more time consuming, more consistent, and more effective. Without her work in finding and negotiating with the publisher, as well as in creating a marketing plan, the manuscript might well never have reached the public.

Chris Heidenrich transcribed 700 pages of Joyce's interviews and conversations with me. Joyce boiled down that collection of stories, memories, observations, assertions, analyses, and recommendations to several drafts. Multiple rearrangements, selections, editing, and reediting by both of us produced the final version. Thank you to Janet Walker at Brookings and her copy editor, Vicky Macintyre, who patiently and carefully edited our manuscript into Brookings style.

John Deutch, Walt Slocombe, and Dick Cooper, each of whom has been my colleague and friend over several decades, took more of their valuable time than I could reasonably have asked to read the manuscript at various stages. All three made extensive comments and provided additional insights that improved the final product. I am deeply grateful to each of them. I appreciate the help of my assistants, Will

Schaffer and Clare Richardson-Barlow, with research and fact checking. My thanks go also to Dr. Edward Keefer, who is in the process of writing for the Historical Office of the Secretary of Defense the official history of my time as secretary of defense, for supplying useful documents from that office.

PROLOGUE

It was raining the day of the Joint Armed Forces Farewell Ceremony that signaled the end of my service as secretary of defense, and that of my deputy secretary, W. Graham Claytor Jr.

General David Jones hosted the farewell program on Monday, January 19, 1981, at Fort Myer, Virginia. I had chosen Dave, an air force general, to be chairman of the Joint Chiefs of Staff. That choice troubled some. It didn't follow the usual practice of rotation among the services. His predecessor had also come from the air force. Some people grumbled that I picked a "purple-suiter." They meant someone who did not invariably support the particular interests of his own branch of the military service. I saw the phrase as denoting a wider perspective on the entire palette of national security, transcending parochial loyalty to only the green of the army or marine uniform, or the blue of the navy and air force. I had given a strong push to the prestige of a career path in joint military service, which had been greatly undervalued.

During the fanfare and nineteen-gun salute, I thought back to my first days in office. My desk sat directly under the portrait of America's first secretary of defense, James Forrestal. His psychological problems, surely exacerbated by the high stress of the job, ended in suicide. Forrestal jumped from a window at the Bethesda National Naval Medical Center, located a few miles from Washington. Early on I determined to stay fit and ease stress by swimming many afternoons. After the swim I'd hurry back to the third floor, taking a shortcut over a low wall and climbing a flight of stairs. Coming down the corridor those first days I'd see the name plaque on the door to my office—"Harold Brown, Secretary of Defense"—and think: is this real?

It certainly was. The 8 a.m. Legislative Affairs and Public Affairs (LAPA) meetings with my deputy, first Charles Duncan and then Graham Claytor, and our key staff, including then military assistant Colin Powell, focused attention on the external threats and turmoil America faced and the domestic influences on national security. Overlapping in time, the former included the nuclear balance with the Soviet Union and later its invasion of Afghanistan; the war between Somalia and Ethiopia; a buildup of tensions in the Mideast culminating in the Camp David Peace Accords; relations with China and meetings with Deng Xiaoping; the Iranian revolution, overthrow of the shah and return of Ayatollah Khomeini from Paris, and the capture of and failed attempt to rescue American hostages in Iran. The domestic debates were almost as contentious.

At the LAPA meetings, we discussed our ongoing programs and plans. Assistant Secretary for Public Affairs Tom Ross and Assistant for Legislative Affairs Jack Stempler briefed us on what bullets from Congress or the media would fly in our direction that day or the rest of the week. Then the special assistant—a post that consumed three successive occupants (John Kester, Togo West, and Peter Hamilton)—told us what the White House was thinking. Over the past fifty-odd years, I have never become used to "the White House says," as if the White House were a person.

At the farewell ceremony, the colors were paraded and posted and the national anthem played. I stepped to the microphone to say goodbye. Early that morning I'd received word that the Iran hostages finally would be freed and coming home. Like the rest of the country, I had heard Walter Cronkite on the evening news intone the number of days the hostages remained in Iran—from 1 up to 444. I considered the failed rescue attempt my greatest regret and most painful lesson learned.

It had not been an easy four years. When I was sworn in as defense secretary on January 20, 1977, an ambitious Soviet Union was pointing nuclear warheads at the United States and threatening European stability. America's continuing security depended on deploying innovative technology to counteract the Soviet threat. That, in turn, depended on a healthy domestic economy that could provide a defense budget sufficient to augment U.S. conventional forces after the Vietnam War.

No one with a technological background had been secretary of defense before me, though Charles E. Wilson had trained as an electrical engineer. My experience in government, civilian, and academic spheres had prepared me for the position of secretary of defense in steps that Tom Ross captured in the ceremony's program notes: "Brown was born in New York City on September 19, 1927, attended public schools, and graduated from Columbia University with an A.B. in 1945, an M.A. in 1946, and a Ph.D. in physics in 1949. In 1952 Brown joined the University of California at Berkeley Radiation Lab as a research scientist. He moved to the E. O. Lawrence Radiation Lab at Livermore shortly after it was established." (Ernest Lawrence and Edward Teller—the latter widely credited as the father of the hydrogen bomb—had used their influence to establish the lab. Herbert York was its first director, Teller its second, and in July 1960, I became the third.)

"From 1956 to 1958 Brown was a member of the Polaris Steering Committee and until 1961 also a member of the Air Force Advisory Board. In the late fifties he served as Senior Science Advisor at the Conference on Discontinuance of Nuclear Tests, and in 1969 he was a U.S. delegate to the Strategic Arms Limitation Talks (SALT) in Helsinki, Vienna, and Geneva. Beginning in May 1961 until September 30, 1965, Dr. Brown served as Director of Defense Research and Engineering. In 1961 the Junior Chamber of Commerce named Dr. Brown, then thirty-four years old, one of that year's Ten Outstanding Young Men.

"In 1963 Brown received the Navy Distinguished Civilian Service Award, the Columbia Medal of Excellence, and the Department of Defense Award for Exceptionally Meritorious Service. From October 1965 to February 14, 1969, he served as Secretary of the Air Force; then as President of the California Institute of Technology (Caltech) in Pasadena until 1977 when President Carter appointed him Secretary of Defense. He served as Secretary of Defense all four years until 1981."

At the farewell ceremony, standing before assembled officers and enlisted personnel, I thanked the assembly so deserving of praise: "Graham and I recognize that the hostage ordeal has been felt particularly by Americans who serve in the military. Your colleagues were among those taken and held. Many of the men in your services risked their lives—and eight died—in the valiant Iran hostage rescue attempt. For all of you who wear the uniform, personal danger is an ever-present reality. These past four years have been rewarding and challenging, as will the years ahead. But much has been achieved. Most satisfying of all is that for four years our nation remained at peace despite the world tensions and turmoil that constantly pose challenges to our interests and peace. A second development of great significance is the forging of an historic consensus for increasing our military strength; we've sustained steady growth in our resources devoted to defense and persuaded our allies to embark on a similar course.

"The role of the uniformed military is helping to chart the proper course for America. You must continue to be wise counselors, articulate spokesmen, and loyal executors of national security policy. That is not to say that all of us agreed in all matters. Nor is it likely that military leaders will agree in the future on all such issues. It is the strength of our defense policymaking that this debate is carried on among well-informed advocates who differ on the issues but who have the best interests of their country as a common and abiding goal. The security of our nation requires this of us."

Aside from more general issues such as our concentration on human rights, four specific accomplishments stand out in the foreign policy and international security record of the Carter administration. These were the normalization of relations with China, the SALT II agreement, the Camp David Peace Accords, and the Panama Canal Treaties. In each, the Defense Department contributed substantially. I helped fashion and carry out the military-related provisions of the Camp David Peace Accords where the Defense Department played a supporting role. I was personally involved in the normalization of relations with China, the Panama Canal Treaties, and the SALT II agreement. In these three, the Defense Department's role was central.

The Defense Department was, of course, even more central to our military capability; we turned around the trend of decreasing resources that had been going on for several years. The Defense Department budget in real terms was 10 to 12 percent more when we left than when we came in—not an easy achievement in a Democratic presidency that began with a campaign promise to reduce the defense budget, and with a Congress whose leaders of Democratic congressional majorities were, to put it mildly, skeptical about defense expenditures outside their own districts.

We fostered a set of new technologies, including high-accuracy ballistic and precision-guided cruise missiles, stealth aircraft, advanced satellite surveillance, and integrated communications and intelligence systems. Some of these came to visible fruition ten years later during Desert Storm, which reversed Saddam Hussein's occupation of Kuwait. The Carter administration initiated and developed these programs, the Reagan administration paid for their acquisition in many cases, and the George H. W. Bush administration employed them. In retrospect, I wonder whether any of the administrations would have supported as many as two of the three elements of the process that took three administrations to achieve. We also produced the submarine-launched Poseidon missile, the MX missile program, and the air- and ground-launched cruise missiles. These efforts ensured that the United States maintained its nuclear-deterrent capability in the face of the continued buildup of the Soviet Union's nuclear threat.

We carried out programs that allowed America to provide rapid conventional reinforcements to NATO allies in Western Europe. In fact, we reinvigorated the NATO alliance and pushed NATO's growth in military capability so that it would mesh with America's. We also reached a specific strategic arms control agreement with the Soviet Union. Though never formally ratified, the agreement was adhered to by both parties and limited Soviet threats that our other conventional and nuclear weapon programs were designed to counter.

More than thirty years have passed since I left the Department of Defense. I have continued to be active in matters of national security and on issues that determine the domestic well-being that underpins American strength in the world. In 1992 I chaired a National Academies panel on innovation ("The Government Role in Civilian Technology") and in 2003 a panel on Chinese military power for the Council on Foreign Relations. I also chaired a congressional-mandated study of the organization of the intelligence community. (The Clinton administration implemented some of the recommendations it could without congressional acquiescence but then forgot about them; Congress took no action, least of all on the recommendations for its own organization.)

From 1994 until now I have chaired or served on the Defense Policy Board, which meets quarterly to offer its perspectives to the current secretary of defense. The board is composed mainly of individuals who once served in government. Many have served as secretary of defense or in other national security positions, as members of the Joint Chiefs of Staff, or as members of Congress. Still others come from academia or other parts of the private sector. Over the past three decades I've also been chair or a member of various other U.S. government commissions as well, and of private organizations' commissions and panels.

In the private sector, I have been consultant to many corporations and a member of the board of directors of a dozen, including IBM, Mattel, and Cummins Engine. As a partner in the private equity firm Warburg Pincus LLC, I led reviews and forecasts by outside economic advisers until my retirement from that organization in 2007.

The book of Ecclesiastes says that wisdom is better than weapons of war (9:18), that wisdom is better than strength (9:16), and that the words of the wise are a good inheritance. Here, I look forward with sixty years of accumulated experience in national security—over the terms of ten presidencies—to offer and discuss lessons learned and wisdom hard won in the hope of bridging the past and future to build a stronger and more secure America. One overarching lesson I've learned is that though both the government and the private sector, profit and nonprofit, function differently, all depend, as do the nation's prosperity and security, on healthy, educated citizens and fair opportunities in a democratic society that operates in a spirit of comity.

Oh, Say Can You See

THE VIEW FROM THE TOP

I watched more than a dozen atmospheric nuclear tests, all of them before I became secretary of defense. Only one other secretary of defense (Charlie Wilson) may have seen one. I wanted to see the work of which I'd been part and to make sure the devices did work. At a test in 1956 of a ten-megaton thermonuclear weapon, I was billeted in a cabin on Eniwetok while the test ran on Bikini, 200 miles away. I was in my late twenties. The test occurred an hour before sunrise. The sky was pitch black. In the Marshall Islands, so close to the equator, there is little in the way of dawn. The sun comes straight up. In the predawn darkness the bomb made a light so bright that for twenty seconds I could have read the newspaper on that beach.

On another occasion I viewed the detonation of a six-megaton bomb from an aircraft thirty miles away. I saw the immense fireball expand to a thousand yards in diameter. About two minutes later I felt the shock wave. The fireball expanded into a hot cloud within the first minute and kept changing color as its temperature rose. When the cloud reached the stratosphere, it spread into the well-known mushroom shape.

My reactions watching tests were mostly scientific and professional. I was gratified when designs I'd overseen worked and disappointed if they fizzled. There was a component of deep concern about their power of destruction and a component of satisfaction that convinced me—as it still does—that I was contributing to U.S. security. By the sixth multi-megaton bomb I had no poetic or religious or inspirational sort of reaction. We needed nuclear weapons as a deterrent to their use. After viewing their destructive power, I was determined that so far as I could influence matters, we would never be confronted with the decision to use them.

One way to make sure that the Soviet Union wouldn't use nuclear weapons was to ensure we could deliver our own. For that purpose new designs were necessary. Emotions could not be substituted for actions. I do not pretend to know what a full-scale nuclear war would be like. I remain utterly convinced that it would be dreadful beyond imagination.

During the 1960s and 1970s we coined new jargon in the Cold War: "rapid deployment forces" and "power projections" and "deterrence." America faced an existential threat. There was widespread concern that the United States might be falling behind the Soviet Union in strategic nuclear weaponry. Most Americans were aware of and feared the Soviet nuclear arsenal. Few citizens knew or wanted to know the terrifying extent of weaponry that the Soviet Union and the United States kept at the ready and how the arsenals grew through the 1970s. By 1979 the total Soviet nuclear stockpile numbered about 28,000 weapons, the U.S. nuclear stockpile numbered about 24,000.[1] The potential devastation that could be caused by these thousands of nuclear arms would be catastrophic.

When I became secretary of defense in 1977, the military services, most of all the army, were disrupted badly by the Vietnam War. There was general agreement that the Soviet Union outclassed the West in conventional military capability, especially in ground forces in Europe. Soviet leaders were convinced that they had conventional warfare superiority in Europe and were committed to increasing their influence in Western Europe. I concluded that America and its allies needed to be able to deny or at least reduce Soviet confidence that it could roll over Western Europe in thirty days. We thought that given more than a month of fighting, the Soviet Union's Warsaw Pact alliance would fray.

The disparity in conventional forces loomed over political relations between the United States and our European NATO allies. Because of it we still needed to rely on the threat that we would use tactical nuclear weapons to deter or blunt any conventional Soviet attack in Europe. We had to accept the possibility that our use of those weapons could escalate to a full-blown nuclear war that would destroy the United States, the

Soviet Union, and Europe. That was a terrifying strategy in a tumultuous time. The world was truly divided into "our side" and "theirs."

The United States considered how to change the Soviet calculation that its military could accomplish a blitzkrieg victory in Western Europe. We reinforced our conventional warfare capability. We planned ways to deter a Soviet nuclear strike with our own ability to strike back. At the same time, we negotiated with Soviet authorities on limiting strategic nuclear arms. The constant Cold War competition raged hot during the Carter administration and preoccupied me throughout the four years.

One telling incident occurred after the Soviet Union collapsed and before Chief of General Staff Sergei Akhromeyev committed suicide. Shortly before his last act, he confided to a friend of mine his belief that the Soviet forces could have fought their way to the English Channel in thirty days in a conventional war. "But," he added with a nod to our nuclear deterrent and the Soviet system's internal failure, "then what would we have done?" Our deterrent and global reach prevented Soviet expansion and military domination. The containment we engineered made the Soviet authorities confront their dysfunctional system and helped to bring it down.

In the four years of my tenure as secretary of defense, I also focused my attention on North Korea. President Kim Il-sung, grandfather of that country's current leader, Kim Jong-un, had authorized attempts to kill the president of South Korea and members of his cabinet. Kim's army had already assaulted and killed American soldiers in the demilitarized zone. Even as we dealt with those pressing concerns, the Carter administration was to find that still more security issues would define the president's term. They included the normalization of relations with China, and the Panama Canal Treaties, as well as Mideast conflicts, and ultimately the Iran Revolution and the subsequent hostage crisis.

From where I sat, the panorama of challenges was complex and the penalty for mistakes was severe. I called on experience I'd gained from my former positions. With each one, my perspective had widened. When I directed Livermore Laboratory, I'd overseen the development of thermonuclear weapons and considered them paramount for national defense.

Next, as director of defense research and engineering (DDRE) in the Defense Department, I became concerned with efficient acquisition of entire weapons systems, nuclear and nonnuclear. I tried to select the ones that made the most sense in terms of cost-effectiveness and mission relevance. In that job I quickly understood that in a situation of mutual deterrence, Soviet and U.S. nuclear weapons in effect canceled each other out. That greatly increased the importance of conventional armament.

Later, as secretary of the air force, I considered one aircraft program versus another for the war in Vietnam. Planes can have up to fifty-year life spans so I looked at them with an eye not only for their immediate use but also for how they would weather time and serve military purposes that could differ and change drastically over decades. Taken together, these vantage points offered an understanding of security issues in considerable detail.

After my first Pentagon service in the 1960s, and before my return as secretary of defense in 1977, I was president of Caltech. During that period I was a member of the negotiating team for the Strategic Arms Limitation Talks (SALT I) for the Nixon and Ford administrations. I understood the need to limit and preferably reduce nuclear arms even as we readied programs for potential conflict or war. I concluded that the goal of a stable strategic balance could be safely sought through agreed limitations on offensive and defensive weapons if they were adequately monitored to ensure the limits were observed. This was a better path than continuing an unrestricted competition in which the perception of advantage, however mistaken, could lead to rash action and even a nuclear war. Our reasoning led to the formulation of the "1,000 strategic warheads" proposal, which the Soviet negotiators dismissed out of hand. So the strategic arms competition continued, only slightly moderated by SALT I.

I still had much to learn about how both my strategic decisions and my daily actions as defense secretary would affect the country's safety and influence the economy clear down to its local communities. I understood from the start that I had to weigh the relative value of various armament systems and of military units and their placement. I compared the value of adding aircraft against adding ships, tanks, or personnel. I considered how aircraft or other weapons platforms and systems might be used not only by America, but also by our allies over the next two generations of those systems. I looked at new technologies under development to select those that provided the most benefit for the cost and would prove effective in combat. And I learned how military capabilities and operations fit into the larger framework of national security.

In high school I had been the kind of kid who went to his room after dinner to read a book. One book, *Bleak House,* written more than 150 years ago by Charles Dickens, concerned a Victorian court bureaucracy in which he'd labored as a clerk. In the frustration and anger that it engendered, it was not unlike bureaucracies of our own day. Dickens wrote of that bureaucracy: "It exhausts finances, patience, courage and hope . . . and overthrows the brain and breaks the heart."

The organization I was charged to lead—the Department of Defense—transcended anything the Victorian mind could have imagined. In 1977 the secretary of defense managed 2.1 million soldiers, sailors, marines, and airmen and airwomen in uniform, and 1 million government civilians—a force much larger than the number of employees in the world's largest private corporation and nearly 40 percent of the civilian employment of the entire federal government. Getting a massive organization like the Department of Defense to focus on the right things wasn't going to be easy.

What So Proudly We Hailed

2

ENSURING NATIONAL DEFENSE THROUGH ITS BUDGET

The Preamble to the U.S. Constitution states that the purpose of our government is to "provide for the common defense, promote the general welfare, and secure the blessings of liberty to ourselves and our posterity." The general welfare includes economic growth, standard of living, jobs, education, and health care. Promoting general welfare entails avoiding or at least limiting class or culture warfare, controlling crime, and minimizing terrorism. Providing for the common defense means deterring war by letting enemies and allies see you're ready to defend American territory and suitably defined American interests, and you're able, if necessary, to fight to win.

The framers of the Constitution deliberately divided power among the branches of the central government, and between it and the states. They accepted the inefficiency of divided power to reduce the risk of tyranny. They sought to avoid faction within representative government, hoping that those chosen to represent the people would surmount or balance particular interests. Surmounting the tyranny of particular interests never quite worked. Political parties—what the framers meant by faction—appeared within ten years.

DEMOCRACY IS MESSY

By 1977 inefficiencies in government caused by special interest groups had become severe (though special interest groups then were nowhere near as numerous or effective as they are now). Conflicts between and within Congress and the Executive Branch sometimes produced flawed foreign and security policies. Opposing viewpoints held by particular interest groups and the many layers of decision makers clawing at domestic policies resulted in contradictory decisions or none at all. Our national security now, as then, depends on our political cohesion and the state of our domestic economy as much as on our military capabilities and diplomatic skills. A failure to face up to and deal with issues in a rational manner risks putting our nation on a course to disaster.

When I was in my early thirties a journalist named Joe Kraft who covered Washington for a long time came to see me. This was in 1961, during my first months as director of Defense Research and Engineering (DDRE). He asked me—maybe because I was so young that the media had dubbed me Child Harolde—"What makes you think you're going to be able to accomplish anything here?" I answered: "I intend to know more about the subject than anyone else in the room and therefore I'm going to be able to get done the things that I want."

How naïve! Of course, by the time I became secretary of defense I'd long since learned that while being smart is good, it's not the same thing as being wise. Wisdom comes from experience and can derive from mistakes as well as from good decisions. Getting things done takes a combination of intellect, personal skills, and judgment, not to mention good luck. No one of them alone gets you very far. As secretary of defense I came to appreciate what is applicable even more broadly in government now: we Americans must close the wide gap between what we say we want our government to do for us and what we're willing to pay or give up to get it.

To make my case, I draw on my particular experience with the defense budget, which directly affects security, domestic welfare, and the blessings of liberty. In this chapter I offer a brief tutorial to illustrate that, supplemented with examples from my particular experience.

THREE MAIN FUNCTIONS OCCUPY
THE SECRETARY OF DEFENSE

The secretary of defense advises the president on national security; manages the Defense Department, including the armed services and the

Pentagon and the defense budget; and is second only to the president in directing the military chain of command—both combat and support.

1. Adviser on National Security

As one of the president's chief advisers on international security, and occasionally on other issues, the secretary of defense offers views that the president considers along with those of the secretary of state, the assistant for national security affairs (usually known as the national security adviser), the director of national intelligence (replacing in that role the director of central intelligence), the Joint Chiefs of Staff, and certain of the president's staff.

Statute puts only four members on the National Security Council (NSC): the president, vice president, secretary of state, and secretary of defense. The national security adviser, the chairman of the Joint Chiefs, and the director of national intelligence are statutory advisers to the NSC. The president can invite others, but they are temporary, not permanent members. (The Obama White House lists up to nineteen attendees. The efficiency of such a crowded meeting is doubtful.) During the Carter administration, the National Security Council usually met informally at Friday breakfasts with five to eight people present. An interesting aside is that President Carter charged us for those breakfasts. He was equally careful with the nation's finances, an attitude less in evidence among his successors.

The advice I offered the president was not only about military matters. I also weighed in on what ought to be included in treaties, negotiations, and certain matters of diplomacy to take into account military need and the inevitably related domestic issues. In many secretaries of defense (SecDefs) there is a secretary of state striving to break out. After all, U.S. military capability is intended to support our foreign policy, and military strategy is part of a larger international security strategy.

The defense secretary meets military security needs through the defense budget, which is much larger than that provided to the secretary of state, although the State Department is charged with broader issues of international relations. I had been deeply involved in arms limitation negotiations with Soviet authorities in various roles both in and out of the government for ten years before becoming defense secretary, so without trying to be secretary of state, I did add my thoughts on that and some other diplomatic issues that affected national security. For example, the

Defense Department became central to the contents of the Panama Canal Treaties. I was also involved in President Carter's decision and efforts in the normalization of relations with the People's Republic of China. I wound up being a principal interlocutor with China, Japan, and Korea.

Of course, all major Department of Defense decisions I made and activities I recommended needed the president's approval. Knowing when to inform him, when to get his guidance before formal coordination with other parts of government—State and White House staff, for example—is something that develops only as you do it and learn. There were substantial glitches. In the case of the proposed neutron bomb deployment in Western Europe, which never happened, Defense, State, and the NSC staff all failed to get President Carter's OK before reaching tentative agreement with our European partners.

2. Managing the Department of Defense

The secretary's advisory capacity can be amplified or preempted by a second major function: the need to manage an enterprise that now consumes 4 to 5 percent (depending on the year) of the country's gross domestic product (GDP). During the thirty-five years from 1977 to 2012 that percentage has varied between 3 percent and 6.5 percent.[1] In principle, the secretary of defense has almost unlimited authority over activities of the Department of Defense, constrained (often severely) by the congressional power of the purse.

America's ability to use military instruments to support its national security depends on the growth and health of the U.S. economy. I cannot emphasize that enough. The economy depends on America's productivity and innovation, the education and skills of the labor force, fiscal and monetary policy, international and economic relations, trade, investment, and the domestic U.S. content of goods and services, whether material or intellectual. At the end of World War II, U.S. GDP was 50 percent of the global economy. America was dominant because of the economic devastation in Europe and East Asia. During subsequent decades, while the U.S. economy has grown by almost ten times, the U.S. share of the global economy has fallen to about 25 percent and America has lost its former economic dominance.[2]

Our economic state has been affected by the wide gap between the services the public demands and the taxes it is willing to pay. This has produced serious fiscal problems, which damage our national well-being. Even as our economy struggles to recover from the financial crisis and recession of 2008, we continue in a war that has lasted more than a decade. America has sustained costs of combat in Afghanistan and Iraq ranging from $33.8 billion a year in 2001–02 to nearly $186 billion in 2008. We spent $155 billion in 2009, and about $171 billion a year thereafter.[3] In the process, defense costs have risen to nearly 5 percent of GDP. (After the end of the Cold War, U.S. defense expenditures ran between 3.5 and 4.5 percent of GDP.)[4] Given our economic challenges, a 5 percent share of GDP is not politically sustainable and hard to justify on the basis of external threats. I believe that a figure approaching 4 percent is justifiable and, if derived as the result of prudent security requirements, politically sustainable.

3. Directing Military Operations

The defense secretary's third major function is to direct military operations. The chain of command runs from the president to the secretary. The secretary issues orders to the unified and specified commanders (now called combat commanders) of forces in the Pacific, Europe, and other geographic areas, and to the transport, strategic, and other functional commands.

The military departments (of the army, navy, and air force) do not have autonomous control of war or peacetime military operations. Their civilian secretaries (secretary of the air force, for example) do not direct combat operations at all. By law they, and the military service chiefs in their respective military departments who also serve as members of the Joint Chiefs of Staff, are responsible for recruiting, equipping, and training military personnel, but not for issuing deployment or combat orders. Those orders go from the secretary of defense and are generally communicated through the chairman of the Joint Chiefs to the combat commanders both in peace and in wartime. The orders can, however, go directly from the secretary of defense or the president to the combat commanders. The chairman of the Joint Chiefs—the senior military adviser to the president and the secretary of defense—is a transmitter of orders; he is not in the command chain. The military departments need close interaction with combat commanders so they can decide, for example, how to rotate units in and out of combat theaters. With its long history, that relationship works more smoothly now than in past decades, but never works seamlessly.

DECISIONS FOR SHORT-TERM NEEDS AND LONG-RANGE FORECASTS

Part of managing the Department of Defense is deciding force composition and capability. The secretary of defense worries about short-term needs of troops in the line of fire even while formulating long-term program and budget projections for ensuring American interests in all parts of the world. On a daily basis, that means making decisions on all kinds of military matters—recruiting, training, and locating troops, and managing their force structure and equipment. Long-term needs, such as a new weapons system, require various stages of work to formulate, detail, and carry through a coherent program. You try to plan for strategic international situations ten, fifteen, and twenty years ahead because it takes that long from concept to fielding a major new weapons system. Some of them stay in the inventory for forty or more years through modified or advanced versions.

FOUR MEASURES OF CAPABILITY

I had many discussions with the senior military as I determined how to allocate resources. We looked at four measures of capability:

—Force structure, which is the number of divisions, navy vessels, fighter and bomber aircraft, intercontinental ballistic missiles (ICBMs), and more.

—Modernization, which includes the nature and capability of weapons systems and equipment.

—Readiness, which concerns logistic capability, training status of troops, and the status of their equipment.

—Sustainability, which is how long personnel, equipment, and munitions can last in combat.

Troop readiness is more complicated than it first appears. Readiness has to do with how *well* people are trained, how *recently* they've been trained, and how *familiar* they are with the equipment. When new equipment is introduced into a military unit, familiarity decreases. The equipment may be more advanced, but the troops don't yet know how to use it. Therefore you may not be confident that you can immediately deploy them. However, less than complete staffing or equipping of a unit doesn't mean that troops can't fight, but that the unit is below full capability. How far below depends on how incomplete the staffing or equipping or training and in what elements.

Sustainability depends on the stocks of equipment and munitions, how long we can keep people in combat or repeat their tours of duty. The question I went over again and again with the military was how do you best allocate your funds among the four requirements? During the late 1970s, the senior military tended to make force structure and modernization their first priorities because these take the longest to achieve. They reasoned that if a war began they would get money for the rest. That was a doubtful assumption during the Cold War because an armed conflict with the Soviet Union would probably have been short. It is probably a better assumption now. Combat commanders—the heads of regional and functional commands then known as CINCs—had the opposite bias. They worried about what would happen if they had to fight beginning next month or wage combat lasting through the next year. In those cases readiness and then sustainability would matter greatly.

EACH SERVICE DEMANDS ITS SHARE

There is no single answer to where you put priorities. Making judgments requires navigating the push-pull of service parochialism. The air force wants money for its research and development, its weapons, and training for personnel. So do the navy and army and marines (though the marines sometimes rely on the navy for their materiel and logistic support with occasional exceptions like the V-22 tilt-rotor plane). The secretary of defense organizes the defense program and budgets from a functional viewpoint, weighing strategic programs, ground combat, command and control, air and sealift, research and development. The defense secretary then deploys the result among the combat commands in terms of readiness, sustainability, force structure, and armaments.

Congress directs its appropriations to each of the armed services by name. Each service competes for its share via its chief of staff, the senior military person in each service branch. Subordinates hold that individual responsible for their cause. When I spoke to a chief in person and in private, he was usually thoughtful and often willing to rise above his particular service's parochial interests for the overall national security. When the deputy secretary of defense and I met with the Joint Chiefs of Staff together without any of their staff present, we could persuade the Chiefs to understand, if not applaud, the most sensible allocation of resources. However, if subordinates were present, the process was more difficult. And it was impossible to get realistic recommendations for force levels if the Chiefs as a group had to provide their recommendations in writing. They would negotiate some version of their individual wish lists, usually by simply adding them together.

An interested secretary of defense can play a decisive role in determining force structure and equipment. I gave a big push to the evolution of joint operations and joint service, which can reduce the degree of service parochialism. I also established a requirement that the combat commanders report to the secretary of defense every quarter with their needs and recommendations. That was a way of producing more balance in the budget between the services and the combat commanders.

SECDEF TRAINING GROUND

What experience can prepare a person for the responsibilities of a secretary of defense? The holders of this office claim a variety of experiences and achievements, but one glaring change over the years is apparent from looking at their backgrounds. Before the start of the Nixon administration in 1969 there had been nine defense secretaries. Of those, one had been a five-star general. Three had been investment bankers, all with previous civilian service in the defense establishment. Three had been business executives with no civilian government service. Two had been lawyers active in politics and had seen previous government service. Neither they nor any of the others had been in elective office.

Starting with the Nixon administration, there have been fourteen SecDefs (counting Donald Rumsfeld twice). Of these, whatever else their careers have included, seven had served in Congress and two others had been elected to office in their own states. An obvious conclusion is that elective political experience and the presumed skills associated with it have, beginning in 1969, loomed larger as qualifications for the Office of Secretary of Defense in the eyes of presidents who make the choice. A more speculative inference is that defense and national security have become more politicized beginning with the Vietnam War, and that feature has survived the end of the Cold War.

HOTLINE TO THE PRESIDENT

Seven appointed positions in the executive branch carry a great deal of weight independent of who occupies them. Four of these positions are the secretaries of the State, Treasury, and Defense Departments and the attorney general—the four original cabinet positions. These people deal directly with the president. In addition, the White House chief of staff, the national security adviser, and the director of the Office of Management and Budget interact almost continuously with the president. Other cabinet members might too, if they have a previous personal relationship or because of what happens to be hot. Generally, most cabinet officials aside from the "big four" understand that they first talk to the president's staff.

The secretary of defense can't function in that mode. My phone had a button that sent my calls directly to the president's phone. I was not a particular confidant of President Carter's; he had few. Nonetheless, I had no problem getting him on the phone or going to see him whenever I wanted, and alone, if I felt strongly that was necessary. I spoke with him by telephone about a third of the days we were in office. A week would not go by without calls from me to him, or from him to me, and I would see him at least a couple of times most weeks. When one or another of the incidents described in the chapters of this book was under way, we would be on the phone several times a day.

My most frequent other substantial interactions with senior members of the Carter administration involved about half a dozen people. Chief among them was Secretary of State Cyrus Vance, a longtime friend with whom I had worked as a colleague early in Robert McNamara's tenure and later worked for when Vance was deputy secretary of defense in the Johnson administration. I interacted as often with the president's national security adviser, Zbigniew Brzezinski, who was friendly though at times prickly. Others who occasioned frequent meetings were the director of the Office of Management and Budget, first Bert Lance and then Jim

McIntyre, with whom I had good relations (though not with all their subordinates); and President Carter's principal political advisers: Hamilton Jordan, his chief of staff, and Jody Powell, one of his most trusted advisers and his press secretary. Inevitably, the real rivalry in the national security area is usually between the president's national security adviser and the secretary of state. Although feuds between the secretary of defense and the secretary of state have occurred commonly in many administrations, in the Carter administration it was Vance and Brzezinski who followed a contentious tradition.

STAYING INFORMED

Before I took office in January 1977, outgoing Secretary of Defense Rumsfeld, as well as former SecDef Melvin Laird, told me to make sure that I was informed right away about any important international or domestic happenings relevant to Defense Department responsibilities. Otherwise, they said, other people will have the information and you won't. I found that advice useful because information about immediate events is important even if wrong. In fact, the first reports are almost always wrong; accuracy suffers at the beginning of an unfolding event. Still, it's important to get "the word," though at first you have to deal with uncertain knowledge of facts on the ground.

An operations center in the State Department informs the secretary of state of important news; a set-up in the White House makes sure the national security adviser hears it. Of course, as secretary of defense I had to sign off on all significant deployments of forces. That was one reason to be kept informed. Another reason was that the president might call on the SecDef for advice. The general or admiral on duty (deputy director of operations—DDO) at the National Military Command Center was charged with informing me in real time of any crisis. A DDO is on duty at all times. He would be the first to hear of anything needing immediate attention and would relay it to the chairman of the Joint Chiefs and to me.

My usual connection with the Joint Chiefs was with its chairman, first George Brown and then Dave Jones. When the chairman was away, another of the Joint Chiefs would act as chairman, often with less detailed knowledge of the issues. That awkward situation has since been remedied by legislation in 1986 creating a vice chairman of the Joint Chiefs, over the objections of then Secretary of Defense Caspar Weinberger and all the Joint Chiefs at that time.

THE TYRANNY OF THE IN-BOX

Sometimes we learned of an event too late to deal with it from an informed position before it made its way into the news media. The news of the day bullied its way to the top of our in-boxes to the detriment of more important programs that required our attention. A lesson we all learned (but found hard to put into practice) is that every effort needs to be made to insulate major objectives and initiatives from the day-to-day static of events.

I confess to having been driven more than I should by the in-box, partly because of my personality. I find it difficult to ignore problems. By contrast, Defense Secretary Jim Schlesinger was famous for letting stuff pile up and not paying it attention because he thought he had more important things to do. That leaves a lot undone but has its advantages.

Failure to insulate high priorities from the in-box tends to divert attention from main objectives, benefiting opponents who want to prevent them from being achieved. I offer this lesson learned to future administrations: to enable staff to keep focused on important ongoing programs no matter the contents of the in-box, divide staff into teams that tackle either short-term problems or long-term ones. That way, a certain amount of attention will be devoted to long-term challenges even when the in-box is hot. The drawback of assigning long-term problems to a separate set of people, however, is that they are likely to be diverted to highly demanding short-term problems, or ignored, or downsized to a vanishing level. But if you insist from the beginning of a presidential term that you're going to devote some fraction of senior staff attention and best people to long-term problems only, the in-box won't claim all of them.

The Defense Department's Office of Net Assessment, set up by James Schlesinger almost forty years ago (in 1973) and headed ever since by Andrew Marshall, has successfully concentrated on long-term issues.[5] In line with the risks mentioned above, its output has not always achieved the attention it deserved, at least within our own government. The Chinese appear to have been very interested in the output of Andrew Marshall's office.

In my tenure as secretary of defense, budgetary and program control proved to be my most persistent and frequent areas of concern. I managed to make time for strategic planning and innovative development of weapons systems. On occasion, however, all else was superseded by an operational situation that needed my immediate decision. The key is to keep enough control over operational situations when not in crisis so that you reduce the chance there will be a crisis. That is more easily said than done. For one thing, the secretary of defense is by no means the preeminent controller of U.S. actions. He has even less control over the behavior of other countries, big or small. Nonetheless, the secretary of defense needs to make sure our country doesn't stumble into crisis as a result of loose rules of engagement or sloppy maneuvers.

PROGRAMMING AND BUDGETING
FOR NATIONAL SECURITY

President Dwight D. Eisenhower understood that the Department of Defense required not only clear objectives but also the programming and budgeting process to carry them out. In his letter to Congress on May 16, 1958, he wrote that "the safety and solvency of our nation" require "technological advances in weapons and other devices of war" to "have a posture ready to react unerringly and instantly to attack."[6] He said the "unprecedented costs of maintaining in peacetime a massive defense establishment demand the utmost economy and efficiency in all its operations. Our goal must be maximum strength at minimum cost."[7] Ike asked for specific legislation to achieve that and got it. Subsequent legislation has built on this foundation.[8]

In the broadest sense, defense works in support of foreign policy. In principle, the defense budget flows from foreign policy objectives. The secretary of defense tries to figure out a way to achieve military force structure, readiness, modernization, and sustainability suitable for the nation's defense needs at least cost. Bob McNamara put it this way: if you avoid war by modernizing and readying a military you don't have to use, you're "wasting" money in the most efficient way. The goal is to deter war by reassuring your allies even as you ensure your position against your opponents. That's easier to assert than to follow, as McNamara himself—and his successors—found out.

PLANNING, PRIORITIZING, EXECUTING

The Defense Department sets plans for national security programs in three stages. First, it decides on the plans for weapons systems, the force structure for both strategic nuclear and conventional war in different geographies, long-range projections, and short-term needs. This is or should be based on a national security strategy that lays out the military capability needed to support U.S. foreign policy and security objectives in various parts of the world. Next, the Defense Department prioritizes programs and decides how much funding each will receive and for how many years. Specific allocations result from a bottom-up addition of what you think you need and from factoring in limits set by what the exigencies of the overall federal budget demand. The third leg is the execution of the program, budget line item by line item, and program by program. Compromise plays a big part as funding for individual programs gets pulled like taffy by local political pressures. In my experience, the existing defense plan is only a starting point, though it purports to lay out a five-year program. You add or subtract numbers depending on how the world, and our view of it, changed from the previous year. The resulting defense budget is a consequence of past decisions, immediate and short-term foreign policy demands, world events, and anticipation of events.

HISTORY OF HOW DEFENSE BUDGETS
HAVE BEEN DECIDED

The history of how defense budgets have been decided provides important lessons. In the 1950s the comptroller in the Defense Department was a powerful and experienced individual named Wilfred McNeil. He was the first assistant secretary of defense (comptroller). After everyone else in the department had put together a defense budget he would look at it and make decisions that might have little to do with programs or objectives, and his bottom line would be the budget for the year.

His successor at the end of the Eisenhower administration was Franklin Lincoln, whose motto was: the budget starts from zero. That is, every budget should be an accumulation of real needs, and each item in the budget should be considered as if no programs were already running.

During the Carter administration, a similar zero-based budgeting idea was interpreted like this: look at each program every year and ask is it worth continuing? Should we change it or abolish it? (Seldom at budget time did I ask whether we should increase it.) The problem with zero-based budgeting is that it can be inconsistent with long-range or even medium-range planning. If you change a program too often, you diminish its efficiency and in fact increase its cost.

Bob McNamara introduced a big change into the planning of the defense program and budget by introducing the idea of a five-year program for major defense categories: strategic forces, general purpose forces, R&D, and five other categories. Along with Charles Hitch, the Defense Department comptroller who had advocated that approach while at the RAND Corporation, he evaluated ongoing programs using established benchmarks to measure progress against projected results.[9] McNamara claimed that his defense budget was built from the bottom up using foreign policy objectives and military requirements with no other constraints. That was a dubious assertion even from the beginning. The Vietnam War took so much money off the top that over subsequent years the rest of his budget could not be assembled on that basis at all. At best, McNamara's five-year plan worked for two. Thereafter, each outlying year saw decreasing resemblance to the original plan. Eventually every five-year plan looked very different from the previous year's five-year plan. That's been a risk ever since.

NEED FOR A FIVE-YEAR PLAN

To my way of thinking, a solid five-year plan that underpins main defense objectives is as critical now as when McNamara introduced that concept. For example, we currently need to consider and plan for the possibility that North Korea will collapse or threaten to use nuclear weapons; that China will wield its considerable economic and military powers as an adversary; that an Iran emboldened by its nuclear program will become more aggressive, and that extremism and terrorism in the Middle East could ignite regional conflicts. Absent a five-year plan, each year's objectives are deflected by what the media makes hot in any given week. That does not prepare us for the future.

HUBBUB, NOISE, AND CONFLICTS

Now, the president with the advice of the director of the Office of Management and Budget and other White House economic and political advisers sets a top number or at least a range for the defense budget. That top number is limited by the overall national fiscal situation and when submitted gets tinkered with or revised by Congress. The Constitution gives Congress the power of the purse, so the congressional role, however dysfunctional in practice, is perfectly legitimate. The budget then becomes vulnerable to Congress's multifarious collection of interests, prejudices, and occasional insights and wisdom.

Rarely is a major weapons systems program conceived, developed, and fielded during a single administration. Because that usually requires a long period of time, continuity of major objectives can be interrupted by how Congress bakes the national fiscal pie. The president exerts his will, but that, too, becomes a trade-off with special interests represented within his administration and through intervention from members of Congress. Political polarization makes the defense budget a political football. As administrations change, continuity fades and commitment to ongoing programs wanes.

MORE TINKERING, LESS ACCOUNTABILITY

The line items setting the amounts appropriated for the various categories—personnel, maintenance and operations, ships, and missiles in each service—totaled about fifty when I first came to the Defense Department as DDRE in 1961. Now more than 2,200 line items crowd the defense budget, and Congress has increasingly expanded its own intervention into the details of more and more line items as a result of the Vietnam and Watergate years.

There used to be individuals on both sides of the aisle in the House and Senate who were very knowledgeable about national security matters and were deferred to by other members of Congress. At various times these legislators included such Democrats as George Mahon (Texas), John Stennis (Mississippi), Richard Russell (Georgia), Sam Nunn (Georgia), Carl Vinson (Georgia), Mel Price (Illinois), and Les Aspin (Wisconsin).

Republicans knowledgeable about defense matters included, at different times, John Warner (Virginia), John Tower (Texas), John Buchanan (Alabama), Jack Kemp (New York), Gerald Ford (Michigan), Melvin Laird (Wisconsin), and Leverett Saltonstall (Massachusetts). Mel Laird became secretary of defense in 1969. John Tower was nominated by George H. W. Bush to be secretary of defense in 1989 but was rejected by the Senate. John Warner had been secretary of the navy before he was elected to the Senate, and of course Gerald Ford became president.

There's a good deal to be said for legislators whose long tenure and concentration on national security has brought useful experience and the authority to use it to influence executive branch behavior. We don't have that nearly so much now. Instead, Congress has quadrupled its supporting staff since the 1960s. During the 1960s and 1970s, congressional staffs were smaller and stayed in their jobs longer, often over a whole career. They were correspondingly more experienced and knowledgeable and often not as partisan as staffers today.

Today, the wider breadth of issues and details in legislation ranging across health care, the environment, social legislation, defense, and more have forced members of Congress to delegate decisions concerning them to their staffs. Congressional staffers come and go as part of their own career moves, some trying to make the biggest possible splash, whether by listening to what contractors or special interests say or by getting a reputation for being tough, mean, or intransigent. Loyal only to their respective congressional bosses or to some segment of their party, and lacking the broad perspective of national security as a whole, congressional staff exert great influence, but no staff are held accountable for national security results. Yet their considerable influence has direct impact on weapons systems, bases, and deployments.

A classic example concerns the ballistic missile early warning system the Reagan administration was considering during the 1980s. It required a decision about whether to use long-wave infrared sensors or short-wave ones. One faction of Congress wanted long-wave; another wanted short-wave. Congress voted on the issue on the basis of staffers' recommendations, which represented their respective connections to, or information from, a long-wave contractor or a short-wave one. When I see that kind of behavior, I do wonder if that's what the framers intended in the Constitution. It's one thing to forego efficiency to reduce the risk of tyranny. However, lowered efficiency in the service of private and narrow interests is not the opposite of tyranny.

It's interesting that Congress seems to want to cut everything but itself. If you meet a member of Congress in the hall these days and address him or her as Mr. or Ms. Chairman or Ranking Member you'll be right half the time. Every committee now has many subcommittees, and each of those has a chair, ranking member, and corresponding staff. When added to the overlapping jurisdictions of committees, this means that almost everybody can say "no," but nobody can decide what to do. Clearly, we need to reduce the many levels of decisionmakers so we can get important work done, and done knowledgeably.

WHAT SIZE DEFENSE BUDGET IS ENOUGH?

After the Soviet Union dissolved, each year's subsequent defense budget in the absence of major combat operations was smaller than the last. That was called the peace dividend. Overall, the defense budget fell by about a third. Contrary to what many people may think, a diminished defense budget does not necessarily produce infusions into domestic health care and education or alleviate poverty. The money goes into tax reductions, or ethanol production, farm subsidies, or "McMansions" via federal loans as a result of the usual political pulling and hauling, of which defense is but one claimant.

When we look at the defense budget now as a percentage of GDP, it's slightly lower than when I was secretary of defense. During the hottest parts of the Cold War the defense budget was 8 percent of GDP. During my tenure the defense budget was about 5 percent. It rose to over 6 percent during the Reagan years and fell to 3 percent after the end of the Cold War. Now, including expenses for the wars in Iraq and Afghanistan, the defense budget is just under 5 percent of GDP, the peace dividend has been spent, and in share of GDP we are back to where we were during the Carter years.[10]

During his 1976 campaign, President Carter criticized defense spending in the Ford administration and promised cuts in the range of $5 billion to $7 billion. "There's so much waste," Carter said. He mentioned that when he was a navy lieutenant he saw a lot of "ridiculous stuff."

That stuck in his mind. Within a few months of taking office at the beginning of 1977, I suggested a series of amendments to Ford's proposed fiscal 1978 budget that cut it by almost $3 billion but still allowed a Total Obligation Authority (TOA) increase of more than $8 billion over the fiscal 1977 budget.

Since every piece of waste in a defense budget is in somebody's interest, the goal is to identify things at the margin and delete items that are less important than the rest of your programs. Congress accepted the amount of my proposed cuts to the fiscal 1978 budget. But rather than cut the programs I had suggested, it took money from various programs I considered a higher priority, including training, readiness, and spare parts. I learned a lesson from that: make sure both sides of the deal are agreed upon before you sign off.

Carter was loath to increase the defense budget's share of GDP during his presidency. Yet given the Soviet Union's nuclear threat and its powerful conventional force strength, I was able to achieve a reasonably well-observed policy of a 3 percent annual real (net of inflation) increase in the U.S. defense budget. That also served to press our European allies to do the same. Called the Three Percent Solution, its purpose was to fund more arms and increase rapid deployment of U.S. and allied forces to Europe so Soviet troops couldn't roll over the continent.

DEFENSE BUDGET CUTS CAN HURT
MUSCLE RATHER THAN REMOVE FAT

As I told the Budget Committees of the House and Senate in 1977 when presenting the Carter administration's fiscal 1978 defense budget, effective defense programs provide a product that is invisible when it works: support for our foreign policy and deterrence of attacks on our interests. Still, the defense budget is a favorite target for cuts because it is regarded as relatively controllable. Cutting it only *seems* free of risks. The 1978 defense budget we proposed represented not what we would like, I told the committee, but what we seriously needed. Reductions would slice into muscle, not fat. Cuts would hurt.

Then, as now, there is no neat and simple formula for determining defense spending. We need to examine our basic interests in light of trends in the international environment, clarify our national security and defense objectives, and relate missions, forces, and resources to those objectives. Military power continues to be a major factor in the resolution of international disputes; it influences the attitudes of friends and adversaries during peace as well as in war.

In 1978 building up our own and allied forces in Europe to counter possible Soviet intimidation of Western Europe became an early objective of the Carter administration. We tied the defense budget to shoring up NATO. To give concrete examples of how the budget meant to fortify American and NATO security, I include here some main line items of the 1978 budget and their purpose:

—$39 million to buy seventy M60 tanks to fully equip one additional armored battalion. There was a big disparity in numbers of tanks between NATO and the Warsaw Pact.

—$35 million more, making a total of $200 million in 1979, for the procurement of ROLAND air defense missiles to provide low-altitude defense of rear-area targets, particularly at air bases. A joint French and German consortium developed the system. It was an element of a program to increase interoperability with the systems of our allies in Europe. Unfortunately, as it later turned out, the U.S. Army decided to "adapt" the system to the point that it became a new development program. (Only one Army National Guard battalion was deployed.)

—$40 million to modify the commercial production of civilian wide-bodied aircraft to airlift troops to Europe should our allies be attacked. Acquisition of roll-on, roll-off ships would allow the transport of equipment and materiel to the potential or actual combat theater. With prepositioned or rapidly delivered stocks then immediately available, we needed to be able to fly troops over fast to match up with them.

—$20 million for full funding of tooling, start-up costs, and long-lead procurement for the ground-launched cruise missile, the best response to the rapid Soviet buildup of long-range nuclear forces.[11]

It was challenging to get our NATO allies to build up their own defense efforts in a way that meshed with ours. Much has changed in the world, but my remarks to the House Committee on Armed Services in 1978 seem equally appropriate today: "We Americans are allied in a common objective. Allies do not always agree about everything, but they continue to respect each other and to work together. Allies remember the common threats they face, and what is at stake."[12]

CARTER'S DEFENSE BUDGET

Because the Soviet Union was seen as an existential threat to the United States, Congress generally accepted President Carter's defense program, cutting it marginally in a gesture of parsimony or increasing bits to benefit local interests, especially those of senior members of relevant committees. In the Carter administration we initiated some things, carried on and modified some programs, and terminated some. I didn't have a political base the way some previous secretaries of defense like Mel Laird or Clark Clifford did, so I could not contend with political people on political grounds. Given that difference, I think I got remarkably little undue pressure, which may have been a consequence of President Carter's own character. He preferred to wait to introduce political considerations until the end of his decisionmaking process. He began his term by telling his cabinet: "You figure the merits. I'll decide the politics." Inevitably that formula eroded as time went on, and politics showed up early in more and more issues.

THE CHICKEN-AND-EGG DILEMMA

Crises that truly threaten the United States, like the Soviet threat, are a basis for substantial defense budget increases. Absent that, the best and most sensible thing to do is avoid big ups and downs. There is a chicken-and-egg argument here: the less military capability you buy, the less you're able to do. Do you tailor your security commitments to your abilities, or do you tailor your abilities to your commitments? Senator Richard Russell, one of the wisest members of Congress about national security (his deeply rooted racial bias thwarted his presidential ambitions), had looked askance at the Johnson administration's plan to develop the roll-on, roll-off ships. (Still in use, they can store an entire military division's equipment.) Russell said: "When you're better able to go places and fight, it's more likely you will. I'm not convinced that's a good thing."

What Russell meant was that to a hammer, everything looks like a nail. That is not a reason to discard hammers. Instead we need to think carefully about whether a hammer (intervention) is the most appropriate, or least bad, tool, and what is likely to happen if we use it. Having the capability may encourage the United States to intervene, but once we do it's not so easy to deal with the consequences, or even to walk away from them. That's what happened with Iraq. There were good or at least defensible and bad reasons for the United States to go into Iraq, but one reason was that we could. In part, the Obama administration is reacting to that by not going into Syria to overthrow its government. When we don't know how getting in would end up, we need to think about the chicken and the egg together. That means we either have to increase our capabilities or decrease the amount of intervention. Even if we have the capabilities doesn't mean we have to intervene.

The size of the defense program and the resulting budget should be set on the basis of our foreign policy and national security objectives and the level of risk that we are willing to take to meet them. That approach includes four variables. Each can be a matter of contentious judgment:

—What do we regard as vital or as lesser but important security interests?

—What level of risk are we willing to accept, depending on which category of interest?

—At a given level of expenditure, what military capabilities would be the most cost-effective way to achieve the acceptable set of risks?

—In the light of other demands and fiscal constraints, what level of military expenditures can we afford?

The process of balancing these criteria in the context of conflicting political interests and strategic views is what makes the secretary of defense post "the graveyard of political reputations." In chapters 7 and 8, I'll answer the questions posed above.

PUTTING THE U.S. DEFENSE BUDGET INTO PERSPECTIVE

The U.S. economy is so big that our defense budget is more than all our allies' defense budgets put together. In 1978 the defense budget totaled $116 billion; in 1979, $124.7 billion; in 1980, $141.9 billion, and in 1981, $175.5 billion.[13] (In 2012 dollars, these figures would be between two and two and a half times higher.) These rising amounts reflect high rates of inflation as well as the need to further strengthen and modernize our conventional forces neglected after the end of the Vietnam War.

FIGURE 2-I

Health, Education, and Defense Shares of U.S. GDP, 1960–2010

Shares of GDP (percent)

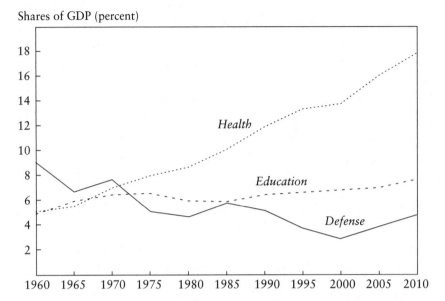

Source: Alan Sager, Professor of Health Policy and Management, Boston University School of Public Health. Data compiled from: Office of the Actuary, Centers for Medicare and Medicare Services; Bureau of Economic Affairs; SIPRI Military Expenditure Data Base, 2011, and National Center for Education Statistics.

What was produced through some of that funding also helped us respond to serious challenges in the Middle East and elsewhere.

There are several ways to put the current U.S. defense budget of about 5 percent of GDP (4.75 percent in the 2012 budget request including Afghanistan and Iraq) into perspective.[14] Of our Western allies, the British spend about 3 percent of their GDP on defense, the French about 2.5 percent. Counting items excluded from their official figures, the Chinese spend about 3 percent.[15] On the other hand, health care expenditures in the United States are 18.3 percent of GDP. Education expenditures are about 8 percent. Since 1980 the defense share of U.S. GDP has varied between 3 and 6.5 percent.[16] Of course, all of the defense costs, about half of the health care costs, and a much smaller fraction of education spending appear as expenditures in the federal budget. But I think of them as shares of the overall economy, defining our priorities, costs, and benefits (see figure 2-1).[17]

America is the only country that accepts a global security responsibility. No other country does. Implementing the recent United Nations Security Council resolution that resulted in the targeted allied bombing of Moammar Gaddafi's military strongholds could not have happened without U.S. capabilities and participation, even though the U.S. decision was late and unenthusiastic. At the level of that conflict, we can afford to continue assuming a similar role, even though (as was the case with Libya) our most important interests are not immediately involved.

MILITARY HEALTH CARE INCLUDED IN THE U.S. DEFENSE BUDGET

The U.S. defense budget includes things that most other countries' defense budgets don't. It takes care of active duty personnel, their families, and retirees. Altogether, personnel costs account for a third of the defense budget; the other two-thirds are for research and development, procurement, maintenance, operations, and military construction (bases). That two-thirds will shrink badly if we do not rein in the health care portion. The military TRICARE program provides health care for the military's uniformed personnel and retirees and eligible family members and survivors. More than 9 million people are eligible in 2012. That costs the Department of Defense about $51 billion in health care in 2012; the figure is projected to rise to $59 billion by 2016 and to $92 billion in 2030, nearly double the amount now.[18] We need to rein in the military health care budget or it will overwhelm us. It represents part of the much bigger national problem of health care costs. The issue here is how much of the military health care cost for those not active personnel should fall on the Department of Defense.

The health care portion of our defense budget now is about a third of what the entire (nominal) defense budget was when I was secretary of defense. That's not a fair comparison because the inflation factor makes the dollar worth only half of what it was in 1981. Still, the military health care portion is more than double our entire foreign aid budget of about $20 billion. Foreign aid is less than a fifth of 1 percent of our GDP.[19]

TRIMMING DEFENSE NOT A
QUICK FIX FOR THE ECONOMY

The U.S. GDP was roughly $15 trillion in 2011. Our current annual defense budget is nearly $700 billion, including the military health care portion and about $170 billion for the wars in Iraq and Afghanistan.[20] Defense is a substantial driver of the U.S. federal budget along with Social Security, Medicare, and Medicaid and the interest on the national debt. At about 4 percent of GDP (apart from war costs), defense is about half of what is called "discretionary government spending," the part of the budget that excludes the so-called entitlement programs. Those are not subject to the congressional appropriation process under the laws creating the entitlements and are spent automatically.

When we try to deal with America's budget deficits by cutting the defense budget, or by cutting the costs of health care in the civilian sector, we generally fail to deal with them in proportion to their respective weights in the economy. With defense (excluding the war costs) at about 4 percent of GDP compared with health care at about 18 percent, it is clear that trying to solve the overall problem of funding health care by slimming the defense budget is not the solution. As fiscal constraints tighten (and they should not in the near term), trade-offs between defense and social programs will become more pressing. That is demonstrated by the nature of the legislated sequestration.

Here's an interesting statistic: compared with European countries, the United States on average spends about 4 percent of GDP on defense (excluding war costs) while Europe spends 2 percent, yet we have far more than twice the military capability they do. That's because we're one country and more efficient and adept at defense than Western Europe. On the other hand, and in broad numbers, Europe spends about 9 percent of its GDP on health care and in addition funds a strong social safety net while the United States spends about 18 percent on a less effective health care system as measured by health outcomes and has a far weaker safety net. So which is the main problem: health care spending or defense spending?[21]

American health care has been tied to jobs since WWII because there was a freeze on pay then but not on benefits. It's been that way ever since. Another factor is that health care insurance and much of its provider structure is a for-profit industry in the United States while it is a nonprofit industry in Europe. The profits plus the extra paperwork and claim juggling among providers and insurers that go with the U.S. system probably add 20 percent or more to U.S. health care costs. Health care and defense together account for about 22 percent of the U.S. GDP, but about 12 percent in Europe, which means Europe has 10 percent more to give to other things, like the rest of its social safety net. With America's defense budget about one-fourth the size of our health care budget, the obvious solution to our health care expenditures is one we're not taking—namely, revising our health care system in the direction of greater efficiency.

DEFENSE A BLUNT TOOL FOR ECONOMIC STIMULUS

The defense budget can be a tool to stimulate the economy, though a blunt and inefficient one. In the short run, changes to the defense budget can't provide a quick fix, either by increasing the defense budget to act as a stimulus or by cutting it to reduce the deficit. Far quicker and more effective tools for stimulating the economy would be to change tax rates so people have more dollars to spend, or to extend unemployment insurance for the same reason, or to temporarily reduce contributions to Social Security, all of which President Obama has done recently.

As I write this in 2012, Secretary of Defense Leon Panetta is planning to cut back troop numbers almost to what they were before the Iraq and Afghanistan wars, slightly more than the level in 2001.[22] That's a savings, but not a major one, and even those personnel cuts take a couple of years to implement. Procurement actions, especially for major weapons systems, have an even slower effect. Sometimes the defense budget spins off its research and development into the civilian sector, which creates manufacturing jobs around new products or commercial adaptations for military ones, a very long-range effect.

THE MULTIPLIER IMPACT ON THE ECONOMY

In practice, the most important effect of the defense budget on the economy as a whole is its impact on overall fiscal and budgetary policy. All government spending stimulates the economy and does so in various ways. Like most other federal expenditures, the defense budget has a multiplier impact on the economy as recipients re-spend their defense income. At a party many years ago hosted by Charlie Schultze, former director of the Office of Management and Budget, Paul Volcker and I got into a discussion about the effect of defense spending on the rest of the economy. He seemed to think of defense as a cost and Social Security payments as a stimulant through the multiplier effect. They are both stimulants, although Social Security may have a larger multiplier effect than defense spending. In a hearing on defense appropriations during the late 1970s, Senator Warren Magnusson (D-Wash.) challenged my factual statement that Social Security represented bigger government expenditure than defense. He said: "But we spend Social Security on ourselves." What he missed is that when you're not fighting a war overseas, the great bulk of defense expenditures goes into the economy. We spend defense money on ourselves with second-order effects that stimulate the economy at large as well as serve its primary purpose of protecting national security.

For example, defense contractors use the money to build factories, planes, and tanks or to do research and development that often spins off military products into the commercial sector, enhancing it greatly. Classic examples include the Global Positioning System (GPS), purely a defense program originally, or the Internet, which was not created by Defense but is an outgrowth of the Defense Advanced Research Projects Agency's DARPANET. Now, of course, both GPS and the Internet have very wide commercial applications and have created entire industries.

Defense spending puts military bases into local communities and benefits their economies. Bases employ a lot of people who spend money directly into the economy just as Social Security recipients do. Some local people may not like the disruption when you open a base, but they're even more upset when you try to close one. It's interesting how politicians react. Legislators who vote against a program are suddenly for it if it's going to exist in their district. Is all that a reason to spend more on defense? Of course not, but it is something to keep in mind.

The question of which benefits the economy more is itself misstated. Social Security and defense spending each aim at an important national interest, though they compete for taxes and expenditures, as does any other national interest. The economic stimulation is of a second order and should not be a deciding factor in the allocation of expenditures between those two functions. Defense spending should be determined by what national security requires. As to the civilian byproducts of defense research and development, in principle if our government could foresee what civilian technology the country may need, the government should invest in that technology directly. But it can't; the government is poor at choosing what civilian technologies to support and how to support them. Spin-offs from defense are a useful byproduct, but no substitute for private sector innovation.

INVEST IN MY CONSTITUENTS, PLEASE

What defense spending surely stimulates is politics. Some elected representatives press for costly added or duplicate programs, casting them as insurance against failure when in fact local interests motivate them. When I was secretary of defense and the F-16 air force fighter aircraft was under development, some members of Congress asked us to develop two separate engines for the same plane. Some think it good to have such an alternative for two reasons: new engines sometimes have problems; and even if the first engine works well, having two engine contractors compete can force the price down. In fact, developing and procuring two different engines costs more in the long run. In my view, the decision to develop an alternative should be based on the amount of risk posed by innovations attempted in developing the preferred engine.

We completed development and began deployment of the F-16 during my tenure as secretary of defense. Pratt & Whitney had the contract for the engine but fell behind schedule. In 1979 GE offered to provide an alternative that we did not include in the defense budget.[23] If approved, GE would build the alternative engines in Lynn, Massachusetts. I got telephone calls from Tip O'Neill, then Speaker of the House, and Ted Kennedy. Both men represented Massachusetts and both men had voted against the F-16 program. They each called to say how important it was to fund an alternative engine for the aircraft they had voted against. Tip was shameless about it, Ted polite and slightly amused at his inconsistency.

The result was that as Pratt & Whitney busily fixed its engine, the GE alternative gradually overtook it in the fighter plane market. Year after year Pratt & Whitney and GE engaged in a competition dubbed "the great engine war" that culminated with GE winning 75 percent of the F-15 and F-16 engine markets.[24] The lesson learned is that congressional pressures, even when based on parochial interests, sometimes lead to good results. That's what the framers of the Constitution may have hoped for when they mandated separation of powers. I regard this case as an exception to the dysfunction more usually engendered by local interests.

More typical is the situation that occurred in 2011, and with a different outcome. An alternative GE engine was proposed for the F-35 Lightning II fighter aircraft. Defense Secretary Robert Gates believed that the plane was needed, but he called its alternative engine "an unnecessary and extravagant expense." GE asked the Senate to restore money for development of the engine in Ohio and Indiana, saying that early development had already cost it and Rolls Royce $3 billion so far and would require another $3 billion to complete. In a February 2011 vote in the House, all nine Republican freshmen from Ohio and Indiana, along with current Speaker of the House John Boehner from Ohio, voted to save the GE alternative engine though these same legislators had stated their commitment to reducing the federal budget and eliminating waste. In the end, the House voted 233 to 198 to cancel the alternate engine, which both the George W. Bush and the Obama administrations had tried to kill during the past five years.[25]

The applicable lesson here is that as our government haggles over the budget and scours it for areas where significant cuts can be made, the proper criterion for decisions is efficient funding of programs necessary for national security even as we eliminate waste. (In the case of the F-35 aircraft, 1,000 jobs involved in producing the alternate engine in Ohio were cut.)[26] Too many weapons systems suffer from cost overruns and duplications of effort mandated by political pressures. That plus contract delays can push costs past estimates by many billions of dollars, so it's important to weed out systems that don't work or are just not needed. What we should do is treat national security as national security and not as a jobs program. We don't want to go down the road of most European countries where defense production, personnel, and basing are little more than another part of a domestic employment program determined by local political factors.

KILL BAMBI

When I arrived in Washington in 1961 as director of Defense Research and Engineering, my predecessor, Herb York, used the word "baroque" to describe systems that are complex, prone to fail, and of limited utility except to their producers. He said it was important to rein in "baroque" weapons systems. One perennial candidate for the "go for baroque" pile was BAMBI, an air force program to shoot down ballistic missiles from orbiting satellites. A proposal for the program has been put forth in every decade since it was first introduced, including as part of Ronald Reagan's Star Wars. BAMBI was again pitched as an antiballistic missile program to the George W. Bush Defense Department. The problem with BAMBI, aside from its possible destabilizing effect on disarmament agreements, was (and for its descendants is) that it is complicated, expensive, and ineffective. It is a good thing that we've never done it.

Baroque systems infect more than defense thinking. Some of our current economic and fiscal problems stem from complex, failure-prone, and opaque systems in the banking industry. Complicated financial instruments of doubtful value to the economic system are deeply implicated in triggering and exacerbating the recent financial crisis and deep recession. It is a serious mistake to tinker with and protect such instruments and practices that produce baroque systems rather than deal with the insufficiency of demand that holds back business investment and growth. As America struggles to regain its economic footing, it's worthwhile to note lessons from the financial sector as well as from our military history.

SETTING LIMITS ON BUDGET EXPENDITURES

Beginning with the Nixon administration, Congress established ceilings on budget expenditure categories through a budget resolution. It set limits for each budget category as an instruction to the authorizing and appropriating committees. At one point in 1978, while those congressional budget committees debated various limits, I indicated my belief that Congress and its committees should act to support President Carter's budget requests. The chairman of the House Budget Committee, Robert Giaimo of Connecticut, had no problem with this. However, Majority Whip John Brademas (D-Ind.) convinced Speaker Tip O'Neill that Congress should make an issue of my statement. O'Neill told President Carter that my words amounted to an infringement on congressional prerogatives; the secretary of defense should not interfere with an internal consideration of how the budget resolution should instruct congressional committees.

The president called and asked me to "lay off." I suggested that for me to be seen as not supporting the president's budget was odd. But I came to understand that this was a tempest in a teapot triggered by significant disagreement between congressional committees about the appropriate numbers for defense. Several committee members I spoke to confided that the issue of whether the executive branch should interfere in congressional budget decisions was a fake argument. Some committee members just wanted me to keep quiet so they could pass what they wanted.

THE AUTHORITY INVESTED IN THE OFFICE

That brought home what may seem an uncomfortable truth: the separation of powers that is constitutionally mandated makes the American presidency a weak office. In fact, the president has far less intrinsic power over the government as a whole than the secretary of defense has within the Department of Defense. In practice, part of the secretary's authority rests on the fact that the military are accustomed to obeying orders from their own military superiors. Habits carry over. In principle the military accepts civilian authority, though that acceptance can be somewhat diluted. Within a military service, the chief of staff can, in a pinch, get almost anything done that he wants. The degree to which a Service Secretary can do the same depends largely on his personal relationship with the chief of staff and other military officers.

By and large, the president has *more* control over factors *outside* the federal government than a CEO has over factors external to his company. The president has *less* control over the government, especially over the other two branches, than the CEO has over his company. Some individuals have managed stronger presidencies, but the office itself doesn't automatically enable that. A CEO of a private corporation who aspires to become a U.S. president would have a terrible time dealing with far less authority than he is accustomed to in the private sector.

Harry Truman once famously remarked that Ike would have a terrible time as president because as a general he was used to being in charge of armies. Truman warned that Ike would say, "Do this and do that" and nothing would happen. Truman may have underestimated what

Eisenhower was able to do as president, but Truman was essentially right. A president can say, "Do this," but a lot of other people can say "no." Even on foreign policy, an American president's authority is less than that of a French president.

STAY FOCUSED ON THE PROGRAM

The moral of this chapter is that cohesion and continuity are essential to planning for what we want our military capability to be in the long run. The secretary of defense makes budget recommendations accordingly. Meanwhile our country reckons with problems that drive the morning's headlines and usurp the focus from major long-range objectives. The importance of keeping focused may sound like a banal lesson, but it's especially important now given a fractious Congress, faster news cycles, upheavals in the Middle East, the depletion of natural resources, and climate change. All of this affects national well-being and security in a future not far off.

PIVOTAL POINTS FOR NATIONAL SECURITY

When I became DDRE, I believed that the strategic nuclear balance was the pivotal point for national defense. And that was correct in the late 1950s when our country thought itself to be in a "missile gap" with the Soviet Union, as well as in an adverse balance in conventional forces. I concluded that we would need to address both of these challenges through technology. In the case of the conventional force balance, it made sense to work on technology and weapons systems in close cooperation with our European allies. The United States had instituted what was called the Mutual Weapons Development Program. For example, we funded the development of an engine in Britain for the Harrier aircraft, a plane with vertical takeoff and landing that we eventually introduced to our own forces.[27] Many people have seen those aircraft at air shows.

As DDRE, I met my "armaments director" counterparts in Europe and found that some of their military-industrial complexes were disproportionately large compared with their militaries. Their armaments industries relied then, as now, on exports to keep them going far more than those of the United States do. We encouraged the Norwegians to develop a short-range missile that could be fired from a small ship, and they did. Projects in small scale worked. But the United States was unable to bring Europeans together to rationalize their industry and share the work to enable larger-scale activities. That still is far from accomplished, though they have made some progress in the case of military aircraft.

Using technology to address disparities with the Soviet Union guided my government service through the 1960s and continued to be a central element through the 1970s. In fact, the United States did maintain nuclear deterrence through our technology. We also worked to offset the Soviet advantage in the size of conventional forces through a combination of technology and training at all levels of our forces. The Soviet military had a top-down approach; our forces emphasized initiative in our junior and noncommissioned officers.

Today, as the United States confronts irregular and unsophisticated forces like the Taliban and terrorists like al Qaeda, technology still plays a large part, as illustrated by our use of drones. So does troop training. However, now we're even more dependent on intelligence, surveillance, and reconnaissance and on the greater roles played by nonmilitary activities. Help to the local civilian structure and economic development in contested areas must function in alignment with our military to support local governments against insurgents. If all those elements don't work in harmony, it doesn't matter how good our technology is, or how big our military. We're now dependent on how well the State Department and other U.S. agencies operate together against terrorism (let alone in the debatable activity of nation building) with the military. Multiple levels of government and every level of human interaction are in play, which makes for a more complicated universe.

Stripes and Bright Stars

3

HOW THE TEAM AT THE TOP
AFFECTS SECURITY POLICY

A joke goes that when a new secretary of defense takes office he finds three envelopes in his desk that were left by his predecessor. They're to be opened when he gets into trouble. There's a crisis. The new secretary of defense opens the first envelope. The letter inside says: "Blame the other political party." And he does. There's another crisis a year later. He opens the second envelope. Its letter says: "Blame the media." A third crisis happens. He opens the last envelope. That letter says: "Prepare three envelopes."

Friends come and go in Washington; enemies accumulate. Four years is enough time for them to accumulate. For defense secretaries who stayed more than four years (Robert McNamara, Caspar Weinberger, and Donald Rumsfeld each stayed six years or more), the job generally ended badly. At the other end of the spectrum, half the secretaries of defense held office fewer than two years, which is too little time to get much done. Mel Laird stayed four years as secretary of defense and managed to come through fairly well. Charlie Wilson stayed a little longer than four years and was pushed out after the Soviet Union's *Sputnik* was successfully launched in 1957. I stayed all four years of Carter's presidency, one of few of his cabinet-level officials to do so.

Some say my longevity was a result of my previous experience and my lack of interest in high visibility. I am by nature an introvert and sought to solve problems I had with others in private. During my last two years in office I had little choice but to become more visible, trying to speak effectively in support of the administration's national security policies. That inevitably eroded my public image of technocratic nonpartisanship. I admit that the increasing political polarization of the subsequent three decades has not left me unaffected. Remaining a Democrat, I have a lower opinion of both parties.

HOW CARTER CHOSE HIS CABINET

President-elect Carter made a thorough process of choosing his cabinet officers. He considered several potential candidates for each job and invited them to Georgia, either to his home or to the governor's office in Atlanta, and interviewed them. His list included people whom he had met before, but also many he had not. My appointment as secretary of defense began with a series of interviews Carter held at Pond House on his farm. My wife, Colene, and I were at a conference in Aspen, Colorado, in July 1976 when I received a call saying that Jimmy Carter wanted to convene a meeting of national security advisers to his campaign. I was one. It was clear to me that this was to be more than just a meeting on issues; Carter was thinking about who might join his administration if he were elected. Before the "defense meeting"—I knew the other half dozen people there—Carter had held a meeting with a group of other people on the topic of foreign policy.

That autumn, Carter asked me to come to Atlanta for an individual meeting at the governor's mansion. He asked me how I would work with other people in his administration without reference to what job he might offer. His approach to assembling his team was more methodical than that of most presidents. He went to great pains to ask potential candidates whether they thought they could get along with each other. Of course, they all said they could. He also wanted to get an idea of the views of the people he was considering. I believe he felt that whatever differences he saw from his detailed interviews, and he did see them, he could manage. It is appropriate for a president to want a variety of views, but there is a limit to the range.

During this process, I remembered that back in 1967 when I was air force secretary, Defense Secretary McNamara had come up to my office on the fourth floor of the Pentagon. Cyrus Vance had just left as deputy secretary of defense. McNamara said to me: "I really want to make you deputy secretary of defense with the idea that you might later succeed me. But I have to make Paul Nitze deputy secretary because he will leave otherwise. I want you to think about moving over to be assistant secretary of defense for international security affairs because that would help prepare you."

That position was lower in protocol rank than secretary of the air force, but more involved in the diplomatic and policy issues (although in an advisory role) than any Service Secretary. That was the first time the thought of becoming defense secretary had ever entered my mind. I went to see Vance who was in the hospital. He had left his job partly because he was having severe back trouble. He encouraged me to make the move. I decided not to; I was happy where I was, and the future seemed too iffy. Lyndon Johnson might not get reelected. Had I accepted the position, I would have been far more involved in the endgame of the Vietnam War during the Johnson administration, and advising on negotiations with the North Vietnamese and related domestic political issues. That would have made me more prepared to be secretary of defense, but perhaps less likely to get the job. You never know.

In the end Paul Nitze didn't make it into the Carter administration because of his performance at the Pond House interviews of defense advisers. As Carter continued to ponder his choices for cabinet officers, he telephoned me about what jobs I would be willing to take. He asked if I'd be willing to be a deputy secretary. I said: "Only for Vance. Not for anybody else." I'd known Vance fifteen years by that time. I told Carter I thought it would be inappropriate to have both Vance and me at State, since we'd both come out of Defense.

Early that December, after Vance had been selected to be secretary of state and was assembling his team, he said to me: "You ought to start thinking about who you'd take with you if you're picked." The position of secretary of defense was still open. Just before Christmas, Carter offered it to me. That very week I flew to Atlanta, stopping in Houston to get to know Charles W. Duncan Jr. whom Carter wanted as deputy secretary of defense. The president announced our appointments the next day with both of us present.

When Carter was sworn in on January 20, 1977, I was sworn in the same day at the Pentagon in an unusual sequence of events (the tag on the back of my chair from the Cabinet Room mistakenly says January

23). The plan was to swear in on the following Sunday all cabinet members who had received Senate confirmation. That gave the Senate time to act. In my case they had acted immediately following President Carter's inauguration. It's easy to forget now, but the Cold War was hot then, hot enough to keep the previous secretary of defense in office until the new one was sworn in, as happened again when I left office four years later. The previous secretary of defense was Donald Rumsfeld. I learned that my special assistant, John Kester, called the White House and asked: "Do you really want Rumsfeld with his finger on the nuclear button any longer?" Carter did not. So I was sworn in on the 20th of January and again at the White House on the 23rd.

At the beginning of an administration, the new secretary of state usually is formally commissioned into office before any other cabinet members and countersigns their commissions after the new president signs them. (Curiously, the secretary of state also receives a president's resignation. In fact, the Spiro Agnew and Richard Nixon resignation letters were submitted to Henry Kissinger!) The relevant cabinet secretary then countersigns the commissions of lower-ranking confirmed officials in the department. The challenge is that somebody has to countersign the new secretary of state's commission, thereby formally putting him or her into office. (In the famous case of *Marbury* v. *Madison,* the new secretary of state, James Madison, refused to sign the commission of William Marbury, whom President John Adams had tried to appoint to a judicial office in the last hours of his administration.) Walt Slocombe relates that in 1993, on the morning of Bill Clinton's inauguration, he witnessed Acting Secretary of State Frank Wisner wryly asking if he would "stay secretary of state forever" if he refused to sign Warren Christopher's commission.

Though long tradition dictates the secretary of state to be sworn in at the beginning of an administration, the decision to have me in place as soon as possible took precedence. The State Department was unhappy that the tradition would be broken and dragged its feet for several hours. In the end, Under Secretary for Political Affairs Philip Habib, as acting secretary of state, signed my commission shortly after the president was sworn in at the Capitol. That unusual beginning taught me something about relationships among the different departments. It was a lesson that would continue as Defense and State worked together over the next four years.

CABINET OFFICIALS AND WHITE HOUSE STAFF

When it came time to staff the White House, Carter relied almost entirely on individuals who had served with him in Georgia while he was governor or on people who had been part of his campaign. In that, he resembled most presidents before and after him. Presidents bring staff that have served them before or have helped elect them and then employ them on the White House staff, especially those who advised on domestic issues. Presidents tend to choose as heads of cabinet departments and agencies people from outside the campaign. This practice has advantages and disadvantages. The president knows and trusts former campaign staff and associates. On the other hand, getting elected is not the same thing as governing. A certain tension exists between the White House staff ("us") and various cabinet officers ("them") that often results in problems. When a president gets into trouble, and they all do, he pulls his staff closer. They circle the wagons. The operating divisions of the government, including cabinet officers, are left more and more on the outside. The tension between them and White House staff can increase as the time for the next election comes around.

Carter was very active and involved in his administration's decisions; in the end he made them himself. He did not foresee and could not solve the fractious relationship that existed between Cyrus Vance, his secretary of state, and his national security adviser, Zbigniew Brzezinski. It undermined the Carter national security policy. Zbig was then a brash, ingenuous, and opinionated newcomer to a senior government office, rather than the elder statesman he is now thirty-five years later. He saw himself as a global thinker and mastermind who could run the State Department and the Defense Department better than any other two people could. Fortunately, the Defense Department was too big for him to try. It was the fundamentals of grand strategy and foreign policy that interested him and not the bread and butter issues of management and technology specific to defense.

Cy Vance fit the traditional mold of secretaries of state. He had deep roots in the New York legal establishment with previous experience at senior levels of government, specifically in the Defense Department. Apart from the fact that he was a personal friend who had been my senior in the McNamara Pentagon, he was well known and deservedly well liked in both the executive branch and in Congress. He had a lawyerly talent for negotiation. At the same time he proved to be defensive of the State Department's leading role in international affairs.

I took care to avoid the arguments that increasingly characterized foreign policy disagreements between Vance and Brzezinski. They were at sword's point from day one. I concluded that two secretaries of state were more than enough. A third was not needed. And I was more than busy running the Defense Department. Apart from defense programs, I also worked on ensuring support within the Defense Department for presidential foreign policy decisions. For example, support from the Joint Chiefs of Staff was instrumental in getting congressional approval for actions like the Panama Canal Treaties and the SALT II agreement.

The personal relations and policy views of the senior national security officials in an administration have a great effect on whether the team operates smoothly and effectively. The willingness and ability of the president to participate and impose his own stamp on foreign and security policy is a necessary requirement; it's not always sufficient. What President Carter may have missed during his selection process is that if the policy views of people differ and their personalities don't mesh, their policy differences become magnified. Add personal rivalry and things go over the edge.

As for me, I had my differences with Stan Turner at the CIA and occasionally with Brzezinski, and quite often with Vance on matters of strategic arms negotiations. Cy and I both wanted an agreement on strategic arms limitation with the Soviet Union, but there were things I was determined *to not have* in the agreement and things I was equally determined *to have* included. From Vance's point of view at State, the balance between getting an agreement and getting one that was adequately favorable to America was different from what I needed from my point of view at Defense. That pulled us a little apart, but our personal relations remained very good.

For example, when an assistant secretary of state for African affairs called the military operations center and told them to move an aircraft carrier because the secretary of state was in charge of what to do about refugees in Kenya, the military operations center called me. I said: "Don't pay any attention to that request" and complained to Vance. There was no problem.

The lesson learned is to have disagreements with cabinet-level colleagues only in private. That's hard to do unless others adopt the same attitude. If only the other side of an argument gets out, it's unlikely you'll refrain from going public if that restraint causes you to lose on the issue.

OTHER ADMINISTRATIONS, OTHER TEAM SPIRITS

Other administrations have displayed as much or more internal conflict than was present in the Carter administration. An exception was George H. W. Bush's national security team. It was especially effective with James Baker at State, Dick Cheney (before his personality transformation) at Defense, and Brent Scowcroft as national security adviser. Their personal relations and their relationships with the president seemed, at least as seen from the outside, to be outstanding. Each person was extremely competent and none was a prima donna. All were experienced in government at the national level and knew each other well.

Relations among security advisers in the Reagan administration were turbulent, partly because the national security adviser's role kept changing. At the beginning, the position was subordinated to a political assistant, Edwin Meese, and the national security adviser reported to him. Subsequently, a string of successors ran into difficulties of one kind or another (including legal), but reported directly to the president. At the very end of the Reagan administration, two very effective national security advisers were in place, first Frank Carlucci and then Colin Powell.

From the start of the Reagan administration, Secretary of State Alexander Haig and Defense Secretary Casper Weinberger did not get along. There was the famous incident of Haig taking the microphone after the attempted assassination of the president and announcing that he was in charge at the White House, presumably mistaking the order of succession to the presidency. Haig was apparently under the misapprehension that the secretary of state was next in line after the vice president (George H. W. Bush was on an aircraft at the time), which was true back in the nineteenth and early twentieth centuries, but untrue at the time. The Speaker of the House was next in line of succession.

Haig's confusion was not the main cause of his difficulty with Weinberger. Each sought primacy in national security affairs, especially when the national security adviser's spot had been downgraded in the White House hierarchy. Haig left involuntarily and was replaced by George Schultz, who had served in the Nixon administration with Weinberger and had known him well when both were senior executives at the Bechtel Group of Companies in California. (Schultz was the company's president and a director, Weinberger its vice president and general counsel, but Steve Bechtel was actually in charge.) Their rivalry in corporate life carried over into the Reagan cabinet, where they differed on almost everything, which made things difficult and complicated. Schultz was not as viscerally anti-Soviet as Weinberger, yet more willing to advocate the use of force in other cases. Weinberger was very much in the extreme Cold War mode, but reluctant to use force. Their different approaches magnified their personal rivalry.

More recently, George W. Bush's first term saw the rest of his national security team notoriously in conflict with Colin Powell at State, making him the odd person out while Defense Secretary Rumsfeld ran his own foreign policy. Differences in personal style amplified their policy differences and the differences in approach natural to State and Defense. National Security Adviser Condoleezza Rice tried to produce a smoother operation without success.

THE CARTER ADMINISTRATION BEGINS

The Carter administration opened with a notebook of hundreds of items to study, consider, and explore so that we could make recommendations concerning them. Brzezinski presumably had helped Carter prepare the national security items that involved both Defense and State, and in some cases other agencies. The notebook launched a series of interagency studies on topics ranging from the relatively trivial—how many generals were necessary—to the very important, such as what size forces the country needed. Since the topics were not well prioritized and the list was long, execution was problematic. Infighting ensued, especially between Brzezinski and Vance over which office would chair which studies and who would make the primary inputs.

The degree of friction depended on which office prevailed. Sometimes the interagency reviews were chaired by Brzezinski's office, sometimes by Vance's, and occasionally by mine. The resulting meetings and papers setting forth the positions and recommendations of the participating agencies fed into presidential decision memos. Of course, what the president thought ultimately determined the outcome. Because Brzezinski was closest to him, Zbig may have had the most influence, especially in the cases where there was disagreement among other advisers. I found that Zbig always included the written positions of the rest of us in what he sent to the president. Carter, given his habit, indeed his obsession of wanting to know as much as possible about a subject before making a decision, invariably read them all before deciding.

The process of gaining information for recommendations depended on how well the bureaucracy in each agency functioned as it did its part of the analysis, and how thoroughly its staff presented their findings to the head of its agency. Because my staff was bigger and at least as competent as the staff of the other offices, I could be very organized about what I wanted and said. I usually knew my brief pretty well. That was partly because the Defense Department has the most horses and is the best organized. The national security adviser's staff is small and elite. That combination can make it, and in the case of Brzezinski's office did make it, quite effective.

State has more people and many more in its most senior bureaucracy than the national security adviser's office, and almost as many as in the defense secretary's office. But State suffers from being process oriented, meaning it's less likely to come up with action-oriented positions. Defense is a "take that hill" organization able to get its way often. People who are used to getting things done tend to have more influence. When it came to decisions on defense programs, the Defense Department's size and detailed knowledge usually carried the day.

In the end, the Carter notebook of tasks had a modest effect on defense programs. It had more effect when a defense program might adversely (or less often, favorably) affect some broader national security interest. Brzezinski, Vance, and I held Thursday luncheon meetings that rotated among our offices. We each brought a set of points we wanted to discuss along with the outcomes desired. That was an efficient venue where we accomplished a lot.

SETTING UP MY DEPARTMENT OF DEFENSE

Defense secretaries both before and after me who had been members of Congress typically brought their senior congressional aides along with them. They relied on their staffers and often ignored the experienced military and civilian personnel in the Defense Department. The results had not always been good. I wanted a mixture of Pentagon insiders and outsiders. Some would be people I knew and had worked with well. I also wanted people I did not know and whose skills would be complementary.

I chose my team carefully. I relied on the opinions of people I trusted to select people I did not know and conducted interviews with the help of Charles Duncan. We clicked right from the beginning. He had been president of Coca-Cola after much experience running large parts of that organization. Before meeting him I had asked two Caltech trustees who knew him well to tell me about him. They had high praise; it turned out to be fully deserved. During our association in the Defense Department and afterward I trusted his judgment. His calm demeanor, ability to evaluate people, and persistence despite obstruction proved invaluable. His skills compensated for my occasional impatience and habit of revealing my reactions through my facial expressions.

We worked so closely together that he was in effect my alter ego, and that was vital. The size and complexity of the Defense Department and its interactions with the White House and the rest of the executive branch, Congress, and even the courts, are daunting. The secretary of defense and his deputy must agree on all key issues and approaches so that the deputy can make decisions as needed. I had that kind of close cooperation with Charles Duncan. I could count on him to make decisions identical, or close enough, to what I would have done, and would not have overruled a decision he made had we disagreed. The value of a perceived alter ego is too important. We could not be played off against each other, as had sometimes happened in previous administrations. We became and remain close friends.

William Perry was my first choice for undersecretary for research and engineering. He said no. I considered other people, and then said to myself, why settle for fourth or sixth best? Go back to Perry and persuade him to take the job. I told Perry the story of Herb York's experience. York (Livermore Lab's first director and my mentor) had considered leaving the lab for an aerospace company, Ramo-Wooldridge, which oversaw the air force's ballistic missile program.[1] York's mentor, Ernest Lawrence, had strongly discouraged him. But when York was offered a senior post in the Defense Department, Lawrence told him to accept. "You'll never regret it," he said.

When I was offered the research and engineering post in the Defense Department, Herb York gave me that same advice: "You'll have a fascinating time, you'll grow, and no matter what your ambition is now, when you leave your ambitions will be at a higher level, and you'll be able to achieve them." I had needed no persuading. I told Bill Perry, "That's good advice for you, too." I got our friend-in-common Gene Fubini to work on him as well. Bill came aboard and neither of us can recall a better professional decision by either of us. Bill and I thought enough alike that our frequent consultations usually made directives from me unnecessary. He later served with distinction as defense secretary himself from 1994 to 1997. The lesson learned from persuading him to join my team is don't take no for an answer.

I relied on Bill greatly for matters of weapons systems and technology. Our close and fruitful collaboration resulted in the development of a series of ballistic and cruise missiles for the navy and air force, ground-force combat systems, precision-guided munitions, and intelligence and reconnaissance capabilities. The intelligence, surveillance, and reconnaissance and command communication and control that link them provide strategic information and battlefield awareness to headquarters and combat units. We also launched the GPS program whose satellites give military operations the capability to hit targets precisely. When Bill and I left office, I was still arguing with the Office of Management and Budget that the three GPS satellites we had put into the sky were not enough. They thought it was, but I wanted a dozen. There are now twenty-four.[2]

Having been an air force Service Secretary, I wanted military Service Secretaries to be more than a mouthpiece for their particular military branch. As a result, Service Secretaries like Navy Secretary (later Deputy Secretary of Defense) Graham Claytor, who could support his service but also make decisions on a broader national security basis, got a lot of my approvals of his recommendations. They were included in my policy determinations.

I put substantial responsibility for strategy and military planning on Bob Komer, my assistant for NATO. "Blowtorch Bob" had been ambassador to Turkey and had a reputation as a hard driver. He later succeeded Stanley Resor as undersecretary of defense for policy.[3] The secretary of defense needs some sort of operations group to work closely with the Joint Staff, which serves the Joint Chiefs. It is up to the undersecretary for policy to work that out with the Joint Staff in a way that enables the chairman and the secretary of defense to function smoothly. I tasked many of the broader issues of national security and relations with foreign countries to Komer and David McGiffert, assistant secretary of defense for international security affairs. Their assistants, Walter Slocombe and Lynn Davis, deftly handled the interagency process with State and the National Security Council staff. Later, each served with distinction during the Clinton administration, Walt as undersecretary of defense and Lynn as undersecretary of state.

John White, who had been the RAND Corporation's vice president, took on the logistics and manpower role as my assistant secretary of defense before becoming deputy director of the Office of Management and Budget in the Carter administration, and later in the Clinton administration as a deputy secretary of defense. His management skills and careful judgment have served each post well.

I hadn't known Tom Ross, who had headed the *Chicago Sun-Times* bureau in Washington, D.C. He became my assistant secretary for public affairs and kept me from many stumbles. Jack Stempler, who had been my assistant for congressional relations when I was air force secretary, resumed that role for me in the Defense Department and similarly helped keep me out of trouble on Capitol Hill.

The military services weighed in through the Service Secretaries and the Joint Chiefs. On force structure and program issues, which were major arguments between the military services and Office of the Secretary of Defense (OSD), the focal point was the Office of Program Analysis and Evaluation (PA&E) headed by Russ Murray. He had served in that organization during McNamara's time as secretary of defense. I decided arguments in favor of the military services about 85 percent of the time, though they best remember when I didn't.

The competition from PA&E greatly improved the military services' own analyses, proposals, and recommendations. PA&E loses influence when Republican administrations take office, announce big defense build-ups, and defer to service aspirations. More thoughtful defense secretaries like Mel Laird think better of PA&E and eventually restore its influence. The oscillation has not been helpful.

I double-hatted two assistant secretary positions to work their own shop and to act as deputies to their undersecretaries of defense. Rather than create more layers of responsibility, each of the assistant secretaries functioned, or was supposed to, as the alter ego of his undersecretary. At the same time, I reduced the number of people reporting directly to me from thirty to twenty. When you have thirty people reporting to the secretary of defense, many of them don't really report to anybody. I eliminated some positions and realigned others so more people reported to Charles Duncan. He had the managerial capability and force of personality to handle that.

STREAMLINING TO SPEED DECISIONS

I tried to create clear lines of reporting with enough military and civilian people around me I trusted so I didn't have to deal with all the details myself. I am a detail person, so I had to minimize that temptation, though it wasn't wholly avoided. I reorganized the Office of the Secretary of Defense to have fewer direct reports and more done at a lower level, especially for less critical items.[4] I adopted a practice of sometimes dealing directly at lower levels when an issue required it, while informing intermediate-level officers. I wasn't a hall-walker (except for exercise), though on occasion I would show up unannounced at people's offices to ask questions if a matter's urgency required that. I wanted others to feel they could just as easily come to me for urgent matters without an appointment.

CUT 576 POSITIONS

Early in 1978 I took action to trim the meta-bureaucracy in the OSD and in incremental steps pared 576 positions. That reflected a White House initiative to trim the headquarters budget. Some positions were reassigned to other Defense Department agencies; some positions were eliminated. Right from the beginning, I had clarified roles within the OSD, made a single deputy secretary of defense position from two former ones, and renamed the director of Defense Research and Engineering (the position of DDRE that I once held) as undersecretary for research and engineering, increasing his responsibilities beyond that scope.

Ideally, the relationship of the defense secretary with the president involves close cooperation and agreement on issues, as is the case with the secretary and deputy secretary of defense, although it is never as close as being an "alter ego." During the existential dangers of the Cold War, I felt it critical that there be no public differences—no daylight—between

President Carter and me on his decisions, though at times my interrogators in Congress tried hard to get me to express disagreement with some presidential decisions. On the rare occasions I disagreed with the president, I did not indicate it and always explained and justified his decisions in public and to Congress.

Streamlining the OSD enabled my office to make immediate decisions on Soviet and other world events and crises without short-circuiting a parallel system for longer-range planning and projects. I've been asked how a secretary of defense keeps details of various crises clear. My office started each day with the Legislative Affairs and Public Affairs (LAPA) meeting. I met daily with the chairman of the Joint Chiefs and also held meetings I'd scheduled into the calendar for longer-range projects, though any of those could be displaced by a crisis. The LAPA meetings let me get started on an immediate crisis, formulate some course of action, and then hand off details to someone who would deal with the crisis minute by minute, reporting back to me as necessary. That let us make decisions quickly if need be.

HEARING AND COORDINATING
ADVICE FROM THE MILITARY

To receive critical advice from military leadership, my deputy and I met almost every week with the Joint Chiefs of Staff in their conference room known as "the tank." We discussed current and specific problems, long-range defense policy, and any other topics they or I wished to bring up. These military professionals substantially influenced my views but were not the only inputs to my judgments. My own staff in OSD and other parts of the executive branch, not to mention Congress, had views of their own.

In addition to holding consultations with the chairman and the other Chiefs, I established regular and close interaction with the senior military leaders next in the statutory chain of command, the commanders-in-chief (the CINCS, later renamed combat commanders by Don Rumsfeld, who apparently thought there would be confusion with the president's designation as commander-in-chief of all the armed forces) of the eight Unified and Specified Commands, to take full advantage of that important source of military advice. While traveling inside or outside the country,

I met with CINCs some twenty-six times to pinpoint specific problems and to probe more deeply into matters raised in their quarterly reports. I instituted the requirement for those reports to gain the CINCs' judgments on what they needed to fulfill their military missions and I encouraged their candid comments.

MAIN MANAGEMENT TOOLS

In setting up my office at the Department of Defense, I used two main management control tools. One got people's attention right away; I insisted on making a few decisions soon after taking office. One example was accelerating U.S. procurement of AWACs (Airborne Warning and Control System) aircraft and urging NATO to buy some. This, like other decisions I made, was not arbitrary, but well justified. I read relevant material, talked to people, and asked questions. Then I made my decisions. It was easiest for me to exercise quick influence over military hardware, a matter I had come to know well. I made it very clear that I knew something about it.

The second tool was to select staff people who knew things I didn't, and who could assemble information and produce a tentative set of policies or programs with alternatives for my decisions. I did that heavily in the "policy" area, which really meant operations and international affairs. I'm not a great believer in ad hoc committees of outsiders. I preferred to rely on a few experienced outsiders I knew well and trusted for advice. I did use one advisory board, the Defense Science Board, and broadened it to include retired military not necessarily oriented toward technology. The goal was to introduce an operational element into its considerations.

Both of these management tools worked well. I was able to choose a few things I thought important and get them done. That's not to say there weren't conflicting pressures from contractors, the military services, Congress, and political influences within the administration. I found that most individual members of Congress did not then regard themselves in as preeminent a role on military hardware decisions as in policy arenas. Their staffs and constituents and their constituents' companies took a more detailed interest in weapons systems and military bases, pressing their views on their congressional representatives. Most members of Congress, absent the need for campaign funding and reelection, might have preferred to concentrate on issues of public policy, domestic and international. But campaign funding needs exist, as their staffers reminded them.

Congressional members told me when they wanted aircraft for international trips, and preferably aircraft with windows, though some converted tanker planes without them had been outfitted for executive travel. One of the most adamant in this regard was Majority Whip John Brademas, who was also one of the most vocal critics of the Department of Defense and what he termed its "wasteful spending."

The senior military are jealous of their prerogatives, especially if they feel the secretary of defense lacks professional expertise in military strategy (which is usually the case) or in weapons of war. They will resist the secretary's use of his own staff regarding operational matters, though the secretary is by law second only to the president in the chain of command. I went to great lengths to organize and staff my office to minimize that resistance.

On issues that involved political and diplomatic as well as military factors, the senior civilian leadership of my Defense Department had a great deal of experience, but some senior military officers did as well. The Joint Chiefs understood that I was very experienced in quasi-military matters and respected my judgment despite my not being a military professional. Because I spent a few hours most weeks meeting with the Joint Chiefs of Staff as a group, they came to regard me as somebody with whom they would at least level even if they didn't always agree with me, and they would accept the decisions I made.

I invariably sought advice from the successive chairmen of the Joint Chiefs and on occasion from their special assistants. One of the latter was Willie Y. Smith, who had been my military assistant when I was secretary of the air force. I also turned to my military assistants, Vice Admirals Staser Holcomb and then Thor Hanson of the navy, and to their successor, General Carl Smith of the air force. I inherited Holcomb from Don Rumsfeld. I felt it important to hold over on my staff someone from the previous administration. Subsequently, the military services offered very good people for my staff.

I GAVE A BIG PUSH TO JOINTNESS

The National Security Act of 1958 formulated by President Dwight D. Eisenhower had emphasized the need to focus on joint operations.

An army man himself, Ike did not change the Title 10 functions of the Military Department Services (under the civilian Service Secretaries) to "recruit, organize, supply and train" forces. But the act made those powers subject to the "authority, direction and control" of the secretary of defense, and it set the stage for joint operations under single unified and specified commanders. Eisenhower's unique combination of presidential authority and personal military history enabled him to override the parochial interests opposing the act's changes. No single subsequent step has been as consequential.

Jointness describes how units from the air force, army, navy, and marines function together in combined organizations. By extension, it can even include elements from beyond the armed forces like civilian infrastructure experts and diplomats, or even elements from allied nations. I wanted to pursue jointness and made it one of my major initiatives. I didn't do it for the sole purpose of involving all services. That could be counterproductive. I did it because most situations call for various kinds of capabilities, expertise, and experience, and many call for a combination not found in a single service.

When I came to office, there was a long way to go to enable military units from different services to train together and operate seamlessly as a team. I wanted to make that kind of jointness not only a reality, but also a career path. In 1977 the epitome of jointness was the Joint Staff, which reported to the Joint Chiefs, not to the chairman. Service on the Joint Staff was not a route to promotion except for a few positions near the top—Joint Staff director and director of operations, three-star positions. Unit and service loyalty appropriate at junior officer levels did little to foster the broader understanding of joint military operations.

As a result, the most promising junior officers were seldom assigned to the Joint Staff and their service in Unified Commands was often a dead end. With no career path for joint service, the best and the brightest did not choose it. The Marine Corps did not send its best people to the National War College where officers on the fast track studied joint service issues. No marine headed any Unified Command.

I determined to create a jointness career path in part because of reasons that began when I was DDRE in the early 1960s. My job was to advise the secretary of defense on major weapons systems and their acquisition. Two weapons systems under consideration were especially contentious;

one dealt with joint use. The struggle over those systems taught me how each branch of the military inspired its most able officers to lead its service, yet restricted their view on broader national security needs.[5]

The two weapons systems under consideration were the Air Force B-70 bomber and the TFX Joint Air Force Strike and Navy Fleet Air Defense fighter. Secretary of Defense McNamara canceled the B-70 and pushed hard for the joint TFX. The air force tried to revive the B-70 aircraft by recasting it as a vehicle that could seek out and destroy movable targets. That campaign, which failed, was led by Air Force Chief of Staff Curtis LeMay. He assigned the task of selling the program in the Pentagon and Congress to Colonel David Jones, a bomber pilot who accumulated 300 hours on missions over North Korea and who served as vice commander of the Seventh Air Force, and later as LeMay's executive officer in the Pentagon.[6]

The navy fought equally hard to break out of the joint TFX program and create its own separate design. After a bruising two-year battle, the navy succeeded. Chief of Naval Operations George Anderson led that opposition to McNamara's decision along with Captain Ike Kidd. Kidd was Anderson's executive officer; his father was an admiral who had been killed in the Japanese attack on Pearl Harbor. Both Jones and Kidd were tough, intelligent, and dedicated to their respective services. I had strong adversarial interactions with each of them as I defended McNamara's decisions, with which I strongly agreed. At the same time, both men impressed me as very able and intelligent.

Fifteen years later, when I was secretary of defense, the Joint Chiefs chairman, General George Brown of the air force, became fatally ill with cancer. I had to decide whom to recommend to President Carter as Brown's successor. I looked at both Jones and Kidd for the job of chairman of the Joint Chiefs. There were several other candidates.

Army officers thought the chairmanship should cycle to their chief of staff, General Bernard Rogers, because the two previous occupants had come from the navy and the air force. Al Haig's hat was also in the ring. He had served as supreme allied commander, Europe (SACEUR), leading NATO and U.S. European commands. His service as Nixon's White House chief of staff complicated his candidacy, especially after he described himself as "acting president" during those final days of Nixon's term. Except for Eisenhower's 1953 choice of Admiral Arthur Radford, then commander of the U.S. forces in the Pacific, to be the chairman of the Joint Chiefs, the position had always gone to one of its sitting or retired members.

I thought that unified and specified commanders, including Haig, ought to be eligible. In the end, I narrowed the pool of choices to Jones and Kidd, two men I had come to know well in the previous two years. By that time Jones was chief of staff of the air force after service as commander of U.S. air forces in Europe. Admiral Kidd headed the NATO Atlantic Command as supreme allied commander (SACLANT) and the U.S. Atlantic Command, which included forces from each of the services.

I selected Jones. I based my decision on the centrality of the arms competition with the Soviet Union. I thought (correctly, as it turned out) that Jones's experience and views would be a promising addition as we went through the process of strategic arms limitation. President Carter ratified my choice. How was it that I viewed both Jones and Kidd, once my determined, difficult adversaries, as highly qualified, thoughtful, effective implementers of policies and decisions by the secretary of defense? Had they changed, or had I?

What happened was that during the elapsed fifteen years, the loyalty and focus of the two men shifted from their respective military branches to broader views of national security issues. Perhaps that resulted from their service in an Atlantic-wide context. Each man had experienced the military purposes of armed forces at the cockpit of the U.S.-Soviet Cold War. The U.S. and Soviet ground and air forces faced each other in Europe. The balance of those forces influenced the political behavior of both superpowers and America's European allies. It was through the Atlantic that reinforcement from the United States would have to come to take on Soviet ballistic missile-equipped submarines.

PURPLE-SUITERS

Both Jones and Kidd had served in four-star military positions. Kidd dealt with his service and controlled a major portion of its combat units. He also commanded units from other services and worked with European units and civilians in his NATO role. Jones had dealt with European military and political leaders in an earlier position in Europe. Later, as chief of staff of the air force, he was a principal military adviser to the secretary of defense and the president.

Both men held a wide view of national security. Yet because of their wider roles and their personal attitudes, colleagues of similar rank in their respective services did not always trust them. Their colleagues called them "purple-suiters," which implied that the two men were insufficiently oriented to their own service and too wedded to joint planning and joint operations. It was precisely that jointness quality that put them at the top of my list.

The role of chairman of the Joint Chiefs was and remains a delicate one. The chairman is supposed to be a neutral spokesperson, transcending the interests of any particular service. That's difficult because when a chief of staff, the senior uniformed person in a military department, perceives one of his main interests overridden or inadequately represented, he finds journalists and congressional outlets to help him seek reversal. The chairman of the Joint Chiefs knows that if the Chiefs' views are split, they will have less influence as a group. So the easy way out is for him to endorse each service's wish list. In operational matters as well, the Chiefs often seek a common denominator rather than make hard choices.

I thought that both Jones and Kidd could make the required hard choices because their perspective had changed as a consequence of their broadened experience, just as mine had in all my previous positions. As the saying goes, where you stand depends on where you sit. When I became secretary of defense, I saw how the world geopolitical situation drove the requirements for U.S. military capability. Our political commitments, as well as our military capabilities, influence the political behavior of our allies and adversaries. Political and economic ties are important in joining us into a common security posture.

Jointness is now essential in modern U.S. military operations, but it was not then and does not now occur easily. Just as differing cultures, goals, methods, and histories divide allies in a coalition, they also divide U.S. military branches. To be sure, there are similarities among tasks, but initial training and loyalties begin and end with one's unit. Only later, in more senior positions, can dedication to joint activity be inspired. In 1978 I made joint service a precondition for promotion to flag or general officer rank—admiral or general. And in the area of weapons systems, we advanced interservice commonality. For example, on Bill Perry's advice, I instituted a Joint Cruise Missile Office to manage both navy and air force cruise missile development.

The military tried to claim that any officer who worked at a senior level in a particular military service automatically dealt with people from the other services and therefore met the joint service requirement. I didn't buy that because those dealings were often adversarial. The senior military have always been sensitive about the SecDef's participation in promotions to top ranks or criteria for them. They admit the secretary must play a major role in selecting the Joint Chiefs of Staff. But go one level below that to the vice chief level and the chief will tell you, "I'm the man who's going to have to work with this guy. I should select him."

That argument has weight. On the other hand, the chief is not the only person who will work with the vice chief. The same applies even more strongly to unified and specified commanders who report to the secretary of defense, not to a service chief or the Joint Chiefs. I gave a pioneering boost to the value and reward of a career in joint service so that it would become more desirable and attract better people.

Things changed slowly. I increased the influence of the unified and specified commanders who managed joint operations. I was the first to ask them for quarterly reports to include their thoughts about organization, force, and materiel needs and the political-military situation in their geographic and functional areas. I also invited their inputs on budget decisions.

I began to rely more heavily on the Joint Staff and on the chairman of the Joint Chiefs, though George Brown and Dave Jones knew they could not afford to get too far ahead of their colleagues. The Marine Corps began to send its best people to the National War College. Marine generals began to command joint forces beginning in 1980 with P. X. Kelly in the Rapid Deployment Joint Task Force, which became the Central Command in 1983.

Over time a joint command was established to provide training for joint operations in recognition that the training function of services under Title 10 can't go very far beyond the "undergraduate" service-specific level without requiring some element of jointness. Eisenhower might be pleased with how his initial idea progressed, but I doubt he would be satisfied.

THE GOLDWATER-NICHOLS ACT

In 1986 the Goldwater-Nichols Act formalized changes for jointness. The act was passed by the Senate Armed Services Committee in March with a 19-0 unanimous vote. In May it passed the Senate 95-0. In October Ronald Reagan signed the legislation.[7] The act grew out of proposals made by senior military officers, including Dave Jones after he had retired, to further the steps that he and I had initiated to advance the processes of joint planning and operations. A meeting of former defense secretaries (including James Schlesinger and myself) and retired four-star officers (including former Army Chief of Staff Edward "Shy" Meyer and Admiral Harry D. Train III, former CINCLANT [Commander in Chief, Atlantic]) at Fort Lee in Virginia during the mid-1980s came up with detailed recommendations, which formed a basis for congressional hearings and the resulting legislation.

Senators Barry Goldwater (R-Ariz.) and Sam Nunn (D-Ga.) and Representative William Flynt Nichols (D-Ala.) were the leading formulators of the act, which overcame the opposition of the then Joint Chiefs and defense secretary in 1986. Since the passage of the act, U.S. joint warfighting capability has improved and built on the foundation of my own efforts, carrying them further. The act established a Joint Officer Specialty in the personnel system; specified minimum tours of duty; legislated the requirement that I had instituted for joint service for promotion to general or admiral (and added it for promotion to one grade below that); made the chairman of the Joint Chiefs the specified military adviser to the president, secretary of defense, and National Security Council, and put him in sole charge of the Joint Staff. The act also added a vice chairman who was senior to the service chiefs. It strengthened the authority of the unified and specified commanders over units of each military service within their command. The act also required their recommendations for resource allocation. All these changes followed the direction set during my tenure in the late 1970s.

The results on the operational side have been an outstanding success, as shown by Desert Storm and the Obama administration's mission that led to Osama bin Laden's end. The improvement in decisions on allocation of resources is less noteworthy. The combat commanders do, appropriately, have more influence in that arena than was the case in the past, generally to good effect, though their shorter-range perspective will always compete with the longer view and correspondingly slower pace of response of the military services. Budgets are still submitted by the services. The chairman of the Joint Chiefs submits his preferred priorities to the secretary of defense, just as Dave Jones did to me. However, the Joint Staff, even though it now has a section that deals with programs, is not the initiator of budget submission. Melding, prioritizing, and improving the efficiency of the programs, systems (and their procurement), and acquisition processes remains a difficult work in progress. We need to make that more responsive to the requirements set by the various military tasks that constitute or support combat.

There are some who now think that once a top officer reaches flag rank he or she should take off the military uniform and wear only the "purple suit." Canadians, with a far smaller force than the U.S. military, have unified their particular services. They adopted and later abandoned a common uniform of a single color. I feel that goes too far for our military. Some of our top officers function within their respective services. Their uniform is important for identity and morale in their relationship to subordinates. To me, it's more important to act as a purple-suiter than to look that way.

THE NEED FOR COMPATIBLE EQUIPMENT

Achieving effectiveness in joint operations carries two prerequisites: joint training and compatible equipment, including software. In terms of training, the 1980 attempt to rescue the Iran hostages suffered from involving all military services before they were used to working together. A later attempt to deal with that shortcoming was to establish the Joint Forces Command. It promoted joint training as its own rehearsal. Last year it was disestablished and its joint training functions were transferred to the respective Unified Commands, now presumed able to carry out the training function themselves as they are closer to "the tip of the spear" and are unified. We shall see.

As for compatible equipment, I recall two outstanding examples of its lack in the late 1970s. One was the incompatibility of in-air refueling systems between the air force and the navy. The other was the inability of combat aircraft to communicate across services and with ground forces.

Remarkably, Air Force KC-135s could not refuel navy fighters. Ground observers sometimes could not direct air strikes. Airborne Warning and Control Systems (AWACS) could not direct all combat aircraft. The air-refueling incompatibility was corrected while I was in office; much of the communications incompatibility still exists and needs correction.

Given the long life span of some major equipment, we need to ensure compatibility for joint operations and flexibility of use from the very beginning, when decisions about which systems to design or procure get made. This is especially important for weapons whose use will likely span forty years or more from initiation of development to retirement of equipment. For example, B-52 aircraft built in 1962 are expected to remain in inventory until 2018. The planes have undergone replacement of almost all of their parts. The uses of the aircraft have ranged from strategic deterrence to air support and sea surveillance.

One path to greater efficiency in weapons system procurement and a way to solve the equipment compatibility problem would be to establish a separate civilian-military service of systems development and acquisition personnel. This corps would be dedicated to the design, development, and procurement of all major systems, especially those relevant to joint operations across all military services. The French have done this in their procurement service, called the General Directorate of Armaments. On a lesser scale, the U.S. Navy does this with the Marine Corps. I discuss this concept more fully under "Establish a Separate Uniformed Procurement Service" in chapter 8.

A JOINT SUPERORGANIZATION NEEDED

In this age of failed states, non-state actors, terrorism, and nation building, we would be wise to apply jointness beyond the Department of Defense. We need a joint operations superorganization that incorporates elements of the State Department, Treasury, the intelligence community, law enforcement agencies, and other sectors to protect our security interests. This may be a near-impossible challenge (though perhaps easier than most ambitious international coalition efforts) but one that is rapidly becoming a necessity. Both the current secretary of state and the previous national security adviser have embraced this idea and taken tentative steps in this direction. But neither the State Department nor its

Agency for International Development (AID), nor the Justice Department has anything like the Defense Department's resources and tradition of action-oriented involvement. It is not clear how to redress that. Simply transferring funds from Defense to these organizations, though it could be helpful, is not enough. In the meanwhile, it must be remembered that jointness is not a panacea to all things military. Sometimes an operation, usually a minor one, is best carried out by a single service.

MY INFLUENCES, HEROES, AND MENTORS

The right people well placed within the right organizational framework can make a difference; so can the right influences and mentors. I came to the Pentagon with the benefit of having had good professional mentors and a supportive, stable family. As a child I'd grown up in a Democratic household, so Franklin D. Roosevelt was an early hero. I used to think of Thomas Jefferson as a man of the people and Alexander Hamilton as "the villain." I've changed that view. I now think of Hamilton as someone who understood how to make a government work, though many of his political views from a different era are not applicable and indeed are distasteful today.

Jefferson is usually seen as a great democrat and Hamilton as an advocate of aristocratic government. But it was Jefferson who was the aristocrat and Hamilton who came from lowly origin. Hamilton was the abolitionist. Jefferson essentially lived off his slaves' labor, sold their products, and then sold the slaves. Jefferson was an inspirational advocate and great theorist of democracy, but a practitioner of aristocracy. Hamilton was a theorist of aristocracy, but a product of democracy. I do recognize, however, that applying our current sensibilities and conditions to an earlier era can be misleading.

Herb York

My first mentor was Herbert York at Livermore Lab. He was great fun to be with and had a variety of interests that paralleled mine in history, science, politics, and people. Over some sixty years—until his death on May 19, 2009—we frequently got together and loved to talk about anything and everything. I eventually succeeded Herb as Livermore's director (after Edward Teller), and immediately succeeded him in Washington as director of Defense Research and Engineering when Herb went off to be the first chancellor of the University of California at San Diego.

He was one of the closest friends I ever had. A rough diamond at Livermore, he was loud and boisterous. Sometimes people thought they heard us arguing in his office; it was mostly laughter and Herb being typically robust. I learned from Herb York how to lead a group of high-intellect people toward a particular goal. We never envied each other the accomplishments we'd not ourselves achieved. I never founded an institution; he had fathered several. On the other hand, he never rose as high in government as I did or engaged as much in the nonacademic private sector. When I first came to Livermore Lab, I admired both York and Edward Teller. Teller's knowledge of and facility with physics and the profusion of his ideas greatly exceeded mine. He was a product of high culture in a way that York wasn't. Teller played the piano; York was tone-deaf. But in the end York was just as intelligent and wiser.

By 1958 I'd held several positions at the lab that prepared me to be its director, moving from group leader to division leader to associate director. When Teller retired from his directorship, I was named. I probably would not have become director had Mark Mills, who was my senior in the organization, not died in a helicopter accident. And if Eisenhower's probable first choice for director of Defense Research and Engineering (DDRE), Jim McRae, had not suffered a fatal heart attack, York probably would not have become DDRE, and I probably wouldn't have succeeded him there. Or it all could have happened anyway, but later. Contingency matters enormously with respect to career events in addition to what is determined by oneself.

In May 2009 I spoke at Herb's memorial assembly and said that "his life was an unsurpassed record of achievement in science, education, and national security. He played the leading role in creating a series of innovative and crucial institutions—a nuclear laboratory, the Defense Department's Advanced Research Projects Agency (DARPA), a University of California campus, and the Institute on Global Conflict and Cooperation. In the national government, in California, and in international meetings and negotiations, he was dedicated to peace while being realistic about security needs. Beyond the public record, all of us who knew him as a friend appreciated his omnivorous interest in the world around him, dedication to his family, great sense of humor, and zest for life."[8]

Gene Fubini

The son of Guido Fubini, a famous Italian mathematician, Gene came from a family that had immigrated to the United States in the 1930s. Gene was one of Herb York's deputies at the Directorate of Defense Research and Engineering. He signed on shortly before Herb left and came to California early in 1961 to see if we would get along well enough to work together when I became director. I reminded him that we'd met at dinner a dozen years earlier. He didn't remember, but I did because he was memorable: short, volatile, very intelligent, and interested in almost everything.

He had a wide network in the technological community and later became my principal deputy when I was DDRE. Gene's title was assistant secretary of defense. He oversaw the Defense Department's intelligence agencies. His contributions to command, control, communications, computers, intelligence, and surveillance and reconnaissance—the brain of modern military capability—have not been equaled.

When I became secretary of the air force, Gene left to join IBM and later had a decades-long career as a consultant and frequent adviser to Defense Department officials. When I became secretary of defense, I named him to head the Defense Science Board and asked him to help me staff defense departments with technological leadership. He played a leading role in helping me recruit Bill Perry. Gene's background was engineering and was studded with patents, but his work went beyond technical contributions to include military tactics and national strategy. I count him as both protégé and teacher, which made him a valuable colleague. I spoke at his memorial service on August 5, 1997, with gratitude for knowing his infectious, inspiring spirit, ebullience, and commitment to excellence, and with sadness at losing him.[9]

Robert McNamara

A man I would put in a category apart from all others was Bob McNamara. He was enormously impressive, not only to me but to everybody. His way of organizing large enterprises, honed during World War II as an air force officer, had proven successful when he was the leader of the Ford Motor Company. Bob was a model, but also a cautionary example for me. He revolutionized the way decisionmaking is carried on in the Defense Department. He created and relied on a group that developed and incorporated systems analysis as a way of making decisions. Other departments of government have adopted it into their own management, usually with less success.

When I first got to Washington as DDRE, I think McNamara viewed me as just somebody who would oversee research and perhaps the development piece of major weapons systems. He seemed not to think I'd participate in major weapons systems decisions or manage them. But in the first few months of that job some specific issues concerning ballistic missiles and defense against them made it clear that my knowledge could help McNamara make key decisions. That's when he began to see me as somebody who would play a major role.

Herb York had played a similar role for McNamara's predecessors, but McNamara had pushed him aside in dealing with the same issues on which I later became a lead adviser, that is, on new weapons systems and the force structure to incorporate and use them. In giving that advice, I regained the influence of the DDRE position within my first six months and soon wound up in Hyannis Port in a meeting with President John F. Kennedy, just as York had wound up in meetings with Eisenhower.

As time went on, I saw that behind the outwardly assertive manner that defined McNamara as secretary of defense and underpinned his hard-driving career at Ford, he had internal conflicts and was not the automaton that some people thought. For example, at the Monday Armed Forces Council meetings he exhibited a habit that made it clear when he was voicing presidential decisions with which he might disagree: his voice rose in intensity and he pulled up his socks as he spoke. As assertive as he was in his official capacity, he took pains not to act like a big shot during his private time. For example, when he and his wife, Marge, invited Colene and me to join them for an evening at the Arena Theater, he drove his own car there. That's impossible to imagine now.

In private, he was sometimes emotional. Those emotions spilled out at a public ceremony on February 29, 1968, when President Lyndon Johnson awarded him the Medal of Freedom. McNamara broke down as he tried to respond and couldn't continue speaking. The emotions were always there, but hidden. He was extremely loyal to the presidents he served and to the process that enabled the most efficient levels of adherence to their strategies.

He was also good at cultivating people and—as was clear for me and for Cy Vance and Paul Nitze—preparing them for higher office.

In retrospect, it's clear to me that Bob had been grooming me in the 1960s for a possible nomination for secretary of defense. I didn't realize it at the time. For example, more than three years into my DDRE role, he toyed with the idea of recommending me to be the director of the CIA when John McCone left. Later, in 1965, he asked whether I'd consider becoming secretary of the air force, again trying to broaden my experience, and I agreed.

When Bob left office on February 29, 1968, members of his staff presented him with a large globe. The citation that accompanied it said: "To the outstanding public servant of our time." That describes his first four years as secretary of defense. The next three years were a Shakespearean tragedy for him, President Johnson, and the country. His rational approach to issues proved no match for the frustrating behavior of foreign adversaries and domestic groups who marched to their own drummers.

Regarding Vietnam, Bob became skeptical of that war well before he stopped saying how great the outcome was going to be. His accounting approach to casualties inflicted on the enemy missed the underlying reality. His attempt to set up sensors to pinpoint where materiel and fighters came through the Ho Chi Minh Trail was plagued by problems. When I spoke with McNamara about the Vietnam War years afterward, his memories of it were far different from those of other participants and keen outside observers.

A telling detail is that McNamara never spoke at commissioning ceremonies at the military academies. I once asked him why not? He said he only planned to stay in the job as defense secretary for four years and needed to spend his time on more immediate matters. Perhaps four years is as long as anyone should stay in that job. After that, there is the challenge of mistaking for wisdom your familiarity with the issues; in addition, it's harder to clean up your own mess.

Reflecting on Bob McNamara's habits when I became secretary of defense, I recalled that he was a very organized person and wrote in his left-handed scrawl many memos we learned to decipher. I came to use a similar method of penciling my questions and corrections onto staff memos. Bill Perry adopted the same tactic. I also realized that I should try to pay at least a bit of attention to the social role a secretary is expected to play as a communicator and representative of the department.

Back when I was DDRE, Colene and I had gone to two dinner parties a week. I'd gained fifteen pounds and after losing them vowed not to dine out socially that much again. However, as air force secretary dealing directly with uniformed officers and airmen on an individual and personal basis, socializing was an integral part of the office. "Dinings-in," a practice borrowed from Britain's Royal Air Force, was an important way of strengthening personal ties.

Air force experience helped make me a more sociable secretary of defense, though in public life one is not always seen as one truly is, let alone how one wishes to be seen. My own feeling about myself in public life is that I wish I were more at ease in personal relationships. I tend to be introverted and cerebral, which is characterized by some as remote. That may be because of how I work, and how the government works. For example, going back as far as when I was DDRE, my staff would schedule briefings for me from outside contractors or agencies. I'd ask to see the written materials the previous night, go over them, and when the briefers came to my office the next day, I'd say: "Don't bother giving me the slide show; I've read it. Just answer these questions." Colin Powell, who was military assistant to my deputy in defense, saw me almost every day when I was secretary of defense. He wrote in his memoir that I sometimes gave the impression of not wanting people to come to see me, but rather wanted them to slip their briefs under my door. That's not how I felt, but that was his impression.

Colene and Deborah and Ellen

Throughout my time as DDRE, air force secretary, Caltech president, and secretary of defense, my wife Colene's easy warmth at social functions compensated for my social reticence. Colene has maintained our stable home life during our entire career. She used to meet me after work for tennis or a swim before dinner. Colene and I played highly competitive tennis with military officers, legislators, and other government officials. What was said between sets proved as interesting as comments shared in the hallway with my counterparts from other countries as we walked toward a conference table. Social interactions could ease policy resolutions.

Every night Colene laid out my clothes for the following morning. If I appeared well dressed, if my tiepin and cufflinks matched, and I wore long socks rather than short ones, she deserves the credit. We raised two wonderful daughters who inspire me. The older, Deborah, is different from me in her interests, but similar, she admits, in temperament. A fine arts painter, she rereads Proust every ten years and learned Spanish in her fifties. My younger daughter, Ellen, is, like me, a Ph.D. physicist. She has raised two children while holding down a full-time job.

Debbie is married to Eric Ploumis, who combines the professions of orthodontist and lawyer, a juxtaposition of talents I've never been able to figure out. Ellen's husband, Ray Merewether, is an engineering graduate of the Massachusetts Institute of Technology via Texas and Oklahoma. His many inventions include underwater and underground sensors. Ellen's children, my sensational grandchildren, are now in college, one in engineering at Princeton, and the other in East Asian languages and studies at Stanford.

At home, when not reading I love to listen to Bach's "Top Six"—the Brandenburg Concertos—and to Mozart. As George Szell, conductor of the Cleveland Orchestra, once said when asked to rate composers: first Bach, then Mozart, then nobody, then Beethoven, then everybody else. And that's exactly right. My choice of music found its way into my SecDef Office. Music was played there partly to inhibit outside listeners from overhearing high security conversations. Rumsfeld reportedly played country and western music. I played classical composers.

LEAVING A LEGACY IN PEOPLE

My protégés include my friend John Deutch, who is really more the protégé of Jim Schlesinger in government situations but sometimes claims me as a model. John served as deputy secretary of defense and director of the CIA in the Clinton administration. Bill Perry followed a pattern similar to mine, first as undersecretary for research and engineering and later as secretary of defense. He and the others of my team at Defense who went on to higher posts are a matter of pride as well as friendship.

People who serve in the Defense Department change and develop—and people count. It is satisfying that many of those who served with me went on then or in later administrations to cabinet positions of their own. Bill Perry became secretary of defense and Charles Duncan became energy secretary. Graham Claytor was acting secretary of transportation, but for only a few months because the president agreed he couldn't take away my two top people for other cabinet positions. Togo West became secretary of veterans affairs. Colin Powell, who was the military assistant to Charles Duncan, sat in on our morning meetings, so I had worked closely with him and am proud to include him in my legacy. Jim Woolsey, my navy under secretary, became director of the CIA.

OBSESSIONS OF EDWARD TELLER

Some people think of Teller as having been a mentor to me. I'm sure Teller felt that, and with some reason. I was impressed with his intelligence and the breadth of his intellectual interests. He was genuinely apprehensive about Soviet capabilities and intentions, views I shared although not to the same degree. I was first his deputy and then his successor as Livermore's director; he agreed wholeheartedly to both those appointments. He became bitterly disappointed in me when I stopped fully sharing most of his views.

Teller is rightly regarded as the father of the hydrogen bomb. He and Ernest Lawrence pushed the Atomic Energy Commission to set up Livermore Laboratory in 1952 as the country's second nuclear weapons laboratory. Teller wanted a second lab because he and some air force officials hoped to exceed the rate at which Los Alamos was developing weaponry. Teller, following Herb York, was Livermore's director for two years until I assumed that post.

Our work in the lab involved nuclear weapons development aimed at countering the Soviet advantage of larger payloads that their missiles could deliver. The United States needed to make thermonuclear weapons that were lighter and therefore more easily delivered than those that had come out of the original thermonuclear tests of 1952 and 1954. I was head of the division charged with that design responsibility. A similar group was working on the same problem at Los Alamos.

One approach we tried at Livermore in 1954 failed. Before we even began our next design, Edward Teller went out on a limb and promised we could come up with a thermonuclear weapon of a weight that could be delivered in a missile mounted inside a submarine. That seemed nearly impossible. The navy had been told that the weight of the warhead demanded a missile larger than what could fit inside a submarine, so their first approach was a plan to mount it outside. But an outside mount would have complicated and delayed the design and procurement of an appropriate submarine, so in 1955 the navy set up a Polaris Steering Committee to design the whole system. It was put under a Special Projects Unit with a three-star admiral in charge.

I give this example because the solution to the problem illustrates two things: that Teller had an obsessive focus on and knowledge of nuclear weapons, and that a very difficult project (in this case Polaris) with a clear objective, a degree of managerial independence, and a high priority can be accomplished in record time. The Polaris Steering Committee included representatives from the contractor that would build the missile, the contractor in charge of the guidance system being designed at MIT, the contractor for the propulsion system, and two people from different contractors designing the reentry vehicle system. I was a member representing the organization that would provide the thermonuclear warhead. Each of these tasks was challenging.

For example, to fly several thousand miles and hit a target within a fraction of a mile takes a very carefully designed and constructed inertial guidance system. A ballistic missile goes through the atmosphere and far into space around the earth before returning at great speed at the end of its range to hit the target. The friction from the high speed of reentry makes the external nosecone of the reentry vehicle (RV), which contains the warhead, extremely hot. The RV separates from the missile on the way up and needs its nosecone to withstand the high temperature on the way down.

Sputnik's 1957 launch and orbit had frightened the American public because it indicated that the Soviet Union could use similar engineering to attack us with its ballistic weapons. The ballistic missile programs of the navy, air force, and for a time the army were all accelerated after the Soviet Union put *Sputnik* into space. Teller was deeply concerned about the risk of Soviet domination; he believed superior nuclear weapons were the only solution to the threat.

In fact, the Soviet Union did not have the operational intercontinental ballistic missile capability we feared, though we didn't know that then. Until the early 1960s, it had only medium-range missiles that could reach Western Europe, but none that could reach the United States. Just two years after the *Sputnik* launch, we deployed the Polaris mounted inside a submarine. So we made good on Teller's promise.

When I came into Livermore's directorship, managing Teller was difficult. He was highly innovative; his was the idea that enabled the development of thermonuclear weapons. He also held pronounced geopolitical views and was convinced of their validity. In the balance of terror that constituted deterrence, Teller believed that the possessor of the more destructive weapons would determine the outcome of the political competition for the world. He held that view for decades, even after most of us who had worked on nuclear weapons had concluded otherwise.

I, for one, soon ceased to regard nuclear weapons as the solution to everything, or even to most military problems. My perspective, even from before my early days in the Defense Department in 1961, convinced me that advances in delivery systems, not the nuclear weapons themselves, were the most important element in the nuclear balance. I also realized early on that conventional forces and their capabilities were equally if not more important. As I changed my views, Teller and I grew apart, became increasingly adversarial, and had testy exchanges.

What came to trouble me most about Edward Teller's behavior was the way that he described "situations," as he called technical issues. His descriptions became increasingly simplified, reaching conclusions that slid rapidly into what I considered distortion. In his own mind, and indeed when challenged by a government oversight committee, he would say: "I need to simplify to get people to understand enough to come to the right conclusion."

In political life this is common practice and might even be regarded as necessary. But for a professionally trained scientist, this practice goes against the fundamental ethos. This is especially true when the scientifically trained individual purports to be expressing a professional, scientific opinion on a public policy issue. As a government official, I had to simplify my presentation of issues from time to time. But I believe I was always careful not to misstate or distort technical matters to get people to arrive at what I considered to be the correct policy conclusions.

Teller sought and found new influence with some in the Republican Party, though he'd started out as a moderate Democrat. He ended up a Reagan acolyte and sold President Reagan on Star Wars. I thought that one of his many less-than-good ideas. He used to joke that although people thought of him as a monomaniac, he was in fact a monomaniac with many manias. I think he had only two. The first, when I was working with him, was nuclear weapons, which he believed were central to all national security issues. Later, after we had long parted ways, he turned to ballistic missile defense ("Star Wars") as central to national security.

As DDRE and later as secretary of defense, I opposed most of what he believed about the value of thermonuclear weapons over all else. He felt I betrayed him. As a consequence, he essentially wrote me out of history. In his autobiography he describes what happened at the Livermore Lab. I hardly appear in that book, though I was a principal protagonist in many of its events.

As my views broadened, and Teller's narrowed to an extremely hawkish Cold War position, he suggested in testimony to Congress during the debate about a nuclear test ban that I had somehow "sold out." In fact, I simply had what I thought a more balanced view about how to counter the Soviet threat. Long after his congressional testimony in the 1960s and continuing through the 1980s, our views became more and more different. Though I had learned some things from him while at Livermore, I didn't choose to model myself after him.

Many, many years later, both of us far older, I saw a photo of him in the newspaper. He was wearing a cape-like coat and carrying a long staff. I wrote him a teasing note. "Edward," I said, "where are the incised tablets of the law?" He was not amused, and now that he's gone I'm not exactly proud of that particular smart-aleck remark. When I was in my twenties and even my thirties I was full of them, but as the decades wore on they were fewer, and that was an infrequent example.

ORGANIZATIONAL LESSON LEARNED
FROM PARKINSON'S LAWS

British naval historian and author C. Northcote Parkinson has noted that "officials want to multiply subordinates, not rivals" and "officials make work for each other."[10] These observations accurately describe what has happened during the past five or six decades within the Defense Department, the rest of the executive branch, and Congress. As defense secretary, I "made do" with two undersecretaries and seven assistant secretaries. There are now five under secretaries and sixteen assistant secretaries, with deputy undersecretaries and deputy assistant secretaries having multiplied by a similar factor. Each appointee staffs up with a retinue of subordinates.

The same is true in other cabinet departments. Congress exercises its legitimate oversight with increasing attention to detail and an aspiration to correct executive failings, managing through its own multiplied subcommittees and staffs that produce more hearings and demand more reports. Each report requires a response that is rarely read by those who requested it, but that generates tasks multiplying endlessly. The process is self-reinforcing: the number of people needed to respond, anticipate, and outsmart each other mushrooms.

What doesn't mushroom is efficiency. What doesn't increase is the speed of necessary decisions. The entire bloated mechanism disappoints in its attempt to achieve accountability, transparency, and concern for the taxpayers' interests.

My own efforts to tighten organization and reduce the number of its levels were at best a modest and temporary success. When other elements of government, executive and legislative, fail to match such steps, the result overloads the pioneer's ability to respond to demands from the other players. It may be that only a severe fiscal squeeze, which now seems likely, will provide the incentive to reverse swollen bureaucracies. Congressional staffs may be the hardest nut to crack.

The Perilous Fight

4

IRANIAN REVOLUTION AND
THE HOSTAGE CRISIS

Shortly after becoming president, Jimmy Carter made a world tour
in 1977 to the "regional influentials," as Zbigniew Brzezinski referred to
them. Carter toasted Shah Mohammed Reza Pahlavi and called Iran "an
island of stability." But the stability that Carter and Brzezinski thought
they saw in 1977 had eroded badly during 1978. Islamic militants, joined
by laborers and much of the commercial class (the "bazaaris"), had
rejected the shah's modernization efforts and policies. I recall taking a
call from Deputy Defense Secretary Charles Duncan while he was in Iran.
He told me he was unable to get outside his hotel room because mobs
were demonstrating in the streets.

In November 1977 the shah came to Washington. I met with him at
Blair House, which is the guest abode across the street from the White
House. When I met with prime ministers or kings who visited America,
I always met them at Blair House or on their turf in their Washington
embassies. When I met with opposition leaders—the "outs," as Margaret Thatcher and Helmut Kohl were at the time—they came to my office
in the Pentagon. At my 1977 meeting with the shah, he told me he was
interested in command and control. He wanted to know how the U.S.
president controlled his military forces. The shah said he wanted to learn
the most modern way of doing that.

I described our system of unified and specified commands and its hierarchy, including the role of the secretary of defense. I told him that the
Joint Chiefs were transmitters, not originators of commands. I suggested

that the shah consider something along the same lines. He vigorously disagreed. He wanted to be in immediate control of all military units. He did not want intermediaries. He did not want any subordinates entrusted with a major role in decisions.

I tried to dissuade him of that view. I said that it was more efficient to delegate responsibility for carrying out orders, although not for making the most important decisions. He remained firm in his belief that his authority had to be exercised directly, avoiding any chain of command. The contrast between that belief and his behavior during the Iranian revolution could not have been greater.

He spoke like a "control freak" during his Washington visit, just as he had earlier in 1971 when he created an elaborate celebration to commemorate the 2500th anniversary of Cyrus the Great, founder of Persia and a continuous monarchy (eliding the numerous regime changes and successful invasions) in Iran.[1] The festivities were meant to bolster his regime. But later in the decade, when the revolution was in full swing, the shah turned from one prime minister to another to help him try to hold onto power. He was already ill during that crisis, which may explain his weakness without excusing it. Meanwhile Ayatollah Khomeini in Paris was pulling strings to control the opposition.

In February 1979 President Carter sent me on a trip to Egypt, Israel, Jordan, and Saudi Arabia as part of a broader mission to assure our allies that we would support them against Soviet attempts to subvert existing governments. Zbigniew Brzezinski, like the Saudis, thought that the Soviet Union was trying to encircle the region. The theory was that the Soviet Union was working through its surrogate, the Cubans, to spread Soviet influence in Mozambique, Angola, and the broad central part of Africa. Meanwhile the Soviet regime itself was increasing its influence over Syria and the radical government in Yemen.

The U.S. concern was to buck up the region. Part of the reason Carter sent me on the trip, likely on Zbig's advice, was to tell the Saudis in particular that we would be prepared to defend them. I returned from the trip to a snowstorm in Washington so blinding we couldn't land. We had to fly all the way to Charleston, South Carolina, and wait until we could fly back to Washington later that day. When we finally got back, I was taken to the White House in a four-wheel-drive truck because the streets weren't cleared. The reason I had to return as fast as I could was that the

Iranian situation was heating up. The shah had left Iran a month before. Khomeini had returned to Iran, and Prime Minister Shapour Bakhtiar's government was shaky.

At the urging of the National Security Council staff, we had sent the deputy commander in chief of U.S. forces in Europe, Air Force General Robert "Dutch" Huyser, to Tehran shortly before the shah left to see what we could do with the Iranian military. We wanted to preserve some sense of order that would be in our national interest, and to keep them from going over to Khomeini's side. Brzezinski kept urging Huyser to tell the military to take over and pushed for a military coup. At the time, and even in retrospect, that was an attractive idea. The trouble was that he was pushing on the end of a wet string.

The senior military in Iran were split, and few, if any, were willing to stage a coup. The military folded. The shah's insistence that he personally had to exercise direct command all the way down to the bottom levels meant that when he was weakened and even more when he had gone, the country lacked a chain of command to pick up the slack. The non-commissioned officers, called the homofars, joined with the mercantile bazaaris and the revolutionaries to overturn the successive governments.

Just before February 1, 1979, as Ayatollah Khomeini planned to fly from his exile in France back to Iran, we had asked the French to try to prevent or slow his plane from leaving Paris. Almost every day beginning with the liftoff of that plane and lasting well into the year, Chairman of the Joint Chiefs of Staff Dave Jones or I talked with General Huyser over a secure but garbled and intermittently inoperative telecommunications link. We needed to understand whom we could help and what we could do. At the same time, the State Department was communicating with Ambassador William Sullivan, its man in Iran. We found ourselves in a holding operation to try to keep things from going down the drain. The Bakhtiar government named by the shah before he left fell at the end of February. The situation deteriorated though 1979 while all of us in the Carter administration tried to encourage the military and the moderates to resist Khomeini's creeping takeover.

The hostage crisis of 1979 was precipitated by an action both humanitarian and political. The president decided on October 20, 1979, to admit the shah to New York for medical treatment. (Other countries had successively hosted him for short periods and then encouraged him to move on.) I happened to be away the weekend when the president decided to admit the shah to New York. The president had been strongly lobbied by friends of the shah both inside and outside the U.S. government. In Carter's announcement, he said he was making the decision with reluctance after the shah was diagnosed with a fatal cancer. Those of us who heard the president in private knew that "reluctance" was a considerable understatement. Though President Carter informed the U.S. embassy in Tehran that this would occur, the failure to simultaneously decrease the number of our embassy personnel there was a mistake. When sixty-six of our embassy personnel were taken hostage two weeks later on November 4, 1979, the U.S.-Iran relationship entered its most poisonous phase.[2]

Iranian students, encouraged by Ayatollah Khomeini, perpetrated an act that was unprecedented: a host government at peace with the United States supported the invasion of our sovereign diplomatic territory and seized diplomatic staff. There were more surprises to come, in part because a condition of the shah's cooperation with the United States over previous decades had been his insistence that U.S. intelligence agencies not operate in Iran. The president found it "inconceivable," he said, "that the militants would hold the hostages for any length of time."[3] President Carter said he had received assurances from Prime Minister Mehdi Bazargan and Foreign Minister Ebrahim Yazdi that our embassy would be protected. On November 1, Brzezinski had had a friendly meeting in Algiers with Bazargan, who had been installed by Khomeini as a "moderate."

On November 6, two days after our embassy personnel were taken, Yazdi and Bazargan resigned, apparently forced out because they favored the release of the hostages and Khomeini refused that. He demanded that the United States turn the shah over to him. The takeover and refusal confirmed that the new regime was fixed in its hostility to the United States. On November 17 Ayatollah Khomeini announced that thirteen female and African American hostages might be released by Thanksgiving. They were released on November 19 and 20 and reported that they had endured terrible conditions, at times in solitary confinement. On November 18 Khomeini intimated that the remaining hostages would be put on trial. (On July 11, 1979, one more hostage was released owing to illness later diagnosed as cerebral palsy.)

On November 23, I and General Dave Jones, CIA Director Stan Turner, Brzezinski, Hamilton Jordan, and Vice President Fritz Mondale met with the president in the Cabinet Room to discuss what to do. The hostages were not sitting at an airport where we could storm in and get them. Then and subsequently we discussed whether to mine ports, set up a blockade, or take other punitive steps. We could not reasonably predict what effect all that would have on getting the hostages released. Some of those maneuvers, like mining Iranian waters, could have easily resulted in armed conflict. Though rescue plans were discussed, until the end of 1979 nobody thought much could be done.

Then I asked the Joint Chiefs to respond to a White House request about what we would do if Iran started to kill the hostages. At that point we needed to have three parallel military plans: one for rescue, another for pressure on Iran, and a third for punishment. Various plans went forward in tandem. By the spring of 1980, the political pressure to do something punishing was very great. The president and I felt strongly that we should work on other alternatives, too. Nightly news reports kept the crisis in the public eye and included a rash of newspaper stories that the United States was considering possible military action against Iran. Word continued coming in that the fifty-three remaining hostages were being treated badly.

The rescue plan evolved over time. We determined that we would leave it to the military to devise and carry out the plan unless they needed additional instructions from the president. Such instruction might be to abort the plan while it was in process. The president said as much to me, to the chairman of the Joint Chiefs, and to the commander of the Task Force.

THE IRAN HOSTAGE RESCUE ATTEMPT

The worst night of my life was the night of the Iran hostage rescue attempt on April 24, 1980 (April 25 in Iran time, 9.5 hours later there). There's a bed in a separate room off the secretary of defense's office. I tried to sleep but couldn't, knowing that at 10:30 a.m. EST, six U.S. C-130 transport aircraft and eight RH-53 helicopters would enter Iranian airspace. Only a small number of people knew about the mission. We had not notified neighboring countries.

The helicopters were big and had been adapted for special operations of this kind. The C-130 aircraft carried ninety members of the rescue team equipped for combat plus aircrew and had room for the hostages we hoped to rescue. As planned, the helicopters would land at a remote site 200 miles from Tehran that had been pre-scouted out in a CIA operation. We called the site Desert One; it was a salt desert where they were to refuel and prepare for the mission's next stages. We knew the long, arduous trip would tax the capacity of the helicopters. We needed at least six for the rescue attempt. We adopted a suggestion from David Aaron, Brzezinski's deputy, that we use eight helicopters to give us the needed redundancy, spare parts, and efficiency.

Things started to go very wrong over Iran. Two of the helicopters experienced problems in a sandstorm en route. One landed in the desert; its crew was picked up by another helicopter, which proceeded to the refueling point. The second helicopter with difficulties reversed course and landed aboard the aircraft carrier *Nimitz* in the Arabian Sea. Upon arrival at Desert One, a third helicopter experienced a severe hydraulic malfunction, which put it out of commission. The helicopters had flown an unusually long distance—500 nautical miles, which is 600 statute miles—something no other nation would have been likely to attempt.

The flight to the assembly point and the refueling had been essentially successful. But based on criteria we had established, if the number of helicopter failures reduced the chance of success, that would dictate ending the mission. The president canceled the operation on the advice of the on-site mission commander when the number of working helicopters dropped to five. As all our aircraft prepared to depart—this in total darkness—a helicopter and a C-130 accidentally collided and caught fire. Eight of our men were killed. Four others suffered burns. The remaining C-130s took off and departed.

Our U.S. forces had been on Iranian soil three hours when they left. No Iranian military forces were ever encountered. However, a bus carrying about fifty Iranian civilians passed by when the first C-130 landed. They were detained at the site. When President Carter gave the order to terminate the mission, all the civilians were allowed to leave and were unharmed.

I hadn't gotten any rest after the mission was aborted. A few of us met at the White House before dawn. We needed to find out what the Soviet authorities knew and if they'd taken any counteractions. I sat at the president's desk in the Oval Office speaking over President Carter's secure line with Admiral Bobby Ray Inman, director of the National Security Agency. He told me the Soviet Union seemed unaware of the mission;

nothing in their communications indicated they knew anything about the rescue attempt. Of all the times to be at the president's desk and using his telephone, that was not the happiest circumstance under which to do it.

I went back to my office to set up a press conference for noon on Friday, April 25. I worried about what I would say. First, President Carter went on television that morning to announce the mission had failed. I had to go up to Capitol Hill to meet with members of both parties in the Senate and the House and explain what had happened. At the kind of press conference we were about to have, there's usually some sympathy at the beginning; then politics kick in.

I opened the press conference with a statement from me, and then General Dave Jones, chairman of the Joint Chiefs, gave a statement. I opened the floor to questions. Journalist Lester Kinsolving, an Episcopalian priest known as a gadfly in the press corps, asked: "Who will be blamed? Who's responsible for this failure? What are you going to do about it?"

I said, "I was responsible for it within the Defense Department and I will not seek scapegoats. This operation just terminated yesterday. We are examining what happened in detail. It is going to be thoroughly and exhaustively examined."[4] As I later learned, after I said that a cheer went up from members of the Joint Staffs watching on internal Pentagon TV. They applauded, perhaps more from relief than as an indication of admiration for me. Still, it was a gratifying thing for me to learn after that press conference. (Decades later I found out that Les Kinsolving had redesignated himself an Anglican priest after he disagreed with the American Episcopal Church's admission of women to the priesthood.)

On April 27 President Carter, Brzezinski, and I took a trip to the CIA camp where the returned Task Force team waited for debriefing. I suggested to the president that he might wish to get rid of the whole national security team that planned the rescue attempt, and I offered to resign. So did Brzezinski. Though we both meant our offers, neither of us insisted when the president rejected them. Cy Vance, who had opposed the rescue mission, had told the president before the operation that he intended to resign as secretary of state immediately afterward. He did so, and the president accepted his resignation.

The Joint Chiefs set up a group of retired senior military officers to do a post-examination of the mission, which makes sense whether a mission is a success or a failure. Former Chief of Naval Operations James

L. Holloway III headed the group, which rightly found a lot to criticize. When the report came out, then Chief of Naval Operations Tom Hayward told the media: "The Joint Chiefs bear responsibility. You can't blame it all on civilians." In the end, however, Carter got the blame. I bear responsibility for two major mistakes that became painful lessons learned.

LESSONS LEARNED

In terms of operational planning, various people drew differing lessons from the failed mission. Some said we shouldn't have tried a rescue attempt at all because it was too risky. I reject that partly because the alternatives involving the use of punishing force could well have led to war. Others said the failure was a reflection of inadequate funding of the military under Carter. I don't think resources were a limitation. My view now is that too many elements of the rescue team were chosen so that all the services would be represented although they had never worked together before. That was a major mistake.

The pride of the various military services via their chiefs, even more than operational needs, pushed us to include all the services in the rescue attempt. That is a good idea when you've had a lot of experience in a joint service activity. But that had not been the case. Constraints of geography required us to fly helicopters in from navy ships. The marines wanted them to be marine choppers. The helicopters were to meet up with air force tankers and an air force transport that would carry the army Delta Special Forces unit. The helicopters would refuel and take the Delta team to Tehran. The lack of a joint operations structure for an effort of this magnitude made the lack of sufficient practice exercises even more damaging.

Without practice, things fail that could succeed. We practiced pieces of the plan, including helicopter landings in U.S. desert conditions. While the individual elements of the rescue mission trained intensively, they did so separately, and there were no practice exercises of the entire operation with the whole team working together—no full-scale exercises of 500–nautical mile flights from a carrier or rendezvous with a refueling aircraft, and refueling and taking off again. We didn't conduct a full practice exercise for two main reasons. First, the profound media focus demanding action, including a rescue effort, put any rehearsal at considerable risk of discovery, and that would alert the Iranians. In retrospect, I'm not sure that would have happened, but at the time a run-through was seen as a substantial risk. Second, we were squeezed for time. When the plan got the go-ahead, we had already discarded an earlier and very different plan to take over a semi-abandoned Iranian airbase. Nights were getting shorter, and much of our rescue had to occur in darkness. That, too, made it hard to carry out a full practice. Had we practiced enough, we might have known that flying the helicopters unusually long distances, even without a sandstorm, was likely to result in several dropping out.

The initial reaction of the military had been that any rescue attempt was not feasible. Although a year earlier the army had established a special group called the Delta team to handle terrorist and hostage activities, they had not practiced anything nearly as difficult as trying to snatch people out of a city 600 statute miles from the sea in a well-guarded area surrounded by a million Iranians. It seemed an impossible situation for a rescue attempt. Still, the choices boiled down to punishment or rescue.

The lowest level of punitive military action we considered was a blockade or the mining of Iran's ports. Both were doable, but my view was that neither one could solve the hostage situation or excise the heart of the challenge. A dozen years before, as air force secretary, I had looked at target folders during the Vietnam War and knew the limitations of such actions. Indeed, not everyone agreed that any action involving military forces should be taken, as Cyrus Vance's letter of resignation demonstrated. The remaining hostages were released on January 20, 1981, fully 444 days after their capture and at the end of the Carter presidency.

By now the lessons have been well learned. The Joint Special Operations Command that was organized and used by President Barack Obama when he dispatched a team to Osama bin Laden's high-walled compound in Pakistan illustrates that. Continuity in the uniformed military makes it better able than most government departments to learn and adapt. Jointness has become even more necessary to combat terrorism, which can't be fought by any one military element alone. The Joint Special Operations Command now includes elements from all the services, which train, practice, and operate together.

The failure to rescue the U.S. hostages still haunts me. The lesson to keep in mind now, especially as Americans watch the news about turbulence in the Middle East, is that at times political pressure becomes strong enough so that even risky actions appear to be necessary. What happened in 1979 and 1980 shows that it's easy to overestimate America's ability to influence events in a revolutionary situation in another country, especially where our lack of knowledge concerning its turbulent political situation means that almost anything the United States tries could be counterproductive. In the case of the shah's Iran, our willingness to rely only on the shah's intelligence services and our acceptance of his insistence that the U.S. intelligence community not be active in Iran gave us a poor understanding of the situation there.

In any revolution, it's hard for outsiders to have an effect. There are exceptions. In 1954 the United States essentially killed a revolution in Iran. We had much better information then. Of course, if you think you're able to influence things to good effect, you go ahead and do it. But if it turns out that you didn't know enough, or handled the situation ineptly, you're worse off than if you'd stayed out.

During our helicopter ride to the CIA camp after the failure of the rescue attempt, President Carter said he was thinking of naming Senator Edmund Muskie to succeed Vance and asked Zbig and me our opinions of that. Muskie had been a member of the Foreign Relations and Defense Appropriations Committees. Both Brzezinski and I thought Muskie would be a good choice. The alternative would have been Deputy Secretary of State Warren Christopher, who later served with distinction as secretary of state in the Clinton administration. President Carter felt that asking Muskie would improve the president's relations with the Senate, especially when he needed Senate ratification of the SALT II Treaty. While not a bad idea, that tactic seldom works. A senator who becomes a cabinet member may be likely to be regarded in the Senate as a defector than as a friend. We didn't get ratification of SALT II despite selecting Muskie.

PROSPECTS FOR IRAN GOING FORWARD

What light does this history shed on dealing with the prospect of an Iranian nuclear weapons capability? More than thirty years later, the Iranian regime continues to be extremely adversarial to the United States and to its interests. Our necessary responses to the Taliban hosting of the 9/11 planners and our unnecessary overthrow of Saddam Hussein removed the Iranian regime's neighboring enemies and greatly increased

Iranian influence in Iraq and Afghanistan. Unsurprisingly, that has not eased U.S-Iranian relations. The Iranian regime now feels empowered, even though it is still threatened by its dangerous neighborhood as well as by internal dissent.

Iran's program of uranium enrichment is fully consistent with a plan to produce nuclear weapons and much less appropriate as part of a nuclear power program. Getting Iran to stop short of producing weapons-grade U235 is a high-priority U.S. objective. Punitive sanctions may possibly achieve that end and perhaps lead to a broader "grand bargain." A U.S. attack to destroy the uranium production facilities could delay an Iranian nuclear weapons capability by a couple of years. An Israeli attack would be less effective. Israelis have fewer aircraft, less refueling capability, and fewer capable weapons than the United States.

An attack by either country could ensure an Iranian decision, even now likely to get popular support in Iran, to produce nuclear weapons in less vulnerable facilities and to launch retaliatory actions. Those actions could be channeled through proxies or involve mining the Strait of Oman or attacking ships there. We could effectively counter Iranian actions, but only a successful invasion and occupation of Iran, which even the most optimistic promoters of the invasion of Iraq are not likely to suggest, would forcibly prevent Iran from resuming its nuclear weapons program.

The Iranian regime has not acted irrationally, however disruptive its rhetoric and use of proxies. In Iran's war with Iraq in the 1980s, Iran was the attacked party. Both U.S. and Israeli retaliatory capabilities, either of which could completely destroy Iran beyond even the destruction caused by Hulagu's Mongol army in the 1200s, provide a high though less than perfect assurance that Iran would be deterred from using nuclear weapons, should it eventually acquire them.

We currently rely on deterrence—the threat of absolute destruction by retaliation—to prevent a North Korean nuclear attack. We do so even though North Korea is arguably a less rational player than Iran. Iran's neighborhood is less stable than that of North Korea, a better argument for caution than for military action. The experience of 1978–80 should remind us that we have limited knowledge about the internal workings of factions within Iran and a corresponding uncertainty of how any actions we might take would turn out. During the shah's regime, we lacked insight into the workings of the Iranian polity and badly misread the process playing out as the shah's regime and its successors gave way to Khomeini. Given the long time our hostages were kept prisoners and the threats to their lives, a rescue attempt was inevitable, though its outcome was badly damaging to the United States.

I still believe that a punishing military attack on Iran in an attempt to force release of our hostages would have been a worse course of action. As the events of the past dozen years have shown, the use of force without a clear and convincing picture of the endgame is a recipe for a bad outcome. Without ruling out an attack on Iranian nuclear facilities, that experience should inform and caution our future actions.

Rockets' Red Glare and Bombs

5   PLANS, PROGRAMS, AND AGREEMENTS

In October 1961 the Soviet Union exploded a thermonuclear bomb at its Siberian site with no notice of any kind. At 50 megatons, it was the largest bomb ever exploded, then or since. Its explosive energy was 3,200 times that of the Hiroshima bomb and sounded, one faraway observer said, as if the Earth had been killed.[1] The shock wave traveled around the planet three times before it dissipated.

A bomb that big could not be delivered at intercontinental range by aircraft or missile. It was so enormous that it protruded from the plane that carried it and required a parachute to slow its descent so its delivery plane could escape. Nikita Khrushchev later bragged that the bomb carried half the 100-million-ton explosive force his engineers had designed. They calculated that a bomb with that yield would increase all the world's fission fallout since the invention of the atomic bomb by 25 percent, so they replaced uranium with lead in part of the device.

KENNEDY AND THE KING OF BOMBS

Everyone in Washington, even people who suspected the Soviet regime had been cheating on the nuclear testing moratorium, were shaken by the blatant manner in which it dropped "Tsar Bomba"—the emperor of bombs.

With apologies to Francis Scott Key, we have transposed lines of his anthem in chapters 5 and 6 to better explain how U.S. weapons development affected the ramparts we watched.

That deed demonstrated that nuclear weapons had become as much a symbol of political conflict between the Soviet Union and the United States as a factor in military behavior. Until that explosion, John F. Kennedy had continued Dwight Eisenhower's moratorium on nuclear tests, though the United States had made preparation for underground tests if necessary. Now the question of U.S. testing was reopened for debate.[2]

The Summer before Tsar Bomba

In August 1961, two months before the Soviet Union dropped the big bomb, a clever listener—not a CIA operative—at an American communications station picked up a Soviet foreign broadcast. It said that Soviet authorities intended to resume nuclear testing despite the moratorium in effect the past two years. For an hour, nobody believed that message. Then Moscow Radio rebroadcast it, and I helped Bob McNamara write an announcement the White House could issue. But the State Department had already scooped us; President Kennedy issued a statement that morning, emphasizing the potential pollution of the atmosphere. (Two years later the president echoed that theme when urging ratification of the treaty banning atmospheric tests.)

Our first appeal to the Soviet Union that August said: please stop, right away. Soviet leaders responded by exploding a small nuclear bomb in the atmosphere. We issued another request to stop; they exploded another small bomb. I never saw President Kennedy more furious. He said that the United States had to be seen testing something. He had little choice. In August barbed wire divided Berlin. By the time of October's Tsar Bomba, the barbed wire in the Berlin Wall had been replaced by concrete. The emperor of bombs cemented an unavoidable perception that the Soviet Union intended to overtake the American lead in strategic nuclear weapons, a lead the Kennedy administration now correctly asserted and wished to protect.

Still, Kennedy was reluctant to resume atmospheric testing. I think he was convinced that fallout was a menace. It certainly was a serious national and international political problem. I have always felt there were reasons for wanting to do tests for armaments, and reasons having to do with arms limitations for not doing tests. Back when I was at Livermore Lab, I understood that to develop nuclear weapons you had to test them. Nuclear fallout was a concern, but the likelihood of an effect on a given individual was tiny. It was when you multiplied the effects on one person by the 5 billion then alive in the world that the numbers got big and the involuntary nature of fallout effects became significant.

In some ways, global warming from carbon dioxide emissions presents similar problems. Like nuclear fallout it affects everyone on the planet, although not uniformly for statistical and geographical reasons. Nuclear fallout and carbon emissions differ in that the former is decided by governments; the latter by governments and individuals.

Soon after the Soviet scientists detonated their August tests, President Kennedy called a meeting of the National Security Council in the Cabinet Room of the White House. Chip Bohlen, the State Department's expert on the Soviet Union, took a deep breath and said it looked like it would be a brisk fall. I had recently become director of Defense Research and Engineering (DDRE) after years of designing and testing nuclear weapons at Livermore Lab. I knew it would take months for the United States to ready a test, and a weapon of but a few kilotons at that. Kennedy was annoyed that we couldn't respond to Soviet developments sooner, and bigger. He'd endured a bruising meeting with Khrushchev the previous July in Vienna where "Khrushchev beat the hell out of me," Kennedy said. In October, he also had to contend with the gigantic bomb.

To give a sense of how huge the "emperor of bombs" was, consider what the United States had done at its two main test sites from 1946 through August 18, 1958. One was in Nevada, seventy miles from Las Vegas, where the Los Alamos and Livermore laboratories tested fission bombs. There, we could put part of a thermonuclear weapon design into a tower and detonate enough of it to know the rest would work. The other site was a pair of atolls in the Marshall Islands in the Pacific. Of some forty-six atmospheric tests the United States conducted in that Pacific test site through 1958, the most powerful was the test of a Los Alamos design called Bravo detonated on March 1, 1954. It was a fifteen-megaton device that had a yield equivalent to about 1,000 Hiroshima bombs.[3]

In 1957 we at Livermore tested the general design of a much smaller (in size and yield) thermonuclear warhead in a Nevada tower, and in 1958 at its full capacity of a couple hundred kilotons at Eniwetok.[4] That was the warhead that went into stockpile for the Polaris missile we deployed in submarines. Nothing we'd ever tested came close to the power of the tsar of bombs.

Kennedy's Knowledge of Missiles and the Strategic Nuclear Balance

Kennedy had campaigned for president claiming, as many then thought, that there was an adverse missile gap. In fact, as we came to know later, there wasn't. The Soviet Union's medium-range ballistic missiles could reach Western Europe, but not the United States. The space-launchers that had put *Sputnik* into orbit in 1957 could be adapted to serve as intercontinental ballistic missiles (ICBMs) able to reach the United States, but that had not yet happened. However, Khrushchev correctly implied an impending Soviet ICBM threat against the United States. In fact, we had more ICBMs than the Soviet Union, though at that time they were primitive, liquid-fueled, and vulnerable. If a missile gap existed, real or imagined, Kennedy knew he'd have to deal with it when he became president.

The issue of nuclear testing soon became conflated with the question of a missile gap. The U.S. Minuteman intercontinental ballistic missiles, which we planned to deploy in 1962, were smaller than the liquid-fueled versions and therefore would carry smaller warheads. The advantage of the Minuteman was that it was solid-fueled and ready to launch at short notice. The larger, liquid-fueled missiles took far longer to prepare for action.

In May 1961 I was to have my first substantial participation in a meeting with Kennedy. It was scheduled as a two-hour meeting. I'd been DDRE only one month. Two nights before that meeting, I was very surprised to learn that McNamara was counting on me to be the principal presenter of nuclear issues, including testing. He said that I would be presenting to a full Cabinet Room. Attendees would include the secretary and deputy secretary of defense, the secretary of state, the Joint Chiefs, the Service Secretaries, the chairman of the Atomic Energy Commission, and the director of the CIA. I gave what I hoped was a dispassionate account of the potential gains that testing could achieve for the Soviet Union and the United States, and the ways that the Soviet testers might try to cheat without detection. I deliberately did not reach a conclusion on whether or not the United States should resume testing. I think the president was surprised; I had the reputation of being a partisan of resumption.

Kennedy asked me if we needed lighter nuclear weapons. There was a series of them still under development that could improve yield-to-weight ratios. Improvement would reduce the weight of our warheads, making room for more penetration aids against Soviet antiballistic missile (ABM) defenses. Testing the weapons could augment the already robust assurance that we would be able to carry out a second strike if we were hit. I think I made it clear that our existing weapons did not require more testing, but that we could test new designs.

At that same meeting, I got some idea of how President Kennedy approached fundamental issues of national security and thermonuclear war. He asked Air Force Chief of Staff General Curtis LeMay, who had designed and carried out a systematic strategic bombing campaign in World War II, for his evaluation of the current strategic situation. Kennedy wanted a baseline from which to examine what changes might be possible under three scenarios: a nuclear moratorium, a situation in which both the United States and the Soviet Union continued nuclear testing, and a situation in which the United States kept to a moratorium and the Soviet Union did the maximum amount of possible cheating.

Kennedy asked me, and then LeMay, what the casualties on both sides would be depending on who struck first. Our estimates were not very different. The numbers of casualties were in the tens of millions in either case. Different scenarios would determine how many tens. If the Soviet camp struck first, they would probably kill 30 million or 40 million people. We could strike back and kill even more. If we struck first, the Soviet Union could retaliate and probably kill 10 million or 20 million. Kennedy (like his successors, including Ronald Reagan long after him) believed a nuclear war would not be winnable by anybody and must be prevented. I sensed that LeMay had a different view. He thought of a U.S. first strike as something you might have to do and a Soviet counterstrike as something the United States might have to accept, as catastrophic as that would be.

Kennedy went on to ask LeMay if he felt confident that if the Soviets struck first, the United States could be sure of striking back. LeMay said that our strategic bombers would get through to destroy Soviet cities, but he thought that the Soviet Union could overcome the U.S. strategic advantage in as few as two or three years. We planned to put Minuteman missiles in underground silos designed to be less vulnerable to attack; we already had Polaris missiles in submarines at sea. One conclusion that grew from a flurry of meetings over the next months was that if both sides could deter the other from all-out thermonuclear war, conventional wars became more likely.

To be sure of having a survivable strike force, the Kennedy administration increased expenditure on strategic weapons by accelerating the

Minuteman production capability and expanding an improved Polaris program. Kennedy and McNamara also began a program to increase our conventional weapons capability by an even greater amount and paid much more attention to the effectiveness of "general purpose" forces. These had been allowed to languish because they were expensive to maintain. Nuclear weapons were a cheaper alternative. Many people believed that with a thermonuclear capability we'd not use anything less.

An anti-ballistic missile (ABM) program was the single thing that carried the risk of unbalancing the strategic nuclear situation, so Kennedy paid it much attention. He met many times with experts to learn more about ABMs and strategic weapons in general. Before Edward Teller's appointment to speak with President Kennedy, I told Edward that if he was going to offer arguments that the ABM program was a reason to resume nuclear tests (and in fact such an argument existed, though I did not find it convincing), he should be sure he knew quite a lot about the ABM program because the president did. From Teller's recounting of that meeting, Kennedy demonstrated that he knew more about the program than Teller, who then made a considerable effort to get himself up to speed.

The president had a favorite question he would ask at meetings, though he well knew the answer. As some people talked about a U.S. need to develop our own 100-megaton "Tsar Bomba," or as I urged the development of penetration capabilities to ensure we could saturate Soviet defenses, or whenever the general question of the destructiveness of nuclear weapons came up, Kennedy would ask in a seemingly innocent way: "How much was the yield of the bomb dropped on Hiroshima?" That was his way of calling attention to the fact that a 20-kiloton bomb could do a great deal of damage, so that at some point you were reaching the law of diminishing returns on yields and numbers of weapons. Of course, he realized our retaliatory forces had to survive, and to penetrate. He wanted to make sure the whole picture was appreciated: you could do enough to deter the enemy from using its weapons with a comparatively small number of your own if the other side was sure that our forces would survive and reach their targets.

Just before Thanksgiving 1961, Kennedy wanted to be briefed on Nike Zeus, an army-funded ballistic missile defense system. Its possible full-scale deployment was an issue in decisions that would be made that winter for the 1963 defense budget. The army had been pressing for approval to deploy Nike Zeus. Its contractor was Bell Laboratories of Western Electric and AT&T. The army's point man was Major C. J. LeVan, an accomplished briefer, but not a technical expert. I had convinced McNamara that Nike Zeus would not work against a massive attack. McNamara told me to make the case. The day before Kennedy was to leave for Hyannis Port for Thanksgiving, he asked his science adviser, Jerry Wiesner, and me to brief him at the White House.

I had devoted many hours during the previous six months to evaluating Nike Zeus. Its full-scale engineering development had begun under Eisenhower as one reaction to the Soviet ballistic missile program. Development had continued over subsequent presidencies, so there was some momentum behind the army's drive for a decision from Kennedy to deploy it. Though McNamara had been convinced by our analysis that Nike Zeus should not be deployed, its development had been completed. It therefore seemed worthwhile to conduct tests to learn more about the limitations of ABMs as they faced incoming intercontinental ballistic missiles. The tests could teach us more about the radar signatures of nosecones carrying warheads on ballistic missiles so we could discriminate between actual nuclear warheads and decoys or debris.

After the meeting at the White House, the president asked me to join the group coming to Hyannis Port where he was meeting with his senior defense and science advisory teams the day after Thanksgiving. When I arrived for my part of the meeting, Kennedy and his advisers were discussing a civil defense program, part of which became "duck and cover." People who were school children in the 1960s can remember bomb drills that had them duck under their desks, and the advent of fallout shelters dug into back yards. Bobby Kennedy came to the civil defense part of the meeting. He'd been playing touch football in the rain with Paul "Red" Fay, under secretary of the navy who had been a PT boat commander with the president in the Pacific.[5] I remember Joseph Kennedy being very solicitous of Bobby, helping him take off his wet sweater, giving him a towel to rub himself down. I was impressed with the family's devotion to each other, and their vigor.

After talk of fallout shelters, we proceeded to ballistic missile defense. I was sitting near the president when an Associated Press photographer asked to take a photo that appeared in the next issue of *Newsweek*. The president rearranged us: "I want Ros Gilpatric sitting next to me in the picture. He's the handsomest man in Washington," he said. Gilpatric was the deputy secretary of defense. I was amused that the news photo taken of that meeting focused on Kennedy and Gilpatric. I ended up facing away from the camera at the other end of the group.[6] We strengthened Kennedy's conviction not to go ahead with the deployment of the Nike Zeus ABM program. That has been the fate of every subsequent proposal for a massive ballistic missile defense because it is so expensive when considered in relation to its potential effectiveness. ABM systems are much more expensive than the ways other major powers have to defeat them. Against more primitive attacks and poorer and less rational attackers, that logic is less overwhelming, which explains the George W. Bush administration's decision to deploy an antiballistic system as a modest defense capability in Alaska. The system is meant to defend against a possible North Korean nuclear missile attack. Today, we are in the very preliminary stages of thinking about deploying ballistic missile defenses in Europe against a potential threat of medium-range missiles aimed at Europe or the Middle East from Iran.

We completed tests on Nike Zeus that helped us refine components as we made them operable at Kwajalein, an atoll in the Marshall Islands. The tests taught us more about radar features aimed at discriminating warheads from decoys. We did not spend money that would have enabled a deployed version of Nike Zeus since there wasn't going to be a deployed version. That kind of expenditure was cut back and eventually eliminated.

The lesson learned is that just because technology can be accomplished, like a 100-megaton bomb, or Nike Zeus—a system that would cost billions of dollars to develop and many more billions of dollars to deploy (and would even meet its technical specifications)—is not justification enough for doing it. There are only so many dollars and personnel capable of carrying out technological research and development, let alone deployment and operation. Before committing to deployment, you need to factor in a system's effectiveness in terms of cost-benefit ratios, how the other side may react, and the outcome of such a competition. Unfortunately, that is too often done in hindsight.

The Bermuda Summit

Shortly before Christmas 1961, from December 20 to 22, I attended the Bermuda Summit with the president. I'd gotten a call from the chair of the Atomic Energy Commission, the Nobel Prize winner Glenn Seaborg. I knew him from the University of California's Radiation Laboratory. He said President Kennedy wanted me to join him at his meeting with Prime Minister Harold Macmillan and Foreign Secretary Alec Douglas-Home of Britain to discuss issues of strategic nuclear warfare. "We're going to be talking about the nuclear test ban and ballistic missile defense and you're the expert," Seaborg said. "You're the person in the administration who is most engaged on these issues."

We met in Palm Beach because the president was staying at the home of friends there. They hosted a reception that evening. Cocktail glass in hand, I stood near enough to President Kennedy to hear him tell Secretary of State Dean Rusk that, sadly, his father, Joe, had suffered a devastating stroke the previous week—not long after I'd seen him in Hyannis Port. Rusk asked the president how his father was doing. Kennedy said: "Well, he is alive but that is about all. When I go, I want to go quickly. I don't want that slow death to happen to me." That comment burned in my memory after the president's assassination.

In that chilly December in Bermuda, summit participants sat in chairs grouped around a fireplace. Prime Minister Macmillan displayed an avuncular demeanor toward Kennedy, with some right to that relationship. Macmillan's wife's nephew had been married to Kennedy's sister, Katherine. The nephew was killed in the war and Katherine was later killed in an airplane accident. At the session I attended, Macmillan claimed a major role for the United Kingdom in strategizing the nuclear balance, noting that in case of a Soviet attack, Britain's V-bomber aircraft would be among the first to retaliate; they were closest. In fact, in the case of a Soviet first strike with missiles, none of those British bombers would have survived. The group discussed the issue of nuclear testing yet again, as well as ballistic missile programs, land- and sea-based, and U.S. weapons programs the United Kingdom might join. Britain had been counting on the Skybolt, a U.S. ballistic missile then in development that was to be launched from aircraft. Launching Skybolt from the V-bombers would have solved the problem of penetrating Soviet defenses but would have done nothing to help the bombers survive a first strike while they were on the ground, even with ground alert. So when the Skybolt was canceled in 1962, we offered the United Kingdom Polaris missiles for their submarines.

By 1963, as the whole country was discussing nuclear testing, Kennedy again displayed his keen grasp of nuclear weapons and their delivery issues,[7] this time at a lunch in the White House family quarters to which he invited Jerry Wiesner, Adlai Stevenson, and me. Stevenson, then the U.S. representative to the United Nations, had pushed for an end to nuclear testing during his 1956 campaign against Eisenhower. (Eisenhower declared a moratorium on nuclear tests in 1959.) We went through the usual arguments for and against testing. As before, I took the position that the new weapons designs would have only marginal influence on the strategic balance. High-altitude tests earlier in 1962 had told us much of what we needed to know about the particular effects of those nuclear weapons. Kennedy pushed for and finally achieved a ban on atmospheric testing by the United States, the United Kingdom, and the Soviet Union on September 24, 1963.[8] Other countries did test in the atmosphere.[9]

THE LYNDON JOHNSON YEARS AND VIETNAM

In July 1965, shortly before I became air force secretary, President Johnson called a meeting of the National Security Council to discuss what to do about Vietnam. Deployments had begun but not yet reached substantial levels. Johnson asked the Service Secretaries and Joint Chiefs to join the Council in expressing their views. He invited me too. Though not yet air force secretary, I had been nominated for the position. We were all seated around the big table in the Cabinet Room. Johnson went around the table asking what each man thought was the proper response to North Vietnamese pressure on the South Vietnamese.

General Wallace Green, commandant of the Marine Corps, said that winning the war would take 500,000 ground troops and five years. No one in the room wanted to face that prospect, and no one chose to agree or disagree by a direct comment. When the president came to me, I said that we should continue to try to interdict the flow of materiel from North Vietnam to the Viet Cong in the South, and that I thought we could. Johnson kept pushing me by asking, "And then what?" I said, "Well, it seems to me that we would probably have to deploy more ground troops." And Johnson said, "And then what?" I had no good answer. Neither did anyone else. Then the president asked whether everyone agreed that he should continue to pursue the conflict and deploy ground troops. No one objected. My view then and now is that Johnson wanted to make sure that no one could later say that he had gone against the counsel of his advisers.

My Assessment of Vietnam

In October 1965 as air force secretary, I joined Stan Resor, then the secretary of the army, on a weeklong trip to Vietnam to make our own assessment. We arrived in the early evening after a twelve-hour flight that refueled at Anchorage. Though dead tired, we decided on being briefed right away. That seemed to annoy General William Westmoreland, the commander of MAC-V (Military Assistance Command–Vietnam). The general presented what amounted to a "Command Briefing," a term that denotes a canned slide show of the organization, its objectives, needs, and the tactical or strategic situation. That kind of show usually is given to visitors with influence but modest knowledge, like members of Congress. Resor and I were not encouraged by what we heard. We saw no evidence that supported Westmoreland's optimism for U.S. prospects in dealing with the Vietcong. (Later, in the Carter administration, Resor served honorably for two years as under secretary of defense for policy.)

That was not my first visit to Vietnam. I had visited as DDRE in 1962 to see what technology might be able to contribute to South Vietnamese military operations. At that time there was no direct U.S. involvement in combat. Later in the 1960s, when U.S. forces were engaged, we began an attempt to set up surveillance of the Ho Chi Minh Trail. That was the so-called McNamara Line. The technology of the day consisted of relatively primitive sensors, communications systems, and inaccurate weapons delivery systems.

As air force secretary, I inherited the air force part of the project, which was to collect the radioed information, analyze it, and use those data as the basis for determining where and when to bomb the North Vietnamese and Vietcong supply lines along the trail. In the air force, I had pushed for some studies of the bombing campaign's effectiveness and believed their conclusions that, in theory, bombing could greatly limit the North Vietnamese. Still other studies commissioned by the CIA drew a different conclusion: the North Vietnamese could prevail in supplying their troops in the South with or without an air campaign that tried to stop them. The CIA studies turned out to be right, although a bombing campaign with wider scope might have produced a different result. It also might have brought the Chinese into an active combat role.

I had the chance as air force secretary to carry further some developments I had started as DDRE. These included precision-guided weapons that made air attack more effective. Had we today's far more sophisticated technology, rather than the sensors and munitions we had back then, the McNamara Line and bombing campaign might have had the sort of success displayed in the Gulf War of 1991. As another example, the effect of NATO airpower on Serbia in the 1990s suggests that more sophisticated technology might have worked in Vietnam, at least temporarily. But in Vietnam in the 1960s, the combination of jungle rather than desert terrain, the background noise in the foliage canopy that thwarted hearing human movement, and the skills of the dedicated North Vietnamese might still have managed to defeat our efforts.

The key issue became whether to bomb not just the Ho Chi Minh Trail and its capillaries, but also the heart of that communist country. President Johnson imposed severe restraint in bombing the North Vietnamese heartland, fearful that such an action might draw in the Chinese or Soviet forces in a more explicit way. That concern intensified in 1967 when Andrei Gromyko turned up at the United Nations with a shell that had been retrieved from the deck of a Soviet ship in Haiphong Harbor. The shell had almost certainly come from a U.S. attack aircraft, which wasn't supposed to be shooting at vessels there. Johnson decided not to bomb the Vietnam heartland. What might have happened had he decided differently is one of history's unanswerable questions.

By late 1967, laser-guided bombs I helped develop closed off North Vietnamese bridges for more extended periods. The unguided bombs used earlier in the war had failed to take out those bridges despite many sorties. I personally pushed the idea of arming C-47 aircraft with heavy machine guns to provide close air support to ground forces in counterinsurgency operations. Since then, we've upgraded to C-130s with sixty-millimeter cannon; that capability continues to exist.

By the end of 1967 I had concluded that the air campaign wasn't going to have enough effect to matter, and that the war was not winnable. I had come late to that view after overestimating the effectiveness of the available technology. Others, including the military leadership, had overestimated the effectiveness of the counterinsurgency program. I, along with the rest of the national security establishment (except the CIA), had underestimated North Vietnamese determination. Our gradual increase of bombing was intended to signal that we could ratchet up the pressure to unbearable levels. Instead, the North Vietnamese concluded that they could take whatever we might dish out. The gradual escalation of the air war had inured them to our bombing raids instead of pressing them to negotiate an end to the war.

Whether an all-out bombing campaign would have changed that is unknowable. The issues around its legitimacy and valid concerns about the risk of a Soviet and Chinese response ruled out such an action. I concluded that the government of South Vietnam, lacking the support of its people and a strong political base, could not defeat the Vietcong insurgency, which made a continued, massive commitment of U.S. forces fruitless and unjustified. In 1968 Clark Clifford succeeded McNamara as secretary of defense. Though Clifford was regarded as a hawk when he served as a foreign policy adviser to President Kennedy, his advice to President Johnson early in 1968 to negotiate and wind down the U.S. presence in Vietnam was sensible. By then many of us had started to think differently about China. Before that, the mistaken fear that China was using North Vietnam as an instrument in a wider game had been one reason for U.S. persistence in Vietnam.

Henry Kissinger and James Schlesinger assert that by 1973 we had won the Vietnam War. They say that after withdrawing our troops all we needed to do was pour money into Vietnam and the South Vietnamese government would have survived. ("For a decent interval," Henry has said.) The assertion that we won is essentially a stab-in-the-back argument because Congress cut off funds to South Vietnam. Even so, the South Vietnamese had a great deal of equipment and forces when they gave up to the North's army. In my view, the South Vietnamese suffered a collapse of morale. They gave up because their government was rotten and they lacked the morale to support it.

TECHNOLOGY CAN'T OVERCOME
CORRUPT GOVERNMENTS

Looking back on the Vietnam War from my current perspective, I learned lessons that are applicable to Afghanistan. For the first three years of active U.S. participation in the Vietnam War, I saw it as a way to push back the

Chinese attempt to take over all of Asia. But by late 1968 I had begun to see China in a different light. In December 1968, before Richard Nixon's inauguration, I privately told Mel Laird and Henry Kissinger that my advice was to get out of Vietnam as fast as they could. In testimony at a classified hearing on the budget to the House Defense Appropriations Committee just before the Nixon administration took over in January 1969, I told the committee that "I as an individual, and we as a nation, ought to have learned that the Vietnamese government did not have the loyalty of the people and therefore success in the Vietnam War was not achievable."

That I had learned that lesson myself became public testimony during my January 1977 appearance before the Senate Armed Services Committee when I was nominated as secretary of defense. I said that "we should be very cautious in expanding our foreign policy commitments beyond our vital security interests. Military action by the United States should be treated with extreme caution. A weak political base in an area outside the U.S. almost ensures that our efforts, particularly military efforts, will be fruitless, and that if there is also a weakness here at home in political support for such activities, then they have no chance of succeeding."[10]

I think the same now of our efforts in Afghanistan. The current Afghan government is unable to control the whole of the country. That is a result of the government's corruption and the lack of a functioning state that can provide cohesion among families, clans, and tribes. Those are the units to which loyalty is given. Without that cohesion, nation building is all but infeasible.

Our willingness to fight in Vietnam might have had a beneficial side effect for Indonesia. A communist attempt at a takeover of Indonesia in the fall of 1965 caused extreme violence and the ethnic cleansing of many Chinese. At the time, the U.S. buildup of forces in Vietnam was in its early and optimistic stages. Had the United States not been present, or not indicated its willingness to fight in that region, the outcome in Indonesia could have been even worse. Is that enough to justify the Vietnam War? I don't think so, but it is something to keep in mind.

A PERSONAL LESSON FROM VIETNAM

The secretary of a military department becomes part of a family in a way that is more difficult for a secretary of defense to experience. As air force secretary, I was a member of the air force family with all that implies in terms of taking care of each other in times of trouble and engaging in intense, internal disputes. Social activities, also part of my function, helped me form close professional relationships with many officers and introduced me to their wives and children.

I had no responsibility for picking targets in the Vietnam War; air force chief of staff General J. P. McConnell kept me informed of the targets in some detail. My responsibility was to recruit, train, and deploy forces and develop and procure equipment. I remember a painting that still hangs in the stairway connecting the Pentagon entrance with air force offices two floors above it. The painting shows an airman with his family. Beneath them is a quotation from the book of Isaiah (6:8): "Also I heard the voice of the Lord saying, whom shall I send and who will go for us? And said I, here I am. Send me." I am not known as an emotional person, but whenever I saw that painting I choked up. I knew when I saw off a fighter-bomber wing or a Wild Weasel squadron of electromagnetic countermeasure aircraft to operate in Vietnam that some would not come back.

Having been present at departure ceremonies for combat forces affected my attitude during the Iran hostage crisis when the issue of whether to mount a military force response arose. I did not want to be looking at target folders again, not unless it was absolutely necessary. The Vietnam War Memorial in Washington, D.C., holds names of men I knew. I remember our mistakes in the Vietnam War. We keep making more of them, especially ones that spring from a lack of deep understanding of other societies.

MAKING THE ULTIMATE DECISION

Making a decision to send troops into combat knowing some will die is no easy matter. LBJ agonized about sending boys into the Vietnam War, but of course he didn't start with a clean slate. I feel pretty good that no American service personnel were killed in an actual or potential combat operation while I was secretary of defense, with the important and tragic exception of those killed by the aircraft collision at Desert One in Iran. Given my mandate and responsibilities, I did the best I could and therefore could sleep most nights, but not always. No, not always.

President Carter felt strongly that the bar for risking the deaths of American military personnel should be set high. I'm sure that George W.

Bush and Barack Obama, whether their deployment decisions were wise or not, also made those decisions very seriously.

AIRCRAFT DECISIONS AS AIR FORCE SECRETARY

I was air force secretary for forty months. I was responsible for acquisition and contracting for various aircraft. For example, General McConnell and I had to decide whether to select an F-5 or an A-7 tactical aircraft for use in Vietnam. The A-7, developed by the navy, was an attack aircraft. It dropped bombs. The F-5 was a small fighter aircraft that could be adapted to drop bombs. Air force pilots preferred the F-5 because it flew like a sports car and was an air force plane. The A-7 was slower and didn't accelerate fast. It was more like a minivan. If you're delivering many bombs, a minivan is better than a sports car, so we overruled the pilots and chose the navy's plane. (The air force was much more willing to use navy aircraft than vice versa.)

At the same time that was going on, we were urging the F-5 as the right choice upon the Taiwanese air force. The reason was that we wanted to enable Taiwanese air defense, but *not* give them the capability to drop bombs on China. These days, that sort of choice would probably not be made by the air force secretary. It would be made in the office of the secretary of defense, probably by the undersecretary of defense for policy or the undersecretary of defense for acquisition and technology, and would become a recommendation to the president.

DEVELOPMENT OF THE C-5 AIRCRAFT

As air force secretary I completed the full development and began procurement of the C-5 aircraft. It was to be a heavy-lift jet transport that could fly 100 tons of materiel over long distances. There had been two competitors for the contract while I was DDRE: Lockheed Martin and Boeing. Lockheed won, and forty-five years later the C-5 is still in the inventory and used.[11] Boeing lost, but turned its design into the 747 passenger plane.

The lesson learned is that some military hardware programs have fifty-year lifetimes before their products are retired. On the civilian side, only transportation and utility systems last that long. So it's important to get the systems right. The Systems Analysis Office was heavily engaged in the C-5 project. Its job is to compare different ways of achieving a goal with various systems. The office wasn't staffed by technological people, yet some of them thought they could design better than designers. They seized upon this project, and as air force secretary I had to push back against their proposed changes.

In the end, I think the C-5 answered the four main questions I use to determine if a new system is cost-effective: Is it vital? Is it insurance against an adversary? Is it marginal or even foolish? Is it worth the cost? When the C-5 was rolled out in grand style on March 2, 1968, my wife and I rode in a ceremonial parade with President Johnson, Ladybird Johnson, and the president's dogs through Dobbins Air Force Base in Marietta, Georgia. On the reviewing stand, we shared our pride in the huge, new aircraft. The guests included Luci Baines Johnson, whose husband was in the air force and deployed to Vietnam, and the president's grandchild, and many national civilian and uniformed dignitaries.[12]

BY NATIONAL DEFENSE I MEAN MY DISTRICT

Johnson decided to close some Air Force Reserve bases. We had too many; closing bases saves money in defense budgets in the long run, though it strips money out of local communities. Among others, we decided to close an Air National Guard base in Pennsylvania, one in New York, and one in California. As air force secretary I had to call the governors of those states to explain our decisions because they have a special interest in Air and Army National Guard units.

I called Governor Pat Brown of California. He listened. I called Governor Bill Scranton of Pennsylvania. He listened and later became a personal friend. I tried calling Governor Nelson Rockefeller of New York repeatedly and never got through. Had I been secretary of defense at the time, I'm sure he would have taken my call.[13]

ARM-TWISTING

Johnson was known to be comfortable using strong language. When I was in the process of closing those air force bases and speaking with the governors, members of Congress protested. At about the same time, Johnson called me at home to discuss a matter that showed how political pressure can work in both directions. My wife answered the phone and listened transfixed as Johnson used four-letter words to impart his directive to me. In essence, he told me to let a certain Louisiana member of Congress who was dragging his feet on raising the debt limit of the budget know this: if he didn't go along, the president and secretary of the air force would pull a base out of *his* district, too. Colene was shocked at the language the president used. These days, multiple communications channels spread popular culture such that many people talk that way.

DO WE REALLY NEED SERVICE SECRETARIES?

The United States Code provides the legal basis for the roles, mission, and organization of the Department of Defense and each of the military services. Service Secretaries (formally, the secretaries of the military departments) ensure civilian control of the military. They are a layer of insulation that limits the extent to which the military staff has its own direct connection to Congress and the political process. The civilian layer also softens direct inputs from Congress to the military. Title 10 of the Code puts military departments under that extra layer of civilian control as a way to protect our democracy. There is a Service Secretary for each branch of service except the Marines. They are part of the Navy Department (but not part of the navy).

Having served as air force secretary, on balance I'm not convinced we need Service Secretaries at all. The useful functions they serve could be handled within the Office of the Secretary of Defense by a thinner layer of management than the Service Secretaries now employ. The Service Secretary has no combat responsibility and needs to get along with his uniformed chief. At its best, the reciprocal loyalty of the Service Secretary and the military chief can be constructive with the military relying on the Service Secretary to make its case to the defense secretary and to Congress. The Service Secretary can do that even as he or she shapes the military organization (army, navy, air force, marines) to better fit the national security strategy. I believe that J. P. McConnell, who was air force chief of staff, worked that way with me and with my civilian staff. He and his military staff trusted me, believing that if they convinced me to make their case, I could do that better than they could.

That said, it is much easier and therefore more typical for the Service Secretary to become little more than a mouthpiece for his (or her) military subordinates. If unwilling to serve that function, and an issue is important enough to the military, they will go around the Service Secretary to the media or to contractors who have the ear of their representatives in Congress. Over the past twenty years, the training that a Service Secretary gained on the job to prepare for further government service has eroded. During the 1950s and 1960s, six Service Secretaries became deputy secretary of defense; then only one more (Graham Claytor) till 2000, and only two since then. Apart from the first defense secretary, James Forrestal, and later Thomas Gates in 1959, I am the only former Service Secretary to have become secretary of defense. The erosion of status and function of Service Secretaries suggests that a more streamlined and efficient arrangement should be adopted. We can abolish the separate civilian secretariats (designated as such in the National Security Statutes) and substitute a smaller cadre within and under the Office of the Secretary of Defense.

There are currently twenty-one layers of bureaucracy in the Office of the Air Force Service Secretary (titled assistant or deputy assistant of this or that) with corresponding layers of staff. Streamlining all this within the Office of the Secretary of Defense may be one of my more controversial suggestions, one of the most difficult to achieve, and one of the most useful.

TWO PARALLEL NARRATIVES: NEW WEAPONS SYSTEMS AND AGREEMENTS TO LIMIT THEM

As air force secretary, and throughout my career, I continued to be involved in two parallel narratives that describe the U.S. response to the threat of nuclear war. One narrative is the elaborate and dead-serious game of creating weapons systems. Their basing and deployment must enable them to survive a preemptive first strike by an opponent and retain the ability to strike back, penetrate the opponent's defenses, and completely destroy its urban centers, military, leadership, and command structure. The purpose of that capability is to deter a nuclear attack on the United States. That narrative is about delivery systems and nuclear weapon stockpiles and assuring the Soviet Union—and now others as well as Russia—that destruction of their country and their regime would result if they used their weapons. Skeptics describe that strategy as MAD, for mutually assured destruction, but it was and is a sane doctrine that has kept nuclear peace for decades. The second narrative is about approaches to limiting nuclear weapon use and weapon stockpiles through international agreements. That narrative begins with the test ban that Eisenhower hoped would begin the process of limiting nuclear weapons.[14]

History of the Nuclear Testing Moratorium, 1958–59

President Eisenhower had come to office promising to end the Korean War. There is some evidence that he fulfilled his promise in part by letting the Chinese and North Koreans know that the United States would contemplate another use of nuclear weapons. Whether he made that threat or not, they did come to the negotiating table. In 1958 Eisenhower acted on his own convictions about the danger of a nuclear arms competition: he initiated negotiations with the Soviet leadership that preceded four international conferences in Geneva during the summer and into 1959.[15]

The first conference between U.S. and Soviet official delegations sought measures to avoid surprise nuclear attack. That possibility had become more worrisome given the new prospect of ballistic missile deployment. With the second conference, Atoms for Peace, Eisenhower tried to "tame the atom" through a program meant to bring the benefits of nuclear power and nuclear medicine to the world while discouraging the pursuit of nuclear weapons. In practice, however, that program encouraged dissemination of reactor technology, the first step on one path to weapons-grade fissile material, and thereby led to the proliferation of nuclear weapons.

The third conference in 1958, at which I was a junior member of the U.S. delegation while associate director of the Livermore Laboratory, was attended by four delegations from each of the NATO and Warsaw Pact nations. The Soviet delegates sat on one side of a table with those from Poland, Czechoslovakia, and Romania. The U.S. contingent sat on the other side with representatives from the United Kingdom (which had nuclear weapons), France (which didn't have them yet, but got them in 1960), and Canada. (China got them in 1964.) That conference focused on detecting nuclear weapons tests. The key question was: can you hide them? A fourth conference in 1959 with U.S., U.K., and Soviet representatives in attendance, and at which I was a delegate as the senior U.S. technical member, focused on issues of negotiating a nuclear test ban.

When I was at Livermore Laboratory, we had devised various ways to hide nuclear tests underground and in outer space in part to suggest that adherence to a ban could be evaded. Concerns about fallout and to a lesser extent about nuclear proliferation generated public advocacy of a ban. The most compelling national security reason for a reliable end to nuclear testing was to limit Soviet advances on nuclear weapons technology. By the late 1950s most U.S. scientists—but not Edward Teller—believed that America was more advanced. We based our belief on unilateral intelligence. We had ways to monitor Soviet missile and nuclear tests. We saw the missiles they proudly trotted out for parades. When it came to their nuclear weapons capability, we could tell a lot from the debris left after their nuclear test explosions. Our aircraft picked up debris from their test sites in central Asia; when the stuff blew northeast, we collected it off the eastern coast of Siberia.

The nuclear conferences dragged on through 1958 and went nowhere. While they were taking place that summer in Geneva, King Feisal II of Iraq and his prime minister, Nuri as-Said, were killed in an army coup. Nuri as-Said's dismembered body was dragged through the streets of Baghdad. That was a reminder of the importance of limiting the number of members in the nuclear weapons club and of preventing unstable governments from acquiring nuclear weapons. Still, Ike could not get cooperation to end nuclear testing, not at the conference and not within his own executive branch. Secretary of State John Foster Dulles, the Department of Defense, and the Atomic Energy Commission had always opposed a ban. So Eisenhower turned to an outside advisory group, the President's Science Advisory Committee, for support of his view that strategic and political imperatives should trump technological aspirations, and that a test ban was in America's best security interest. In other words, he took charge and overruled his principal national security advisers. As a result, there was no nuclear testing in 1959 or 1960.

The Delicate Balance

There was always the worry that Soviet capabilities could destroy our deterrent systems before we could deliver a retaliatory strike. We thought that a Soviet counterforce strategy would have to include a combination of preemptive ballistic missile and bomber launches, air defenses, and some sort of ballistic missile defense. Late in the Eisenhower administration, the United States began the Minuteman program and later built 1,000 of those small intercontinental ballistic missiles with the solid fuel propellant that could be fired on short notice. The Soviet Union's liquid-propellant missiles took hours to fuel and could not be kept fueled all the time. We were ready with the Minuteman in 1962, which put us far ahead in an ability to launch a nuclear attack. The arithmetical projections recounted in our meetings with Kennedy had affirmed that much.

The definitive word on the workings of the strategic balance among bombers, land-based and sea-based ballistic missiles, ballistic-missile defense, and civil defense came from a study carried out in 1963 and 1964 in my Defense Research and Engineering office, led by Brigadier General (later Lieutenant General) Glenn Kent of the air force with three other officers.[16] It showed that an offense could defeat defenses at lower cost. In analytic terms, the exchange ratio was adverse for the defense. A mix of three offensive forces was most cost-effective in terms of ensuring survival and retaliatory capability. Civil defense could save some part of the population at relatively low cost, but not the structures and resources that create an orderly civilization. In other words, appropriate force planning by both the United States and the Soviet Union would mean that each could destroy the other by launching a nuclear attack, and would in turn be destroyed. Hence MAD—mutually assured destruction—would be the outcome of a thermonuclear war.

As the1960s proceeded, Soviet leaders responded in a worrisome way, first with the deployment of intermediate-range ballistic missiles to Cuba at a time when the Soviet regime had few ICBMs. When the United States forced the Soviet Union to back down during the Cuban missile crisis, one of the Soviet responses was to accelerate its ICBM program. It established radars on the Baltic coast. That seemed to indicate (incorrectly as it turned out) that Soviet authorities were pushing a massive ballistic missile defense capability. We knew for certain that they had an elaborate air defense system, enormously greater than ours, because we had a big bomber force they needed to defend against. We'd had our own Distant Early Warning (DEW) line since the 1950s, which consisted of radars across northern Canada. While I was DDRE we installed much more capable radars in Greenland, Canada, and Alaska and elsewhere in the United States that could track, not just detect, a Soviet bomber force.

AIRBORNE ALERT

The concern that the Soviet Union could somehow launch a preemptive attack, wipe out our bombers, and then have enough air defense left to deal with our remaining capability caused us to establish an Airborne Alert program. In addition to keeping some nuclear-armed bombers on ground-alert, we put a few bombers with nuclear weapons into the sky and continued that practice constantly until the late 1960s. After that, we kept airborne at all times an aircraft capable of transmitting the order to launch a retaliatory nuclear attack. That program operated until the end of the Cold War in 1990.

Early in the Carter administration, when the Soviet Union began to move its submarines carrying ballistic missiles closer to the United States, we heightened the ground-alert status of our bombers. We wanted some of them able to be in the air within fifteen minutes. That was less time than the interval between detection of a ballistic missile launched from a Soviet submarine and its possible arrival at our bomber bases, so those bombers would survive the attack. As the nature of the Soviet threat shifted from bombers to ballistic missiles, we dismantled most of our air defense program, leaving only a modest ability to survey our borders and to track and intercept interlopers.

PENETRATION AIDS PROGRAM

While I was DDRE, I put emphasis on a penetration aids program for getting through missile defense systems. We devised warhead imitators. For example, if you could carry 1,000 pounds on a missile, you'd use half the weight for a re-entry vehicle containing a nuclear warhead. The rest of the weight would be much lighter objects that looked like re-entry vehicles to ABM radars, thus saturating the defense. Still other parts of the payload were designed to jam, confuse, and blind an enemy's radar.

Of course, the best imitator of a warhead is another warhead. So eventually we put three warheads, each weighing less than a standard one, onto ballistic missiles and aimed all three at the same city target. Later we realized we could aim them at different targets. The defender would have to hit all three missiles to defend. A defender has to defend all his targets; the attacker can, at the time of the attack, choose to attack only a subset of them. And the attacker doesn't have to destroy all of the enemy's cities to destroy its country.

U.S. missile guidance systems were better than the Soviet systems. We put three warheads on each Minuteman, independently targeted. It was a good idea, but as time went on Soviet scientists took advantage of the higher payload capacity of their ICBMs. They could put more warheads onto each of their missiles even though their nuclear weapons technology meant that their warheads had to be heavier than ours. Our Multiple Independently Targetable Reentry Vehicle (MIRV) program inspired a similar Soviet program.

By the 1970s, when I became secretary of defense, Soviet missile accuracy had improved. We had to create another survival tactic in addition to hardening the silos that housed our ICBMs. By adopting MIRVing, which the Soviet scientists imitated, we had decreased our security as well as theirs. Current proposals for further limitation and reduction of Russian and U.S. nuclear arsenals include banning MIRVs on some or all missiles. Had we thought ahead to the probable outcome, we might have tried to arrive at an agreement with the Soviet Union not to further develop MIRVs in either country. That probably would have failed. New technologies have a momentum of their own.

SMART BOMBS AND CRUISE MISSILES

In the late 1950s and early 1960s, General Bernard Shriever of the air force managed the development of the first U.S. land-based medium-range and intercontinental ballistic missiles. In 1963, as head of the Air Force Systems Command, he convened Project Forecast to identify prospective technological breakthroughs that could alter military capabilities in a game-changing way. Gordon Saville, a retired air force major general, chaired a group of outside experts who looked at a wide range of technologies and possible systems, from lighter aircraft to intelligence satellites. One major recommendation was to concentrate on Zero CEP, which means hitting a target within a circular error probability of, for example, less than a foot. From that idea flowed generations of increasingly accurate weapons called precision-guided munitions (PGMs).[17]

During my tenure as DDRE, we instituted several PGM programs using optical and other guidance methods, including lasers, and other devices for homing in on radio signals or on the optical contrast created by the edge of a target. Later, while I was secretary of the air force, we developed some of these PGMs to a higher level of accuracy and reliability. During my tenure as secretary of defense, we developed and began deploying terrain-following systems, Global Positioning System (GPS) guidance, and inertial guidance systems for use in PGMs. And we developed a new generation of ballistic and cruise missiles.[18]

After I'd left office, the Department of Defense deployed a new PGM called the Joint Direct Attack Munition (JDAM).[19] It attaches GPS-capability and fins to individual free-fall bombs. We had large quantities of those older bombs stockpiled. The fins and guidance system can alter the path of the bomb toward a target whose location is identified by the GPS system while the bomb is falling. This new generation of weapons and the intelligence, reconnaissance, and surveillance (ISR) satellites we put into orbit—and their improvements—refine our ability to destroy military targets using a small fraction of the attacks and the cost required years earlier. (These weapons reduce, but do not eliminate, civilian casualties.) This history is an example, unfortunately rare, of a well-thought-out, decades-long program, one that I was able to guide through the 1960s and 1970s and that continues to this day.

One of the first issues that I had to deal with as secretary of defense was the future of the cruise missile program. By the mid-1970s two technological developments had made cruise missiles more promising strategic arms than the comparatively crude versions we had during the Eisenhower and Kennedy eras. One development was a small, efficient turbine engine that enabled small cruise missiles to reach long ranges reliably. Because the missile was small, it could have a low radar cross-section that made it hard to detect, even before incorporating advanced stealth technology. The other development was the terrain-following radar system that could be incorporated into the missile for accurate targeting. It was accurate to a few meters; now GPS can make the cruise missile accurate to within a few feet. That means these missiles can be armed with conventional (nonnuclear) warheads and be effective against various military targets.

I considered it essential to maintain the triad of ICBMs, submarine-launched ballistic missiles (SLBMs), and strategic bombers. An important extra strategic capability was nuclear-armed cruise missiles that could be launched from bombers. Taken together, these weapons enabled our strategy to strike, penetrate, defend, and strike back after being hit. In addition, ground-launched or submarine-launched cruise missiles with conventional (nonnuclear) warheads also proved important in the Gulf War.

1961. Harold Brown (right), director of Defense Research and Engineering; Deputy Secretary of Defense Roswell Gilpatric (seated); and Secretary of Defense Robert McNamara in his office under a portrait of America's first secretary of defense, James Forrestal. Sixteen years later Brown would be in office here.

March 23, 1962. President Kennedy showed keen interest in a ballistic missile early warning system displayed at Vandenberg Air Force Base, California. Brown advised the president and Secretary of Defense Robert McNamara on major weapons systems. (Photo courtesy of Critical Past.com)

December 16, 1969, The Cabinet Room. Meeting of the General Advisory Committee of the Arms Control and Disarmament Agency during the Nixon administration. Brown, just back from the Helsinki SALT I talks, reported on progress. Clockwise from left: Douglas Dillon, Dean Rusk, William Scranton, John J. McCloy, chair, Harold Brown, Peter Peterson, Lauris Norstad, Phil Farley, Kermit Gordon(?), William Foster, James Killian, William Casey, President Nixon, Henry Kissinger, I. W. Abel, John Wheeler, and Cyrus Vance.

1976. Trilateral Commission meeting with President Ford. Members from North America, Western Europe, and Japan promoted economic, political, and security cooperation.

1977. Secretary of Defense Brown (right), National Security Adviser Zbigniew Brzezinski (in profile), and Secretary of State Cyrus Vance met Thursdays over lunch to discuss and debate issues. Meeting without staffs was often the best way to reach recommendations or provide alternatives for presidential decisions.

Brown spoke with the president several times a week. One of few cabinet officials to remain in office all four years of Jimmy Carter's presidency, Brown had a central role in the normalization of relations with China, the SALT II agreement, the Panama Canal Treaties, and the re-invigoration of NATO.

February 1979, Egypt. Five months after President Carter signed the Camp David Peace Accords, and following the shah's forced departure from Iran, Brown visited Mideast allies to assure continuing U.S. support. In Egypt, Brown (right) and Assistant Defense Secretary David McGiffert (to Brown's left) met with, left to right, Vice President Hosni Mubarak, President Anwar al-Sadat, and Foreign Minister Mustafa Khalil.

Israel, days later. Brown with Prime Minister Menachem Begin and U.S. Ambassador Samuel Lewis. Begin and Sadat shared the Nobel Peace Prize in 1978 for forging the first Israeli-Egyptian peace accord. President Carter was awarded a Nobel Peace Prize in 2002.

February 1979. Brown was the first U.S. secretary of defense to visit Saudi Arabia, meeting with Prince Salman, then governor of Riyadh Province and now the Crown Prince, as well as with Prince Sultan, the defense minister (shown here), as part of his Mideast trip to reassure allies of continuing U.S. commitment to peace. Three days later Brown visited King Hussein of Jordan.

Secretary of Defense Harold Brown with the Joint Chiefs. Brown met with the Joint Chiefs weekly and gave a defining boost to jointness as a career path to enable more interservice planning, operations, and compatible equipment, initiatives carried further by the Goldwater-Nichols Act. Top row left to right: Lou Wilson, Tom Hayward, Lew Allen, and Bernard Rogers. Bottom row left to right: Deputy Secretary of Defense Charles Duncan, Harold Brown, and David Jones.

January 1980. Brown, the first U.S. secretary of defense to visit China, meets with Deng Xiaoping exactly a year after normalization of relations with China. Brown initiated military-to-military talks and maintained a close relationship with Chinese officials thereafter.

In 1980 China was decades behind Western technology, as Brown saw when he visited an aircraft engine factory there. He experienced the bitterest cold he'd ever felt viewing ground and air force exercises at a base near Beijing.

May 1983. Brown offers his perspective as the Scowcroft Commission looks at issues of strategic forces, the MX missile, and Star Wars. Sharing a light moment here are President Reagan, and to Reagan's left clockwise, Brent Scowcroft, (unknown), James Woolsey (with glasses), Casper Weinberger, Harold Brown, Richard Helms, Melvin Laird (partially hidden), (unknown), William Clarke (at far end), Robert McFarlane, John Deutch (with glasses), James Schlesinger (with pipe), and Al Haig.

July 29, 1993. President Clinton, flanked by Brown and his wife, Colene, presents Dr. Brown with the 1992 presidential Fermi Medal, one of the most prestigious awards in science and technology. On the left is Hazel O'Leary, secretary of energy. Brown was cited for "outstanding contributions to national security, leadership in development of nuclear weapons and in formulating nuclear deterrence policy during the difficult Cold War period, and ongoing counsel."

January 25, 2006. President G. W. Bush convened a meeting and photo op with former secretaries of defense and other officials and his own team in the Cabinet room. Brown is on the left facing Donald Rumsfeld.

2012. Brown's involvement in government continues as a member of the Defense Policy Board that advises sitting secretaries of defense. Brown chaired the board for five years in the 1990s and continues serving as a member now, offering his perspective to Secretary of Defense Leon Panetta.

THE MX MISSILE PROGRAM

MX was to be a new, big, MIRVed missile (with ten independently targeted warheads on each missile) to provide a cost-effective supplement to the Minuteman in the ICBM component of the strategic nuclear triad. We could strike ten different targets with one MX missile because as its reentry vehicles separated, another small stage of propulsion moved them over a wide enough area to hit ten different places. The MX was designed to address the concern that the fixed-base Minuteman was vulnerable to the increasingly accurate Soviet ICBM force that they would likely use in a first strike.

My support for a mobile-based MX system was an answer for that concern. I simply did not think it made sense to depend entirely on a sea-based force for a survivable missile capability. I thought it necessary for the United States to have a less vulnerable land-based force. At first, President Carter was not a strong advocate of the MX missile program. He committed to it after his decision to not produce the B-1 bomber. That decision, along with the continuing buildup of Soviet missile forces, raised the pressure to modernize the other part of our land-based strategic nuclear forces, the ICBMs. Even as I endorsed the MX land-based missile, I accelerated development of the larger Ohio-class nuclear submarine, the first of which was launched in 1979, and the Trident missile, larger and more accurate than its predecessors, and with more warheads.[20] We carried forward the conversion of Poseidon submarines to a fully MIRVed missile capacity.

Not in My Back Yard

The most difficult issue in the MX program was finding an acceptable basing system for its deployment. The increasing accuracy of Soviet missiles made fixed basing, even in very hardened silos, almost impossible because the large payload of the MX made it an exceptionally valuable target. For the MX missile to survive an attack, we had to establish a basing system that would make it very difficult for incoming Soviet missiles to find it. The same precision guidance and improved accuracy that made our strategic forces more effective were mirrored on the Soviet side. Depending on the yield and accuracy of a Soviet warhead, and the hardness of a silo, the calculated probability of a single Soviet warhead destroying the MX missile in its silo could be about 80 percent. Two Soviet warheads could have a 96 percent chance of destroying it. Several ways around that problem existed. For reasons more political than practical, none of them was successfully implemented. Indeed, the public reaction against MX acquired its own acronym: NIMBY—Not in My Back Yard.

We had considered hiding the MX by having a lot of silos and moving the missile around in a sort of shell game so the Soviet Union couldn't know where it was at any given time. It's much easier and cheaper to build a hiding place than a missile, and our treaty with the Soviet Union limited missile numbers, not their shelters. We wanted to spread out the silos so that one incoming Soviet warhead of about a megaton couldn't reach and destroy more than one MX. That strategy could deter an attack by confronting the Soviet planners with an adverse exchange ratio: they would always have to use more of their force than the portion of ours they could expect to destroy. A rational enemy, if starting from a position of only near-parity, would be deterred from attacking preemptively since one result of the attack would shift the relative balance against it.

To ensure that MX missiles would survive an attack, I recommended that 200 MX missiles be sheltered in Nevada, Utah, New Mexico, or Texas among 4,600 relatively inexpensive silo-like shelters.[21] We called our proposal the Racetrack System. Transporters would move the missiles from place to place so that even if the enemy knew where the missile was yesterday, they wouldn't know where it would be tomorrow. We came up with a number of schemes, several of which I think would have worked had we not encountered so many real estate problems. They relegated the MX to a proposal still on the table when the Carter administration left office. Similar NIMBY problems killed a proposal by the Scowcroft Commission in 1983 to deploy a small mobile ICBM.

Dense Pack

The Reagan administration inherited our proposal and ridiculed it. Reagan's defense team proposed an alternative that theorized what could never be tested. They posited that given the way nuclear weapons work, spacing MX silos close together would require attacking warheads to be close together in space and nearly simultaneous in time to be effective, the latter because otherwise some MX missiles could be launched while its neighbors were being destroyed. The Reagan administration's theory was that the explosion of one warhead could emit enough neutrons to cause another Soviet warhead landing on a nearby silo to fizzle. That theory was called Dense Pack by the Reagan administration and rechristened by me (and others) as Dunce Pack. In the end, the Reagan team deployed fifty MXs at existing silos and didn't try to deal with their vulnerability. After fewer than a dozen years, the MXs were phased out.

On the other hand, the Minuteman first deployed in the early 1960s is still in use and housed in the same silos, though the missile itself is far different from the version that we produced fifty years ago. Now more than thirty years old, almost none of the Minuteman's original elements remain; the missiles have been repeatedly reworked and reconditioned, just as is the case for the B-52 bomber. We now rely in part on the strategic arms limitations agreement we have with Russia to ensure that the Minuteman force cannot be destroyed in a preemptive strike.

Today, both the Russians and the Chinese deploy mobile missiles. The Russians move them on trains and transporter erector launchers (TELs), which are big trucks. The Chinese run the missiles into tunnels underground and then bring them up to ground level at various places. In neither of those countries does public concern, if there is any, pose a challenge. Both Russia and China adopted the very basing methods that we explored for the MX during my time as secretary of defense.

STEALTH AIRCRAFT

Aircraft are vulnerable to detection by radar. The U-2 "spy plane" had survived by flying high enough—80,000 feet at the edge of the atmosphere—to survive surface-to-air missiles. Then the Soviet radars and missiles improved and became a greater threat. A SAM-2 (surface-to-air missile) shot down Gary Powers in his U-2 aircraft on May 1, 1960. (During the Vietnam War, Soviet missiles of this class destroyed many other U.S. aircraft.) Our work with cruise missiles—making them smaller and harder to detect—reinforced our belief that we could do the same for our aircraft.[22]

DARPA had begun a program to reduce radar cross-sections. When I became secretary of defense in 1977, I decided this was an approach worth pushing hard. Bill Perry and I launched development and production of the first stealth aircraft, the F-117.[23] Because the program was carried out secretly, we were able to produce the first full-sized version of the aircraft in 1981 in fewer than three years. These were the tactical-range aircraft that in 1991, undetected by Saddam Hussein's defense air system, destroyed the Iraqi air defenses and other targets on the first nights of the Gulf War. Their stealth was achieved by a combination of the aircraft's shape and a special coating on its surface.

THE B-1 AND B-2 PROGRAMS

Early in 1977 I advised President Carter that it would be a good idea to produce a few B-1 aircraft at a very low rate of production. That way we could keep the B-1 option open without committing to any specific number of aircraft while we saw how our new generation of ballistic and cruise missiles came along, including the MX. I was concerned about the difficulty of getting our aircraft through enemy defenses so I recommended upgrading existing B-52s and equipping them with air-launched cruise missiles. My thinking was that instead of building many expensive, high-speed B-1 bombers to make deep strikes into enemy territory, we could focus on developing highly effective cruise missiles that could be carried aboard less expensive subsonic aircraft like the B-52.

Carter canceled the B-1 program entirely in 1977, but we mistakenly kept the tooling, which allowed the Reagan administration to revive it. The results of that move showed that Carter was right to cancel the B-1, which turned out to have problems both with its range-payload abilities and its electronic countermeasures needed to reduce its vulnerability to ground-based and fighter air defenses. The cancellation of the B-1, as previously noted, strengthened the argument to add the MX missile to our modernization of strategic forces, which led to other problems. Over time, the B-2, which was the more advanced stealth bomber, proved to be a much more effective and lasting capability than the B-1. However, far fewer B-2s were built than would have been optimum from the standpoints of force structure and cost-effectiveness.

Much later, as a private citizen, I recommended to President Clinton that the air force acquire at least thirty B-2s. He explained his decision to the contrary by noting that the Joint Chiefs would not support that suggestion unless the defense budget was raised to accommodate it, and that Congress would not increase the defense budget. In retrospect, the Chiefs should have altered their priorities.

The B-2 development was completed by the Reagan administration, its production was carried out during the Bush senior administration, and it was first used in combat during the Clinton years in attacking Serbian infrastructure. It remains the most capable long-range bomber in the world. Though the B-2 is not capable of supersonic speed like the B-1, the B-2 can get through enemy defenses for attack or retaliation, and that's the important thing. Accordingly, we rely on it for the most challenging use of conventional force, which is to quickly deliver a massive, accurate strike from a long distance. Only a small fraction of the original planned production came about, in part because legislators and editorial writers argued that a military system planned for strategic nuclear use could not be the right approach after the Cold War. Well, so much for amateur strategists. As for the B-52, the archetype nuclear bomber, it has remained in use for conventional wars sixty years after it entered the force.

NEGOTIATING STRATEGIC ARMS LIMITATION AGREEMENTS (SALT)

While in private life as president of Caltech (1969–76), I was involved in strategic arms limitation and reduction issues. That took a fair amount of my time because negotiations were in Helsinki, Vienna, and Geneva, successively. SALT I marked the first instance of a U.S.-Soviet attempt to limit their strategic arms, though at an excessively high level. We soon discovered that the Soviet military kept the actual numbers of their weapons and their capabilities close to its chest. Even officials in the Soviet foreign office were not in the loop. The SALT negotiations not only brought them into the loop but also captured the attention of Soviet leadership as never before. For their part, the Soviet leadership realized that stability was more important than marginal advantages in numbers of weapons or their throw weight—bigger warheads. In 1969 that leadership was in the hands of Leonid Brezhnev, who had succeeded Khrushchev in 1964.

I was a part-time member of the U.S. government's negotiation team at the Strategic Arms Limitation Talks (SALT I) during the Nixon administration. I spent a few weeks every few months in these negotiations. It gave me a chance to use my experience as DDRE, as air force secretary, and as an analyst and strategist of nuclear weapons.

By the time SALT II negotiations reached their decisive stage, nine years after the SALT I talks began, I was secretary of defense. Cyrus Vance, Zbigniew Brzezinski, and I were the principals advising President Carter on the treaty's policy goals and provisions, including those pertaining to force structure and verification. When the time came to defend the SALT II Treaty in Senate testimony, the task fell to me.

Negotiating Ballistic Missile Defense

In SALT I negotiations, the issues included strategic offensive forces (ICBMs, submarine-launched missiles, and long-range bombers). Another important issue always on the table was ballistic missile defense because it was central to the issue of maintaining strategic stability. An effective ability to defend against the other side's missiles would be destabilizing because it could destroy retaliatory missiles that survived a first strike. Thus it could tempt a first strike. A similar but less persuasive argument applied to air defenses in the pre-missile era.

At first Soviet representatives wanted to exclude ballistic missile defense from negotiations entirely. The United States wanted to include it in SALT I. The negotiations went round and round, with both sides reversing their initial positions, and wound up with a strong limitation, but not an outright ban, on ballistic missile defenses. The value of those negotiations and the resulting SALT Treaty was twofold. While SALT I didn't greatly limit strategic nuclear weapons (and allowed far more than was needed in any rational sense), the discussions alone indicated that limits were possible and a good idea. Moreover, the talks opened dialogue and focused the attention of the Soviet leadership on the need for stability.

Limits of Missile Range and Design

The Strategic Arms Limitation Talks (SALT I) during the Nixon and Ford administrations left undecided the range and numbers of cruise missiles that the United States and the Soviet Union would allow. In 1975 President Gerald Ford and Chairman Brezhnev reached a fuzzy agreement at Vladivostok. It left many details incomplete, including how to verify compliance. The agreement never became an agreed or documented treaty. If it had, its text would have limited the range of cruise missiles to 600 kilometers, a dangerous proposition for the United States. To explain why, I need to go back in time.

Well before SALT II, in 1975 while I was at Caltech, I'd visited the Soviet Union as a guest of its Academy of Sciences and its Institute of U.S. and Canada Studies. I told my hosts that the buildup of Soviet ballistic missiles created great concern in the United States. One possible counter, I cautioned, would be for the United States to develop and deploy more sophisticated cruise missiles armed with nuclear warheads. That would pose a very different kind of threat to the Soviet Union, one that it would be unable to counter with its antiballistic missile defenses. A couple of years later in the Carter administration, that issue became an important element in SALT II negotiations. We wanted to revisit the issue of number and range of cruise missiles, but it took considerable effort to overcome the State Department's reluctance to do that.

I wanted to ensure that we could load several cruise missiles onto a single aircraft and give them adequate range. Donald Rumsfeld, the secretary of defense who preceded me (and reemerged in that post twenty years after I left it), had prevented the Vladivostok accord from being incorporated into a treaty. That may have been a good thing. Had it been signed, the agreement might have eased U.S.-Soviet relations, but it would have tied America's hands by limiting our cruise missile range for nuclear and nonnuclear cruise missiles. That would have constrained our strategic capabilities and, more important as it turned out, our conventional warfare forces.

I continue to believe the SALT II Treaty that the Carter administration negotiated was very advantageous to the United States. One reason concerns geography, which, astonishingly, the U.S. negotiators in Vladivostok had ignored. The Soviet position was that 600 kilometers is always a good limit on the range of many things, including cruise missiles. That distance sounds all right until you look at a map of the Soviet Union and compare it to the United States. A cruise (or any other) missile penetrating 600 kilometers past Soviet or Warsaw Pact border defenses would reach relatively few Soviet population centers. Moscow, for example, is about 700 to 800 kilometers from a border we could target. In the United States, on the other hand, some 53 percent of the U.S. population lived within 600 km (or 372 miles) of our borders along the coasts. By 2015 that percentage will translate into about 172 million people.

By setting a range limit, the geographic context of a treaty affects not only strike capability, but also how you research, design, and build the missile. As secretary of defense, I worked most of a year to overcome State Department objections to reopening the issue of range and reversing the 600-kilometer limitation. We were able to extend the agreed range limitation to 1,500 kilometers, which also let us put the heavier conventional warheads on cruise missiles and still have useful ranges. That made them an important part of our conventional war options, as demonstrated by their very effective use in the first Gulf War. If the 600 kilometers had remained as written, we would not have had cruise missiles capable of carrying out those strikes and more recent ones in Iraq and Afghanistan.

Wanna Gang Up on China?

The SALT negotiations made for frequently boring but occasionally interesting theater. In the formal meetings the chairs of both teams made statements. Then discussions occurred among different working groups and in one-on-one social settings. The groups reported back to their home governments and received instructions for how to go forward. The discussions among working groups educated each side to the others' thinking and established a precedent that led to more substantive agreements later.

Those side conversations in SALT I often revealed real reasons behind suggestions, or startling strategies not mentioned formally. In one such conversation I learned that the Soviet negotiators were in effect inviting us to join them in bombing and destroying Chinese nuclear weapon production and deployment capabilities. I came back with that interesting tidbit and discovered it had been floated in other channels, too. I mentioned it at a meeting with President Nixon at the General Advisory Committee to the Arms Control and Disarmament Agency, which I attended as a member of the committee. The Nixon administration declined the Soviet invitation and nobody bombed China. What was especially interesting about the suggestion was that it apparently wasn't an off-the-wall idea. The Soviet leaders were actually contemplating the act and didn't want to do it alone.

THE ROCKY PATH OF SALT II

A stunning example of how distractions can have a negative impact on American defense was our failure to achieve formal Senate confirmation of the SALT II Treaty, an agreement to limit the dangers of nuclear arms competition with the Soviet Union. SALT I negotiations had extended from November 1969 to May 1972 and resulted in a treaty ratified by the Senate within three months.[24] But SALT II, signed by President Carter and Brezhnev in Vienna the summer of 1979, had a rockier path.

SALT II resulted from long, difficult negotiations with the Soviets. An equally difficult and in the end incomplete process fraught with delays took place within the U.S. government. Ratifying a treaty requires a two-thirds vote of the Senate. That process has a tendency to conflate remotely related issues, and this was no exception. Some senators tried to extract concessions or benefits that had nothing at all to do with the SALT II Treaty. As they haggled, time passed. The alternative to SALT II was not some ideal treaty we might have achieved had we been negotiating only with ourselves (we sometimes did that, too.) The alternative was no treaty at all. That would have ushered in an era of greater military and political uncertainty resulting in increased strategic forces on both sides. Apart from the need to limit and stabilize the strategic nuclear arms competition, the SALT process was important to the further development of U.S. relations with the Soviet Union, and to improving East-West relations in general as we achieved a stable global political balance.

A few months after signing the treaty in 1979, we rediscovered a Soviet army brigade in Cuba. It had been there since 1962. Some members of the Senate decided that made any treaty with the Soviet Union undesirable. I pointed out that Soviet troops were in Cuba as part of the agreement reached during the time of the Cuban Missile Crisis to withdraw their missiles.[25] The Soviet presence had no effect on the balance of security in the Caribbean. To persuade moderate Republicans and southern Democrats to ratify the treaty—both groups were amenable to arms control but concerned about the overall balance of U.S. and Soviet military strength—we made commitments to increase the defense budget, including U.S. conventional military capabilities in Europe and elsewhere.

Finally, toward the end of 1979, it looked like we had enough votes in the Senate to ratify SALT II. Then, on Christmas weekend, Soviet forces invaded Afghanistan. That shut down relations with the Soviet Union for the rest of the Carter administration and ended any chance of getting Senate ratification. President Carter withdrew the treaty from Senate consideration of ratification in January 1980. We ended grain sales to the Soviet Union and did not participate in the Moscow Olympics.

The fact that we had a signed treaty, though one that lacked Senate confirmation, made it possible for both the United States and the Soviet

Union to observe its provisions, and both sides did. Yet the failure to ratify marked a downturn in U.S.-Soviet relations that lasted well into the second term of the Reagan administration. Negotiations on the Strategic Arms Reduction Treaty (START I), which was meant to supplant the SALT II Treaty, did not begin until the end of June 1982 in Geneva, and the resulting treaty was not signed until nearly a decade later, on July 31, 1991, five months before the Soviet collapse.

The lesson from all this is clear. "Invented" problems, like the non-threatening Soviet brigade in the Caribbean or a too-slow churn of U.S. internal debate, can badly damage U.S. relations with another country and our own security interests. You can't let things hang on too long. I knew when dealing with Soviet representatives that we were adversaries. As for Congress, we're supposed to be on the same side. Most of these were tactical weapons, which were not affected by SALT or START. Strategic weapons, whose numbers are included in the table, were affected.

TRUSTING ONE'S NEGOTIATING TEAM

In reaching the SALT I agreement that Nixon signed with Brezhnev, the negotiating team was working on details after the fundamental decisions had been reached. All through the negotiations, Henry Kissinger was negotiating directly with Soviet ambassador Anatoly Dobrynin without always informing Gerard Smith, who was carrying on the negotiation in Geneva. As a result, there were loose ends that had to be cleared up at the last minute in Moscow.

That didn't happen with SALT II. There were last-minute telephone calls about verification provisions between Cyrus Vance in Moscow and me in Washington, but we had just one channel of negotiation, not two, which had muddied the waters on SALT I.[26] Nixon and Kissinger tended to trust neither the State Department (even when Henry was secretary of state) nor their designated negotiators—and sometimes less than they trusted the Soviet side.

WORKING WITH HENRY KISSINGER

I worked with Henry Kissinger when I helped negotiate the Salt I Treaty. I first met him in 1959 when he came to give a talk at the Livermore Lab.

U.S. and Soviet Nuclear Warhead Stockpiles, 1945–2002

	Year	United States	Soviet Union		Year	United States	Soviet Union
	1945	6	—		1974	28,170	17,385
	1946	11	—		1975	27,052	19,055
	1947	32	—		1976	25,956	21,205
	1948	110	—		1977	25,099	23,044
	1949	235	1		1978	24,243	25,393
	1950	369	5	SALT II[b]	1979	24,107	27,935
	1951	640	25		1980	23,764	30,062
	1952	1,005	50		1981	23,031	32,049
	1953	1,436	120		1982	22,937	33,952
	1954	2,063	150		1983	23,154	35,804
	1955	3,057	200		1984	23,228	37,431
	1956	4,618	426		1985	23,135	39,197
	1957	6,444	660		1986	23,254	40,723
	1958	9,822	869		1987	23,490	38,859
	1959	15,468	1,060		1988	23,077	37,333
	1960	20,434	1,605		1989	22,174	35,805
	1961	24,111	2,471		1990	21,211	33,417
	1962	27,297	3,322				
	1963	29,249	4,238	START I[c]	1991	18,306	28,595
	1964	30,751	5,221		1992	13,731	25,155
	1965	31,642	6,129		1993	11,536	21,101
	1966	31,700	7,089		1994	11,012	18,399
	1967	30,893	8,339		1995	10,953	14,978
	1968	28,884	9,399		1996	10,886	12,085
	1969	26,910	10,538		1997	10,829	11,264
	1970	26,119	11,643		1998	10,763	10,764
	1971	26,365	13,092		1999	10,698	10,451
					2000	10,615	10,201
SALT I[a]	1972	27,296	14,478		2001	10,491	9,126
	1973	28,335	15,915		2002	10,640	8,600

Source: Natural Resources Defense Council (www.nrdc.org/nuclear/nudb/datab19.asp).

Note: U.S. warhead estimates exclude those awaiting dismantlement and are accurate to a few hundred warheads. Soviet Union/Russian warhead estimates exclude warheads awaiting dismantlement or in reserve status; total number of intact warheads is about 18,000. NEW START, signed on April 8, 2010, went into force February 5, 2011.

a. Signed May 26, 1972; entered into force October 3, 1972.

b. Signed June 18, 1979, but never ratified by the Senate; was nonetheless adhered to, with its most major limitations entered into force in 1986.

c. Signed July 31, 1991; also affected launchers and went into force on December 5, 1994.

A year later we met again at a session on arms control at Princeton. At the time, I was a very junior member (at the age of thirty-two) of a principally technical group investigating whether a nuclear test ban would work, which is to say, would we be able to observe a Soviet failure to abide by it. In 1961, after I had become DDRE, Henry invited me to Harvard to give a talk to his class and took me to dinner at the Harvard Faculty Club (where I decided not to eat horsemeat featured on their menu). Kissinger was very smart, self-assured, and ambitious. He exhibited a historic knowledge and strategic sense matched by few people.

Over the years I got to know Henry well. In 1968, during the Johnson administration while I was air force secretary, Henry came to the Pentagon to give advice on Vietnam. Later that year I was designated to be the number two negotiator on strategic nuclear arms for a prospective U.S. delegation. The number one negotiator was to be Adrian Fisher, then head of the Arms Control and Disarmament Agency. Those negotiations, set by Lyndon Johnson and Prime Minister Alexei Kosygin at their June 1967 meeting in Glassboro, Pennsylvania, never materialized because Johnson didn't run for reelection. The Soviet leadership understandably waited for the next administration, at which point the negotiations did commence as SALT I.

When Nixon came in, all the people changed; I became a part-time negotiator, participating episodically during my new position as Caltech president. That was when my first serious interactions with the Soviet military took place. Though much detail was hammered out during the talks at Helsinki, Vienna, and then Geneva, the gist of the U.S. position came from a backup committee in Washington representing various government agencies. Henry Kissinger was its mastermind. He was the national security adviser then, before taking on additional duties as secretary of state.

I've always been able to be quite frank with Henry and like to tease him. It's easy because he's a calculating person who believes he has a lot of wisdom, which he does, though he adjusts its message to have the desired effect on the listener. In other words, he's telling different stories or different parts of the same story to different people. That may be the essence of negotiation in some circumstances and one of the skills that helped him pull off his Middle East agreements. In contrast, Carter was able to pull off what he did by telling the same story to different people.

I tease Henry by pointing out to him how devious he is. He remains both devious and wise.

MEETING WITH THE PILLARS OF SALT

In mid-June 1979 I flew on *Air Force One* with President Carter to Vienna, where he was to sign the SALT II agreement with Brezhnev. On the flight, Vance and Brzezinski and Dave Jones, chairman of the Joint Chiefs, and I planned what we would try to accomplish. There was not going to be any substantial negotiation on SALT II; only a few t's to be crossed. But we decided that I should meet with the Soviet defense minister and talk about conventional force reductions. If a war with the Soviet Union were to begin, it would probably start with conventional forces in Europe where the Soviet deployments were much larger than those of the United States and the rest of NATO combined. Issues that concern conventional forces can range from where forces could and could not be located during peacetime and at what degree of combat readiness.

I was to meet with Dimitri Ustinov, Soviet defense minister. I would request that our respective military chiefs accompany us. That would be Dave Jones on our side and Nikolai Ogarkov on the Soviet side. I had known Ogarkov for ten years but hadn't seen him for a long time. I'd be on my own during the meeting; the president and Vance and Brzezinski would not attend.

As I had expected, the meeting itself was two and a half hours long, desultory, and didn't get anywhere. I later learned that the Soviet representatives let our people know that I had been willing to go quite far in proposing new ideas and was not just speaking from a list of talking points in a prepared statement. They had not expected that. Though Defense Minister Ustinov was a member of the Politburo and wore a military uniform, he was not a military leader, but a politician from the industrial side of the military-industrial complex in charge of providing military equipment. The story told by a subsequent Soviet chief of military staff is that when Ogarkov, the senior military leader, opposed the Soviet invasion of Afghanistan in 1980, Ustinov told him: "Shut up and do what we tell you." Ustinov was in similar candid form at the celebratory dinner following the signing of the SALT II agreement. He downed vodkas and exhorted President Carter to get me a military uniform.

Harold Brown in a flight suit in 1978 on the deck of the aircraft carrier *Saratoga*. "To take off on an aircraft carrier is an exciting experience and landing more exciting. Night operations are a taxing mixture of technical capability and human skills, as I saw later."

"Your defense secretary needs his own uniform," Ustinov clapped me on the back repeatedly and raised his glass.

As close as I ever came to wearing a uniform was a flight suit I wore in the observer's seat of an A-10 Thunderbolt attack aircraft. I was secretary of defense and we were testing a new infrared sensor. I had initiated that program as air force secretary more than a dozen years earlier. Today, A-10 aircraft are still flying in their close air support role. I have a photo of myself in a similar flight suit on the deck of an aircraft carrier, having just landed as a passenger in another kind of aircraft. I can testify as well to the thrill and the dangers of landing on an aircraft carrier by night. My face after that landing was far paler than my flight suit.

THE CARTER-BREZHNEV HUG

It was at the SALT II signing in June 1979 that Carter and Brezhnev had their famous embrace. Carter said that the Soviet leader gave him a hug. The U.S. media thought it made a better story to say that Carter had hugged Brezhnev. I sat next to Brezhnev that night at dinner. It was obvious to me during the meetings and at the dinner that Brezhnev was losing it. In one instance, he read a prepared statement and mistakenly turned over one too many pages, but kept reading despite the break in continuity. Gromyko leaned over and turned back the page. During the dinner, Brezhnev appeared to be in decline in what he said in conversation and how he ate. Konstantin Chernenko who was prominent in the Politburo and later became president, hovered, and behaved like a go-fer. My conclusion was that Brezhnev had seen his best days.

Brezhnev died four years later, in 1983. Yuri Andropov, who had been head of the KGB, succeeded him and ill himself, died in 1984. (He was only seventy, which now seems young to me.) Next, Chernenko took over and lasted fifteen months until he died. I learned that it was Gromyko, who served as president in the figurehead role of head of state from 1985 through 1988, who pressed for Mikhail Gorbachev to take over because Gorbachev was comparatively young and vigorous. After three geriatric cases, that surely must have been appealing. What the Politburo didn't realize was that Gorbachev believed that the Soviet Union needed bigger changes than others might have wanted. He started to change the country a little; it would change a lot.

START AGREEMENTS

As I write this, the U.S. and Russian nuclear warhead stockpiles are considerably smaller than they were in the late 1970s, when the number of nuclear warheads on each side was in the range of 25,000 or more. The great majority of these were for short-range tactical delivery systems. The SALT and START Treaties both limited, albeit at a high level, U.S. and Soviet strategic nuclear weapons. The agreements kept them from being used, in part, by inhibiting possible competition to gain the ability to achieve a disarming first strike. Without SALT II, the probable ensuing Soviet programs would have made necessary a truly massive U.S. program to thwart a two-decade attempt to target our ICBMs.[27]

START I, signed in July 1991 and put into force in December 1994, barred signatories from deploying more than 6,000 nuclear warheads mounted on a total of 1,600 ICBMs, submarine-launched ballistic missiles, and bombers. START I expired on December 5, 2009.

On April 8, 2010, a NEW START Treaty was signed in Prague by President Barack Obama and President Dmitry Medvedev and gained Senate ratification. It went into force on January 26, 2011, with verifiable weapon limits about 74 percent lower than the limits of the old 1991 START Treaty.[28] The Obama administration showed considerable skill in gaining Senate ratification of the NEW START agreement during the lame-duck session of Congress after the 2010 congressional election. That agreement is modest in its reduction of nuclear arsenals and does not deal with the imbalance between the United States and Russia in tactical weapons. The current agreement limits Russia and the United States to 1,550 deployed strategic warheads each within six years. Under the agreement, thousands more strategic warheads can be kept in storage as backup.

As of September 2012, the number of U.S.-deployed ICBMs, SLBMs, and heavy bombers is about 800; for the Russians it is about 500. The strategic warheads deployed or counted as deployed total about 1,750 for the United States and about 1,500 for Russia. The Russians have several thousand warheads deployed on shorter-range tactical delivery systems; the United States has hundreds.[29]

We have come a long way, but both countries still need to reduce the deployed nuclear warhead stockpiles toward much lower levels. The disparity in tactical warheads will also need to be resolved. That may be difficult because the Russians now see themselves, just as the United States did throughout the Cold War, in an inferior military position in conventional military capability. That invariably argues for the maintenance of tactical nuclear weapons as an offset and deterrent. The absence of those weapons from the START II Treaty will not help nonproliferation efforts, as it suggests that tactical nuclear weapons may be valuable because Russia considers them so. However, the treaty does set the United States and Russia on a useful if slow course toward more significant weapon reductions. Its ratification also helps the United States maintain decent relations with Russia.

PROLIFERATION OF NUCLEAR WEAPONS

In the 1970s India, Israel, and Pakistan acquired nuclear capabilities. The Carter administration worked hard and successfully to keep some additional countries from getting nuclear weapons, an achievement rarely mentioned in history tracts. The Carter administration took the threat of proliferation more seriously than did its predecessors, who had failed to act when the original Big Five (the United States, Soviet Union, United Kingdom, France, and China) saw still more countries try to join the nuclear club. We in the Carter defense administration were especially concerned about plans in various countries to build breeder reactors. In addition to generating electrical power, the reactors could produce and separate out plutonium that fuels nuclear weapons. We stopped a breeder reactor project in Barnwell, South Carolina, as an example to press other countries to stop their reactor projects. However, even our allies failed to follow suit. France and Japan continued their own breeder programs though it wasn't clear they would be cost-effective from an industrial or economic perspective.

To prevent further proliferation would have required U.S.-Soviet cooperation, which the Cold War rivalry denied. Subsequent nonproliferation efforts, though leaky, did not entirely collapse. Brazil, Argentina, and much later Libya backed away from incipient nuclear weapons programs. South Africa dismantled its program. Following the demise of the Soviet Union, several of the breakaway republics—Belarus, Kazakhstan, and Ukraine—gave up not only nuclear weapons but also ballistic missile delivery systems.[30]

The United States and the Soviet Union discouraged members of their respective blocs from pursuing nuclear arms. Japan may not have needed much discouragement. Germany was offered a substitute during the 1960s for an indigenous nuclear capability in the form of the proposed Multilateral Nuclear Force to be operated jointly with NATO allies, though that never materialized. The United States forced the governments of South Korea and Taiwan to discontinue their fledgling nuclear weapons programs by threatening to withdraw our security commitments. The Soviet Union's iron hand and mistrust kept non–Soviet Warsaw Pact members from nuclear weapons programs. The Soviet Union failed to prevent China from gaining nuclear weapons, one reason for the Sino-Soviet split. And the United States failed to prevent an Israeli weapons capability. Five permanent members of the United Nations Security Council continue to have nuclear weapons: the United States, Russia (successor to the Soviet Union), the United Kingdom, China, and France. Israel, India, Pakistan, and North Korea have subsequently joined the nuclear club. The prospect of an Iranian nuclear weapons capability shadows the world scene.

The Atmospheric Test Ban of 1963 and the 1968 Nuclear Nonproliferation Treaty (NPT) helped inhibit some countries from pursuing nuclear weapons. The NPT suffers from a major deficiency: nothing in it prevents a signatory from producing weapons-grade fissile material and exploring nonnuclear components of a weapons program within NPT rules, and then leaving the NPT within three months under a withdrawal clause (Article X) and producing weapons within months. That was the North Korean pattern. Now, the United States offers the North Koreans materiel, trade, and financial incentives to give up their nuclear program. The North Koreans, now adept at extortion, retain their nuclear threat to keep the goodies coming. In effect, they've created an annuity for themselves.

The Paradox of Nuclear Deterrence

During the Cold War, massive nuclear arsenals kept by the United States and the Soviet Union deterred both sides from using them against each other in a direct attack, either by surprise or as an extension of a conventional war. Paradoxically, the arsenals also inhibited direct engagement of their conventional forces with each other for the years of the Cold War. The advantages of a terrifying nuclear balance came with a terrifying price: the real possibility of mutual annihilation. If mutual deterrence failed and conventional war occurred, it could escalate to massive nuclear exchange. That strategy of mutually assured destruction worked and seems to have worked so far between India and Pakistan, though not as well. They have engaged in sporadic conventional combat, although at a much lower level of violence than before both of them had nuclear weapons. As for the United States and the Soviet Union, the two superpowers (mostly the United States) engaged in armed conflict with others.

Motives for Acquiring Nuclear Weapons

For terrorist groups, the wish to inflict maximum damage is reason enough to acquire nuclear weapons. For nations, reasons range from wanting internal prestige to a belief that nuclear weapons will improve national security and their lack will harm it. Some nations, like Israel and Pakistan, saw nuclear weapons as a deterrent to conventional attack by an opponent with overwhelming advantage in conventional forces. That is part of Iranian and North Korean motivations and perhaps reflects

India's concern about China. Chinese concerns about conventional and nuclear attack by the Soviet Union or the United States played a role in China's decision to pursue nuclear weapons. Some countries see the value of a nuclear weapons arsenal to intimidate, threaten, and influence regional rivals and neighbors.

Russia still maintains several thousand tactical nuclear weapons that can be carried on aircraft and short-range missiles. Its leaders say that is to offset an inferior position to the United States and to China's conventional military force. Russia has specifically rejected a No-First-Use doctrine. Notably, that was precisely America's position in Western Europe during the Cold War. The United States has only a few tactical nuclear weapons in Europe that it can deliver in U.S. and NATO tactical aircraft. We keep the weapons as evidence of U.S. commitment to allies (especially to Russia's immediate European neighbors) and as a deterrent to (a very unlikely) conventional war.

Along with Russia's justification for its tactical nuclear weapons, other countries also claim to pursue (or keep) nuclear weapons for their value in deterring an adversary's conventional force advantage. These countries include Pakistan, Israel, North Korea, perhaps India, and potentially Iran, a complex case. Iran fought a punishing war with Iraq that included missile and chemical warfare against civilians as well as troops. Iran is driven by regional animosities, prestige, its own ambitions, the existence of Israeli nuclear weapons, and the perception of an overwhelming U.S. conventional capability that might be used to overthrow the Iranian regime. The U.S. nuclear weapons arsenal has not played a significant role in motivating Iranian nuclear weapons ambitions, though talk of using it to destroy Iran's nuclear facilities could change that.

It is for their own security, as other nations see it, or because of their ambitions, as the United States sees it, that states continue to pursue nuclear weapons. Reducing U.S. nuclear weapons deployments and stockpiles, backing off from hair-trigger readiness, subscribing to more comprehensive test bans, and not designing new nuclear weapons will have little or no direct effect on other countries' nuclear goals. Such policies or actions can help gain international support for other measures that will help thwart nuclear ambitions. There are two other good reasons for these policies: to achieve strategic stability and to lower threats of nuclear accidents or theft.

New Threats

The proliferation of nuclear weapons now held by nine countries, as well as the potential theft of nuclear weapons by non-state actors, means that many nuclear weapons are controlled less well. An apocalyptic leader could cause nuclear destruction if supported by people equally mad. That may not bring about the cataclysmic consequences that would have characterized a nuclear war between the United States and the Soviet Union, but a few nuclear weapons unleashed could cause the kind of damage seen only once before—at the end of World War II. As terrible as that would be, it might take a localized nuclear war to prompt a revision of global governance in a way that would prevent nuclear destruction from happening again.

Safeguards Needed against Bomb-Making

Terrorists could acquire nuclear weapons through deliberate transfer from a state, through transfer from a group within a fractured state, by theft of bombs or fissile material that can be made into a bomb with modest technical and industrial facilities, or much less feasibly by building a bomb from scratch. A few critical masses of weapons-grade uranium can be turned into a nuclear bomb with modest technical facilities. Plutonium takes more advanced facilities. In either case, we probably could tell the source from characteristics of the fissile material or nuclear debris of an exploded bomb. We ought to turn that possibility of identification into an actual capability and punish the source of an exploded nuclear bomb as well as the perpetrator.

There are three ways to prevent, inhibit, or delay the creation of nuclear weapons by rogue states or terrorists. The first is to prevent the intentional or unintentional spread of weapons and technology. Ensuring the security of existing stockpiles is central. A great achievement in that direction was the Clinton administration's ability to persuade former republics of the Soviet Union to transfer their nuclear weapons to the new Russian state. The security and economic carrots that oiled this action were the NATO Partnership for Peace and the Nunn-Lugar Cooperative Threat Reduction program to improve the security of weapons stockpiles and remove fissile material.

The second way to thwart nuclear weapons programs is to employ sanctions and punishments. These can range from financial penalties to international cutoffs of investment, trade, and flow from suppliers to an offending country, and ultimately by an attack on its nuclear facilities. The third way is to offer economic and security incentives to stop nuclear weapons programs.

Control Enrichment Facilities for So-Called Energy Purposes

The way to respond to nations claiming to need nuclear-generated electricity would be to do uranium enrichment and fuel reprocessing for them at internationally controlled facilities. Western powers offered this option to Iran. Various other arrangements could inhibit new aspirants from acquiring weapons-grade fissile materials. These include agreements by states with nuclear capabilities to stop producing weapons-grade uranium, to stop separating plutonium produced in reactors from fission products for use in breeder-reactor cycles, and to control the production and operation of high-technology centrifuges that are the easiest uranium separators to hide.

Imagine a World with No Nuclear Weapons

The United States would benefit most in a world with no nuclear weapons. As the world's dominant possessor of conventional military force, the United States would not see its freedom of action undercut by any use of nuclear weapons against us, though many other limitations on U.S. actions would remain. Countries that now have or seek nuclear weapons to deter or intimidate their neighbors would have to find different strategies. This might not result in more peaceful conditions as compared with continued nuclear proliferation. But the nuclear cloud would not appear.

This miracle is unlikely to occur because even if all nuclear weapons and fissile material were destroyed, the knowledge of how to make them remains. We don't know exactly how many nuclear weapons various states possess. Pakistan may have a hundred; North Korea may have ten. Some nuclear weapons would likely remain in the hands of rogue states, so for the foreseeable future the United States needs to continue to have them along with a rationale and a doctrine for their use. It is not an end to nuclear weapons that will make a peaceful world. It is a peaceful and orderly world that is prerequisite for the abolition of all nuclear weapons. The last decade in which the world was without nuclear weapons was the 1930s. We know what followed.

LESSONS LEARNED

The lessons learned during the Cold War came with the sobering reality of an existential threat. Our country and our allies depend on U.S. capabilities and strategy. The action-reaction element in arms competition remains real. Dialogue between adversarial states is useful. Only an easing of political differences perceived as vital, or a step back from the brink of catastrophe, can ensure conclusive progress on arms limitation.

Economic constraints short of causing economic collapse won't accomplish arms limitation. We should continue working toward further reductions in nuclear armaments and prevent—and where possible reverse—nuclear arms proliferation. It should be feasible to bring U.S. and Russian reductions to below 1,000 strategic nuclear warheads. Other nuclear powers—India, Pakistan, and Israel—need to be brought into arms control limits. That, as well as the inclusion of China, will complicate the process of reduction, which should be pursued vigorously. Strong limits on antiballistic missile deployments need to be set. Russian and U.S. nuclear weapons on short-range systems need to be dealt with as well, reduced to perhaps a hundred.

The United States should attempt to reach deals with dangerous states, such as Iran and North Korea, by providing believable assurance that we will not seek regime change in exchange for verifiable abandonment of their nuclear weapons programs. Because such attempts are unlikely to succeed, the United States should work with other major nuclear powers to deter dangerous states from using nuclear weapons or leaking them to non-state actors by announcing the intent to respond with devastating nuclear force. That should be accompanied by a clear U.S. doctrine that we will not be the first to use nuclear force, but will be free to respond in kind to any use by others, whether the U.S. is the target or not.

The acquisition by North Korea and potentially by Iran could result in further proliferation in their regions. The inhibition of conventional war that results from the fear of nuclear escalation is less likely to apply in unstable, inexperienced states. What worked in a one-on-one situation between the Soviet Union and the United States is less likely to work in the many-on-many case. The major powers should plan now how they will react in the event of a regional nuclear war with intent to then establish an international regime that would control all nuclear weapons and the capability to produce them—and in a less conflicted world, to eliminate them.

COMMAND AND CONTROL
DURING A THERMONUCLEAR WAR

The Cuban missile crisis of 1962 was the closest the world has come to a nuclear war. Opinions differ on how close. Though I was not in the inner circle of Kennedy advisers on the crisis (the "Excomm," as the Executive Committee of the National Security Council was called),[31] I followed the tracking of Soviet supply ships, the U-2 shootdown, and the intelligence collection related to the crisis. Thus I was close enough to be totally apprehensive about its possible outcome. The lessons I draw now are two: first, it is vital for the National Command Authority (the president and secretary of defense) to maintain very tight control over the actions of our military commanders and their troops. Second, lines of communication with the adversary need to be established at the top level as early as possible and well before a crisis starts to unfold.

In the 1962 crisis, the United States was in the fortunate position of dominating the military situation at every potential level of military conflict. But if combat had begun between U.S. and Soviet forces, escalation could well have gotten out of hand. If it had proceeded to a general nuclear exchange on homelands, dominance of the military situation would have lost meaning as both nations were destroyed.

I believe all five permanent members of the UN Security Council understand these lessons well; these nations have had nuclear weapons for decades. It is much less certain whether the subsequent members of the nuclear club, let alone prospective ones, have adequate political and military controls in place. Since the United States used nuclear weapons against Japan, there has been a constant dialogue between military people and political leadership in the United States about possible future use.

America's political leadership has been clear in exerting control and establishing clear lines of command. We have put hardware into our nuclear weapons that prevents the military from using them without explicit authorization and a careful procedure. That is lacking in countries new to nuclear capability. We've offered our procedure to the Pakistanis, who rejected it. They fear taking that kind of advice from the United States will reveal to us the location and vulnerabilities of their nuclear weapons or insert Americans into their decisionmaking system. That illustrates why nuclear proliferation constitutes the most dangerous risk for sudden catastrophe.

TERRORIST THREATS IN GENERAL

When we think about terrorists getting hold of nuclear weapons, we need to remember that there has been no major act of foreign-based terrorism on our soil since 2001, although there have been substantial acts of terrorism elsewhere in the world. It's hard to say why not here. Our safety could be the result of good counterintelligence and policing, the relative remoteness of the United States from failed states, and good luck.

I've always been worried that a group of thirty terrorists sent into the United States could do considerable harm. I imagine fifteen two-person teams shooting up fifteen malls on the same day and killing several hundred people, demoralizing the United States for a while. That hasn't happened either and can be explained in various ways. One is that al Qaeda and its affiliates don't want to follow 9/11 with anything smaller. Bin Laden's letters and e-mails sent to his associates from his compound said as much. Another plausible explanation is that our policing and intelligence have been good at anticipating and foiling schemes. Attacks on al Qaeda leadership have disrupted its command system, leaving smaller and less capable groups to plot attacks. At the target end, the Transportation Security Administration (TSA) airport protection seems to provide more inconvenience than security per dollar. But even a modest risk of detection provides some level of deterrence. Some might add that at the least it's a job stimulus.

6

The Ramparts We Watched

DEALING WITH THE OUTSIDE WORLD

One month after taking office as secretary of defense I turned my attention to NATO. My hope and priority were the same: to reinvigorate the alliance. By 1977 the focus of U.S. foreign policy had shifted from Vietnam to Europe, where the Soviet Union and the United States faced off and where Soviet conventional force strength was generally agreed to be far superior to ours. Though I thought that superiority might be exaggerated, it was indeed real. Even if that had not been the case, the perception of Soviet conventional force strength mattered in the political relations among the United States, Europe, and the Soviet Union.

REINVIGORATING NATO

NATO was established in 1949 to offset the possibility of Soviet attempts to dominate or intimidate Western Europe. After World War II, economic deprivation coupled with communist sympathies, particularly in France and Italy, had fanned Soviet ambitions. That situation, accompanied by the Soviet military threat, produced the impetus for NATO to become the political counterpart of the Marshall Plan that helped revive the European economy. NATO later developed a military component and became an umbrella for incorporating a revived German military capability that had been eliminated after World War II. In 1977 Western Europe together with the United States and Japan comprised the bulk of the world's industry and economy. West Germany stood at the front line of the Cold War. Just across the border was the heart of the Soviet colonial empire and its power.

We had to convince the Soviet leaders that if they attacked Europe with conventional troops and began to overrun NATO forces, the United States would respond with tactical nuclear weapons. We deployed thousands of tactical nuclear weapons as a deterrent and to offset the Soviet advantage in conventional force. That plan was inherently risky. If it did not cause the Soviet authorities to pause, it could act like a powder train leading through escalation to a strategic exchange of nuclear weapons on Soviet and U.S. homelands.

To reduce reliance on a threat of Armageddon, we sought to increase the conventional capabilities of European NATO members. Two months after I took office, I went to a NATO defense ministers' meeting in Brussels and took a side trip to Aachen, Germany. It had been Charlemagne's capital. I reminded myself in his chapel that Europe had once been unified. My goal to unify NATO under a "shared burden of defense" would be easier said than done.

The NATO alliance was composed of the United States and fourteen other sovereign states, each concerned with maintaining indigenous militaries and its own research and development, industry, and employment. We needed to press NATO members, and the U.S. Congress, to augment defense trade and cooperation and the dual production of weapons and equipment that would ensure interoperability in the field.[1]

The "Three Percent Solution"

The United States provided more than 60 percent of NATO alliance defense spending and about 40 percent of the men under arms.[2] My defense department set up a program to increase the size and efficiency of contributions that European members, as well as the United States, would make to a shared defense. We asked NATO members to increase their defense expenditures by 3 percent a year in real terms. That was to respond, at least in part, to the annual rate of increase of 4 percent or more by the Soviet Union for nearly twenty years running.[3]

While keeping President Carter's pledge of a one-time trim of the defense budget, we also asked the U.S. Congress to approve a subsequent annual 3 percent increase focused on NATO reinvigoration. That expenditure, I told Congress, and NATO allies, would include modernization of equipment and rapid deployment capabilities. It would include funding for spare parts, unit training, and field exercises, especially joint exercises with NATO allies—not the stuff of headlines, but exactly what the United States needed to offset the increasing threat of short-warning attacks.[4]

In 1977 the Soviet Union was investing about three times as large a percentage of its GDP in military expenditures as the United States. Though we thought the United States had the edge on quality, we lacked quantity and fielded less than the best equipment for ground forces.[5] Bob Komer, Bill Perry, and I urged NATO and the U.S. Congress to cooperate in defense procurement and research and development, and to remove restrictions on all sorts of defense trade and cooperation. We encouraged production lines, one each in Europe and North America, to reduce redundancy and lower costs for the NATO alliance as a whole. We pointed out that the F-16 aircraft were being coproduced by Europe and the United States, lowering unit costs through longer production runs and in some cases keeping production lines available longer. We needed more cooperation like that.

Congress and the NATO countries understood the need for interoperability; dual production soon benefited the AIM 9-L program introduced in 1978. That program created a version of the Sidewinder heat-seeking short-range missile used by the United States in 1981 against Libyan planes in the Gulf of Sirte, and by the United Kingdom in 1982 in the Falklands War. The ROLAND, a mobile, short-range surface-to-air missile made in the United States and based on the original French model, became a candidate for NATO standardization in 1979.[6] Some 600 missiles of its type were rolled out until the program closed in 1985. But it, like most of our joint programs, suffered from reluctance by one or both sides to accept a system without tinkering with it afterward in a way that undercut the benefits of common use and large production runs of identical equipment.

Though the other NATO countries didn't quite live up to their 3 percent commitments (historically, they rarely if ever did all they said they'd do), they did increase actual defense expenditures, and year to year the U.S. Congress approved what came to be called the Three Percent Solution. Komer and I considered it a major achievement.[7]

Strategic Mobility

By 1980 we had learned of an increase in the number of flights of Soviet reconnaissance Bear aircraft. They flew out of Arctic staging bases around the North Cape of Norway and through the Greenland-Iceland-U.K. gap. There was also an increase in Soviet naval exercises in the Norwegian Sea and in the Arctic. How much of all that was oriented toward a possible conventional conflict on land and sea we couldn't be sure. The Soviet Union and its Warsaw Pact allies had far more tanks and artillery than the NATO forces. Should a war break out in Europe, NATO understood it would be at a disadvantage and in a defensive role.

Therefore we planned ways to put our combat forces, men and equipment, in place in Europe fast by prepositioning equipment, then by use of airlift to deliver soldiers who would join up with prepositioned hardware, and finally by use of a sealift. The right mix of these capabilities would depend on the crisis. We constructed a force of maritime prepositioning ships that could carry equipment in dehumidified storage for rapid deployment. Until full procurement and deployment of all roll-on, roll-off equipment ships, we chartered two existing ships capable of handling armored vehicles, artillery, and other large items of rolling stock. For a NATO contingency, we had 865 available ships, including U.S. flag fleet ships of the national reserve fleet.[8]

AWACS

In the first few days of a conflict, aircraft are key. One notable example of NATO cooperation was the purchase of a half dozen airborne warning and control system (AWACS) aircraft as part of a NATO common infrastructure.[9] One of the first things I did was impress upon NATO the need for standardization of that weapons system and its purchase, which would greatly increase the alliance's ability to carry out air operations. The AWACS aircraft could track planes over a 250-mile radius; its acquisition sent a signal to the Soviet Union that the NATO alliance would not rely solely on a nuclear deterrent.[10] The purchase and joint operation of that aircraft quickly made NATO more useful not only militarily but also politically, because the planes showed the Soviet Union that the United States and NATO had become more integrated.[11]

NATO owns few assets. Its military units belong to their respective nations. NATO consists primarily of command organizations and staffs, along with some common logistic facilities. But AWACS is an exception. Owned and operated by NATO, those aircraft have since been used in every joint operation. Modernized AWACS reinforced NATO's southern flank during the Iraqi invasion of Kuwait. In the 1990s NATO and its AWACS supported missions in the Balkans. AWACs circled New York after 9/11. And NATO took much of the lead in the recent mission to Libya, though its non-U.S. forces could not have operated successfully without major U.S. support.

Basing Pershing II and Cruise Missiles

With Bill Perry's advice, I set goals for the next generation of anti-armor weapons, naval mines, anti-ship missiles, and air-to-ground weapons. These "families of weapons" required standardization and interoperability to increase NATO military strength. Ominously, the Soviet Union had an SS-20 capability, a medium-range nuclear missile that could reach Western Europe. We had nothing to offset that and were in the process of removing from NATO bases 1,000 American tactical nuclear warheads that had become obsolete. We had developed an extended-range Pershing II and cruise missile that could reach the Soviet Union from Western Europe.[12] We had a year-long discussion in NATO, led by Dave McGiffert and David Aaron, who was Brzezinski's deputy: should we deploy those missiles or, as some NATO allies suggested, get the Soviet Union to reduce its SS-20s in return for reducing some of the U.S. (but not the Soviet) strategic nuclear forces?[13]

We decided to deploy with West Germany as a key location for two reasons: Germany stood at the front line of the Cold War, and Chancellor Helmut Schmidt had raised the issue of the Soviet SS-20s as an unmet threat to Western Europe. At first, Schmidt declined to accept the Pershing II in Germany unless we had other bases on the European continent as well. He didn't want to reinforce West Germany's position as the Soviet Union's prime military target. Nor did he want to put himself in the line of fire as a political target. Antinuclear demonstrations in Europe were proliferating along with the Soviet nuclear capability.

On a visit to the German capital Bonn, I cleared most other people out of the room and said to Schmidt: "Look, the U.S. and Germany are allies. The American president can afford to have the German chancellor unhappy with him, but the German chancellor really can't afford to have the American president unhappy with *him*. So, let's try to find a way through this for your benefit as much as for ours."

Schmidt didn't like that conversation, but he understood it. For my part, I think I was too assertive and close to being impolite in a way that I doubt a secretary of defense would be now, though strong language is not unknown in the heat of political argument. The Soviet threat caused and justified my behavior, I thought, because the United States had a responsibility for the security of other nations as well as for itself. When you're trying to avoid Armageddon, you sometimes overreact. We got Italy to agree to base the missiles. That still didn't satisfy Schmidt, who wanted yet another continental European base. In the end, we achieved commitments from the British, the Italians, the Dutch, and the Belgians.

MISSILE DEPLOYMENTS IN 1983

The actual missile deployments, including those in Germany, began in 1983 after both Carter and Schmidt had left office as heads of government; Schmidt continued his service in the German parliament. "Better Red than Dead" demonstrations against our missile systems ensued in European capitals; notably, there was never a demonstration against the Soviet SS-20s. Schmidt, along with Hans Apel and Georg Leber, all three of whom were former German ministers of defense, stood up to the protests. They were members of West Germany's Social Democratic Party, which was out of power by then. Still, Schmidt, Leber, and Apel worked hard to persuade their own party (contrary to its platform) to join the majority Christian Democratic Union and Chancellor Helmut Kohl to support deployment of the intermediate-range nuclear forces. Deployment was approved.

In my view, that decision was significant in convincing Mikhail Gorbachev and Eduard Shevardnadze that Soviet military capability, activity, and threats were never going to help them achieve domination of Western Europe. Deployment was one reason why Gorbachev told Shevardnadze in their famous conversation on a beach: "We've got to change."

Gorbachev realized that a dysfunctional and sclerotic Soviet economy, facing a stronger U.S.-Europe alliance, meant that the Soviet system needed not just retooling but drastic revision. Some claim that it was the Reagan Strategic Defense Initiative (SDI) that did the trick. I think that Soviet perceptions of U.S. superiority, both economic and technological (including military technology), played a key role in Gorbachev's decision to change the Soviet Union's course. SDI may have been a small part of that, but Soviet Military Marshall Nikolai Ogarkov had already bemoaned U.S. superiority in military technology in the late 1970s, well before SDI. He pointed to our precision-guided munitions and integrated surveillance, intelligence, reconnaissance, and communications networks as "a technological revolution."[14]

MARGARET THATCHER AND HELMUT KOHL

In 1979 Margaret Thatcher, whom I had met in London in 1970 when she was minister of education, visited the United States and came to my office. I had been ensconced as secretary of defense for two years. She was the leader of the Conservative opposition and brought with her young Winston Churchill II, one of her defense advisers and grandson of the great prime minister. She pushed very hard for standing up to the Soviet Union, a position that intensified after she became prime minister. Soon after she became prime minister, Britain played an important part in ensuring basing for the intermediate-range nuclear forces. She insisted that Britain needed two bases as she needed to "share the pain." I took that to mean the Brits had their NIMBY problem, too. In fact, one base was not room enough for the full complement of missiles we intended to deploy in Great Britain.

Helmut Kohl, while he was West Germany's opposition leader, also met with me during a U.S. visit. At the time he was much less versed in defense matters than Schmidt. When Kohl became chancellor in 1982, he strongly supported the deployment of intermediate-range missiles. That deployment later led to the Intermediate-Range Nuclear Forces (INF) Treaty of 1987 eliminating that class of arms on both the U.S. and Soviet sides.[15]

I attended NATO meetings of one kind or another several times a year, working closely with Secretary-General Joseph Luns. He was a well-known (and tall) figure in Dutch politics with a jovial sense of humor. He liked to poke fun at his Dutch language, which was intermediate, he said, between other human languages and animal noise. He and I held a press conference after every NATO meeting to describe what had transpired. Those press conferences were one way to continue sending the Soviet Union signals about NATO's increased capabilities. The press conferences also reassured European allies about U.S. commitment and capability. That kind of activity demonstrates why U.S. technical, economic, and security policies have to be viewed in the context of international relations, and relations with our allies.

As I look back, it seems to me that the emphasis I placed on NATO during my tenure as secretary of defense continued to have a good influence after I left. Schmidt and I got along pretty well despite my harsh admonition. He thought I was an economist, which was a high compliment from him. He had served as minister of finance as well as minister of defense in the government of Chancellor Willy Brandt. NATO continues to be a framework for security cooperation between the United States and Canada and our allied European partners—a total roster of twenty-eight member countries now.

LESSONS LEARNED

An important lesson learned is that not only the nuclear balance but also America's high-quality (and NATO-coordinated) military technology enabled conventional along with nuclear deterrence during the Cold War. Soviet military leaders in their doctrinal writings expressed the belief that they could win a blitzkrieg victory in Europe. They took the position that part of their responsibility as soldiers was to be able to win a nuclear war and that they would therefore plan to do so. They were mistaken about anyone's ability to win a nuclear war at the level that U.S. and Soviet arsenals could have unleashed, but what was important was what they believed. We countered that belief so that it never matured into action.

As we go forward, the worsening European economic crisis will continue to distract NATO's European partners from international security issues and will squeeze their defense budgets. Germany plans to reduce defense spending by a quarter over the next four years. Britain plans to slash its defense budget by 7.5 percent until 2015. The defense budgets of some smaller European nations have taken even larger cuts. Since the end of the Cold War, defense spending by European NATO members has declined by 20 percent.[16] Though all the Western European economies put together approximate that of the United States, their defense expenditures are less than half our own. Their military capabilities are less by an additional factor of two or more.

Nevertheless, European contributions, both military and political, remain vital to sustaining U.S. interests in Europe and adjacent areas. European interests in the borderlands between Europe and Russia run parallel with our own and help us stabilize the military and political balance there. In North Africa and the adjacent areas to the south, in the Middle East, and beyond to central Asia and the Indian subcontinent, joint operations with NATO allies bring additional resources, regional and historic familiarity, and political insights. As the intervention in Libya showed, these benefits are worth the complications that accompany alliances.

The increased U.S. attention to the Western Pacific area and East Asia makes closer and more efficient cooperation among NATO allies in other parts of the world even more important. We need to encourage our NATO partners to rationalize their military expenditures to reduce duplication and advance interoperability. We need to ensure that the inevitable decline in their defense expenditures does as little damage as possible to our mutual security interests.

In my role as secretary of defense I took the pulse of various sections of the world and proactively took steps to protect U.S. interests or reacted as needed. These actions yielded many lessons that could guide us in the future.

THE MIDDLE EAST

One lesson learned concerns Israel and the situation in the Middle East now. Until just after the Six-Day War in June 1967, Israel had bought Mirage fighter aircraft from France. The U.S. government had not been a significant supplier of aircraft or other arms to Israel when Yitzhak Rabin, a no-nonsense military person and Israel's ambassador to the United States, came to my office in 1968 while I was secretary of the air force. He told me that France would no longer supply Israel with jets; he wanted U.S. aircraft that might fill the bill. Israel settled on the U.S.

Air Force version of the F-4, which had originally been developed for the U.S. Navy.[17] That was the beginning of a U.S. commitment to supply and fund many Israeli needs for advanced armament. That arrangement continues to this day and represents a deep U.S. commitment to Israeli security. Between 1967 and 2012, the Israelis developed their own high-tech armaments industry. It complements and underpins the country's civilian economy. Most of its managers and export industries derive from the technology of the military sector.

I worked with Israel again, and far less peripherally, when I became secretary of defense, beginning at Camp David in 1978 where I forged military arrangements with the Israeli leadership during negotiations leading to the Camp David Accords. Upon taking office, President Carter had quickly restarted the Middle East peace process that had stalled during the presidential campaign. He used a variation of Henry Kissinger's shuttle diplomacy following the 1973 Yom Kippur War. In the first year of his presidency, Carter met with Anwar El Sadat of Egypt, King Hussein of Jordan, Hafez al-Assad of Syria, Crown Prince Fahd of Saudi Arabia, and Prime Minister Yitzhak Rabin of Israel. Most of them came to Washington. Assad met with President Carter in Geneva.

Working with Secretary of State Cyrus Vance and Zbigniew Brzezinski, Carter advanced a three-objectives peace plan based on the Geneva conference. He outlined them in his most recent book, *White House Diary:* (1) Israel's right to exist in peace; (2) Israel's withdrawal from occupied territories gained in the Six-Day War in ways (reached through negotiations with Arab countries) to ensure that Israel's security would not be threatened; and (3) an undivided Jerusalem.[18] Secretly, the Israelis and the Egyptians had already started to create their own framework for bilateral talks.

On November 9, 1977, Egyptian President Sadat made history by announcing to his parliament that he wanted to travel to Israel and speak before the Israeli Knesset. Israel's government then passed a message to Sadat via the U.S. ambassador and cordially invited him. Sadat's trip to Israel and his address to the Israeli parliament were groundbreaking. He was the first Arab leader to implicitly recognize Israel as a state and the first to extend an olive branch on Israeli soil.

Sadat's actions took the White House and the rest of the world by surprise. Some thought he just wanted to reacquire the Sinai as soon as possible. But his willingness to hear the views of Prime Minister Menachem

Begin, and Begin's willingness to talk with Sadat, soon revealed a different motive: Sadat wanted to leave his communist allies for a stronger relationship with the United States. That gave the peace process added momentum. On August 6, 1978, Begin contacted Sadat with a plan that included returning land to Egypt, a prospect that enhanced Sadat's lagging popularity there.

The next day Vance flew to the Middle East. With President Carter's Camp David meetings with Sadat and Begin set to start in four weeks, Vance wanted firsthand confirmation of the proposed Israel-Egypt plan. A month later, on September 5, and with negotiating teams in tow, Sadat and Begin came to Camp David for what turned out to be thirteen intense days of talks. My participation there focused on airfields, military equipment (and its U.S. funding) for the Israelis and the Egyptians, and monitoring and observation of the Sinai Peninsula. After the 1967 war, the Israelis had built two airfields in the Sinai they would have to relinquish under the proposed Camp David Peace Accords. They were willing to do that if the United States paid for building replacement airfields.[19]

Israel wanted to retain the Etzion airfield near Eilat for two or three years. I worked that out with Ezer Weizman, Israel's defense minister. President Carter called me during those negotiations wanting assurance that I wouldn't give away too much or fund more than necessary. I think I managed that all right. Weizman and I worked on arrangements for observation sites in the Sinai where U.S. personnel would help prevent Arab infiltration.

The Israelis continually expressed their concern about the balance between their own forces and those of Arab adversaries, pointing out that during the Six-Day War Arab opponents had mounted 465,000 troops, nearly 3,000 tanks, and 810 aircraft along Israel's borders. All of us senior members of the Carter administration considered that Israeli concern overblown. In 1967 Israel had smashed its opponents, and later in the 1973 Yom Kippur War repelled an Egyptian attempt to retake the Sinai. With Egypt now agreeing to peace and Jordan cooperating to police traffic across the border, the military balance clearly favored Israel. Still, the Israelis had a point. Their opponents had survived several major military defeats; the chance of Israel surviving even one was problematic.

That was one reason why the Carter administration assured Israel of continued military assistance in addition to our commitment to offset the loss of strategic space that Israel had gained in the Sinai. In addition, Israel would gain a peace accord as a substitute for its military presence in the Sinai. The United States also agreed to give the Egyptians $1.3 billion annually to help modernize their military. The original agreement was to provide that amount (in addition to funding already promised) for three years; more than thirty years later, we still provide it.[20] U.S. financial support to Israel runs at about $2.5 billion a year.[21]

Sadat Threatens to Storm Out

On Friday morning, September 15, the eleventh day of the negotiations, I was in the throes of discussing the military budget with President Carter in his cabin when Cyrus Vance suddenly walked into the room and announced: "Sadat's packing his bags; he's leaving." Apparently, Sadat was concerned that Begin would not sign any agreements at Camp David and would use any issues agreed upon as negotiation points at a later time. Whether or not that was a dramatic ploy, we didn't know. Carter sought guidance in prayer, then changed from casual clothes into a suit and tie and went to Sadat's quarters to talk to him.

Carter had tough choices to make as he walked from Aspen Lodge, the presidential cabin, to Sadat's cabin. He could accept an end to the Camp David talks and meet with reporters who had not been given access to any word of how the talks were going, or he could try to press Sadat to continue negotiating. Carter reportedly told Sadat that if he left it would mean an end to the relationship between the United States and Egypt. Moreover, a hasty departure would be unexplainable to the American people after Carter's heavy investment in a Mideast peace accord and would severely discredit his presidency. Last but not least, the president told Sadat that if he left, he would take away something personally and sincerely precious to Carter: his friendship with Sadat. "Why are you doing it?" Carter asked the Egyptian president and promised to put into writing agreements both sides had reached in the negotiations thus far. Sadat stayed.

That is but one example of why President Carter deserves credit for the Camp David Peace Accords. Without his personal attention, the accords would not have happened. Today some pundits disparage the accords and say they did not ensure the intended peace. But without them, things would have quickly become very dangerous. The Israeli-Egyptian part of those accords has so far held up remarkably well. It brought a cold peace, but a peace nonetheless.

Carter had in mind a more extensive settlement of Israeli-Palestinian conflicts. He was unable at Camp David to get explicit arrangements for Israeli withdrawal from the Gaza territory or a two-state solution. He fully expected progress would follow from what had been embedded in the accords. He became bitterly and justifiably disappointed that it did not, and he remains so. Carter tends to lean toward the underdog and the marginalized. He tries to see things not only from the U.S. side, but also from the viewpoints of adversaries and troublesome or even dangerous players. For example, he tried to ease tensions with the universally distrusted North Koreans. That approach was not a political advantage during his presidency, nor has it endeared him to his successors; it has made his post-presidential career probably the most productive in living memory.

The Camp David Peace Accords were signed at the White House on September 17, 1978. Five months later, in February 1979, on the president's instructions (and probably suggested by Brzezinski), I visited Israel and Egypt before President Carter's trip there in March. Part of the purpose of my February trip was to assure those nations of our continuing commitment to the peace process. We also wanted our Mideast partners to understand that the shah's forced departure from Iran would not affect America's defense commitments; such assurance was very important.

Shoring Up Defense Commitments

On February 10 I set down in Riyadh, Saudi Arabia, the first U.S. secretary of defense to visit that kingdom. I told the defense minister, Prince Sultan, and the cadets at King Faisal Academy that as a matter of mutual benefit "the United States would . . . provide the best training and equipment in the world, and the extra strength to meet a foe from outside the region."[22]

Three days later I was in Jordan expressing my appreciation for the hospitality shown by King Hussein and assuring him that the United States was "prepared to press negotiations for a comprehensive and just settlement . . . and to deter outside intervention in the area."[23]

On February 16 I was in Egypt assuring leaders that "the United States will not be satisfied until progress in the peace process leads to a comprehensive peace." I was grateful to be met at the airport by General Kamal Hassan Ali, with whom I'd worked at Camp David, and to renew our relationship in Egypt.[24] That day the Egyptians toured me around the stone monuments of Luxor. Chiseled in the rock were depictions of ancient weapons of war as well as instruments of farming and trades. Their juxta-position inspired my remarks at dinner that night in Cairo. "It should not seem strange," I said, "that a secretary of defense should see peace in terms of art and human rights and justice as the real guarantors of security."[25]

I next touched down at Ben-Gurion airport, my first visit to Israel. I reassured the Israelis that the United States was committed to Israel's security. I continued the discussions on arms transfers that had begun at Camp David and looked at prospective sites for new Israeli airfields to replace the ones they would abandon in the Sinai. I visited Ezer Weizman at his pleasant seaside home in Caesarea. "Our two countries are great democracies," I said to the Israeli leadership, "and there is great strength in democracy. We have the opportunity and responsibility to use this strength to bring peace and stability to the Middle East."[26]

As mentioned in chapter 4, I returned to a Washington snowstorm that rerouted my plane until I could land there and attend to urgent matters concerning the Iranian situation. Several weeks later I accompanied President Carter's triumphant tour through Israel and Egypt. As the train carried Carter from Alexandria to Cairo, it passed lines of cheering people, the women ululating in happiness at the peace forged at Camp David. The accords ended the united Arab front opposing Israel and gave Israel a major advance in its security. Begin and Sadat shared the 1978 Nobel Peace Prize. Carter's well-deserved Nobel Peace Prize for that and other achievements was not awarded until 2002.

CARTER MAKES A REQUEST OF HIS CABINET

A domestic political postscript: four months after Carter's peace mission to Egypt and Israel, and the month after he signed the SALT II agreement with the Soviet Union, he went up to Camp David for advice concerning his presidency. In that hot, humid July, many advisers external to the administration told him he was perceived as a weak leader. Once back in Washington, he heard much the same from his own political advisers. They told Carter his administration was perceived as ineffective and recommended that he ask all his cabinet members to submit resignations; he could accept those he wanted and regroup. I think his political counselors believed that such a move would show he was in charge and meant to change things.

When Carter asked for the resignations at a cabinet meeting, first orally, later in writing,[27] the two people who told him he was making a mistake were Cy Vance and me. We said: "Look, fire who you want, but asking for everybody's resignation is more likely to be taken as a reflection on you rather than on them. It says you're not sure that your judgment in picking people was right." As soon became apparent after Carter made a few cabinet changes, the strategy didn't work.

Beginning July 17, Carter announced the resignations of Brock Adams, secretary of transportation, and Joseph Califano, secretary of health and human services. In August both James Schlesinger, secretary of energy, and Michael Blumenthal, secretary of the treasury, resigned. Later on, and in circumstances unconnected with the mass submissions of resignation, Juanita Kreps resigned as secretary of commerce in October 1979. Vance resigned as secretary of state before the Iran hostage rescue attempt in April 1980 but announced it just after. I was one of few cabinet secretaries who lasted all four years. The others were Cecil Andrus in Interior, F. Ray Marshall in Labor, and Bob Bergland in Agriculture.

U.S.-Egyptian ties formed with the help of Sadat's statesmanship survived his assassination and lasted for thirty more years under Hosni Mubarak, even as his regime grew more authoritarian and sclerotic. U.S. equipment and training replaced the Soviet equivalents that had characterized the Egyptian military since Gamal Abdel Nasser's time. Many Egyptian officers now in their seventies were trained in the Soviet Union. Those less senior, who now or soon will lead the Egyptian military, were trained in the United States. It is because of that long association with American counterparts that I had hoped the recent Arab Spring would demonstrate that the Egyptian military learned a new approach to military-civilian relations. Perhaps that is now happening. Of course, in a situation in which the secular Western-oriented parties receive only about 20 percent of the vote, the United States may not want the Egyptian military to abandon all of its political clout. For now, the U.S.-Egyptian relationship is strained, and Egypt grapples with widespread turbulence after its elections in May and June 2012. Models of smooth, let alone rapid, transitions away from authoritarian military regimes are hard to find. South Korea's transition took more than fifteen years. Taiwan's one-party regime took even longer. Unfortunately, revolution usually results in suppression, not brotherhood.

NORMALIZATION OF RELATIONS WITH CHINA

In January 1980 I became the first U.S. secretary of defense to visit the People's Republic of China. The trip came almost exactly a year after normalization of relations with that country on January 1, 1979. My initiation of military-to-military talks with the Chinese leadership promoted a strategic relationship. That relationship is very different now, and much more contentious, but it has become more important to the parties and to the rest of the world. The process had begun in the early 1970s with the Nixon administration. Concerned about the position of the United States in the Cold War, Nixon took advantage of the split between the Soviet and Chinese leadership to open a dialogue and establish a U.S. mission in China. Nixon and Kissinger saw that opening as important in itself. They knew it would help the United States in its competition with the Soviet Union.

They were not the first to see it. In a 1967 meeting of the Armed Forces Policy Council, Paul Nitze, then the deputy secretary of defense, remarked that the natural tactic for the United States, the number one power in the world, would be to align with the Chinese, the number three power, against number two, the Soviet Union. That alignment was not the sole or even main motive of the Carter administration's negotiations with China in 1978. Reason enough was the need to end a thirty-year unnatural lack of normal relations with a major power.

With the strong Soviet military presence on the Chinese border, Brzezinski suggested more of a U.S.-China military alliance than anyone else had in mind. (A photo once taken of him brandishing a rifle in Pakistan toward the direction of the Afghan frontier captured his flair for the dramatic.) After a visit by CIA Director Stan Turner, China agreed to joint monitoring of Soviet missile tests from installations in western China. That replaced installations the United States had operated and lost in Iran after the Iranian Revolution. China's cooperation provided more evidence of its willingness to collaborate with us.

A major issue during the Carter administration's negotiations for normalization with China was Chinese insistence that the United States end the Mutual Defense Treaty that we had signed with the Taiwanese nationalist government (called the Republic of China) on December

2, 1954.[28] Gaining congressional acceptance of that termination, which required a year's notice, depended on endorsement from the senior uniformed military. That led to a series of meetings I held with the Joint Chiefs of Staff. They had concerns about losing air and naval bases on Taiwan. We all worried about appearing to abandon an ally if we removed troops and bases.

These concerns were decisively outweighed by the probable consequence of failing to normalize: a rapprochement between China and the Soviet Union. If those countries became less hostile to each other, some forty Soviet divisions stationed at the Chinese border would be freed up and could be moved to Europe. More Soviet troops on the NATO/Warsaw Pact front in Germany could increase the danger that they could quickly roll over Europe. Commandant Bob Barrow of the Marine Corps, who had served in China at the end of World War II, joined the other Joint Chiefs in wanting to avoid that possibility. He spoke strongly in favor of normalization, and the others agreed. The Joint Chiefs' support of normalization eased congressional concerns.

In August 1979 Vice President Fritz Mondale visited China, at which time it signed agreements with the United States on maritime affairs, civil aviation, and textiles.[29] Mondale tentatively arranged a trip for me as a natural follow-up to Deng Xiaoping's trip to America. U.S. State Department officials objected to my going to China. It wanted Secretary of State Cyrus Vance to go instead and focus on easing any dangers that the U.S.-China rapprochement might pose to our relationship with the Soviet Union. Vance was concerned that U.S.-Soviet relations would be inflamed by an appearance of a military or even a strategic political relationship with China and would damage chances for the Strategic Arms Limitations Treaty (SALT II) with the Soviet Union. Those relations were already troubled by Soviet actions in the Third World and by the belated "discovery" of a Soviet brigade in Cuba. Both factors had stalled Senate approval of the SALT II Treaty. Brzezinski, on the other hand, wanted to use China as a lever against the Soviet Union.

My stance on U.S. policy toward China and its relationship with the Soviet Union fell between positions taken by Vance and Brzezinski. Some wanted me to mediate between them. I didn't try; I had my own position—that we should normalize relations with China and not let Soviet dislike of that process interfere. And we should not rub the Soviet Union's nose in what we were doing with China. In a way, I was "splitting the baby in half."

Brzezinski pushed for me to be the strategic interlocutor of the Carter administration to the Chinese. He thought that what I would say would sound more like what he'd say than like Vance. Despite State Department opposition, President Carter approved my trip, which made me an emissary of the United States to China. A week before I left, Soviet troops invaded Afghanistan, an action obviously planned some time before. That invasion heightened the strategic aspects of my visit.

Accompanying me on the plane were my wife, my daughter Deborah, and my associates including Under Secretary Komer, Assistant Secretaries McGiffert and Gerald Dineen, Assistant Secretary of State Richard Holbrooke, and China experts from Brzezinski's and my staffs, Mike Oksenberg and Nick Platt. We celebrated Colene's birthday on the plane with a cake and candles that made that birthday particularly memorable. I worked with my associates during the flight on what we'd say to China's leadership and how we would say it. When we touched down on a cold, dark January night, the Chinese greeted us by playing their national anthem and then "The Star Spangled Banner." My daughter snapped a photo of Chinese military officers standing near me as I listened to our anthem with my hand over my heart.

The discussions that took place in China over seventeen hours during my first few days there were with Premier Hua Guofeng, Vice Premier Deng Xiaoping (as acting premier), Vice Premier Geng Biao, Defense Minister Xu Xiangqian, Foreign Minister Huang Hua, and other Chinese officials. Arms Control and Disarmament Agency Director George Seignious and Vice Foreign Minister Zhang Wenjin held the first formal discussion between our two countries devoted to arms control matters. China was going to participate for the first time in the Committee of Disarmament in Geneva in February.

Talks began with a tour d'horizon—an exchange of views about the strategic situation in Europe and the Third World as well as in East Asia, Afghanistan, the Middle East, and the Persian Gulf. We discussed the military balance in various parts of the world, the strategic nuclear balance, and China's concerns about Soviet forces on its own border. What emerged from those meetings with China's senior military leaders and with de facto leader Deng Xiaoping underscored our common under-standing of the world situation and the risks of Soviet adventurism. Chi-nese leaders used our shared concerns to try to press me for transfers of weapon technologies and military equipment. Before I left Washington for these talks, we had determined to make no firm commitments. I did indicate that technology and materiel might well be forthcoming for such defensive systems as antitank weapons and surface-to-air missiles.[30] I dis-couraged Chinese interest in advanced aircraft and avionics.

After a lengthy and convivial banquet, I engaged in an equally lengthy but contentious discussion with the crusty Marshal Zhang Aiping, who was in charge of weapons systems development and production. He stub-bornly continued to press for technology and equipment transfers. I urged patience. (Years later in 1989, after his retirement, he publicly criticized the suppression of the Tiananmen Square demonstrators. I revised my negative opinion of his assertiveness.)

At another dinner, I arranged for the attendance of Qian Xuesen, the father of China's missile program. He was a Caltech professor in the 1950s, one of the founders of Caltech's Jet Propulsion Laboratory, and had been denied permission by the U.S. government to travel to China during the McCarthy period. Then in 1955 the U.S. government deported him there. I'd been president of Caltech from1969 to 1977. We chat-ted about mutual friends. I noticed that his fluent English deteriorated severely when Chinese officials were present.

Using chopsticks at mealtimes, I found I could nimbly pick up three grains of rice or a single peanut and gained some approval for that. I was not surprised that my wife and daughter charmed our hosts who took them shopping. Over the week of our visit, my family wore lovely Chi-nese garments to the events we shared. The Chinese were gracious hosts. Banquets were lavish. Dinner tables were decorated with fresh flowers and colorful cakes elaborately carved into the shapes of exotic birds with long tail feathers. Toasts at dinner progressed in a particular way; I soon got the hang of it. The Chinese practice of charming foreign interlocutors to make them "great friends of China" was on full view.

At meetings, my counterparts and I were seated across from each other, interpreters behind us and our colleagues seated alongside. Bowls of fresh oranges and apples were always within reach. Official photos taken just before those meetings show Chinese leaders in uniform (and

Brown, his wife, Colene, and their daughter Deborah in China.

me in my business suit) seated on chairs festooned with lace doilies and ruffled upholstery. I noticed all that when I recently looked at the photos. At the time, my thoughts focused on the tasks at hand and the military materiel displayed outside to impress me.

How the world has changed in thirty-two years! On that first visit, China was decades behind Western and Soviet technology. Our party visited an aircraft engine plant in Xian (and the ceramic warriors of Emperor Chin Shi Huang) and a naval base at Wuhan. We froze in the bitterest cold I have ever experienced as we viewed an exercise involving ground and air forces. I saw little sign of combined arms from various military services, let alone joint service capabilities. Some ground forces at the exercise rode motorcycles. The jets were of Korean War vintage.

China's civilian economy in 1980 was as backward as its military equipment. Bicycles and beat-up trucks constituted most of wheeled traffic. Clothing had just begun to emerge from the "blue ant" era. I was impressed by the abundance of food in city markets (in contrast to what I had seen in the Soviet Union during the 1970s), but the countryside endured inefficient processing and transport. As we drove to see the Great Wall, we passed wagons carted by mules. The wagons were rickety and overloaded with hay.

The most impressive post-dynastic buildings were those of the pre–World War II extraterritorial Bund in Shanghai. One evening we attended a Chinese circus performance that featured balancing acts both precise and extreme, perhaps a metaphor for China itself, which aimed to become a modern, prosperous, militarily up-to-date nation on the back of what was still a peasant economy. My meetings with Deng Xiaoping suggested that the leadership had sensible ideas for how to make that happen.

China Now

Now, more than thirty years later, the success of those ideas is evident in the rise of China. Indeed, apart from the Soviet collapse and end of the Cold War, China's rise is the most important international development of those years. And the U.S.-China relationship is likely to be the most important factor in international affairs during the next thirty years, eclipsing developments in the Islamic world. China's rise in three decades is as significant as that of the United States, and more than that of Germany and Japan, all of which took place over roughly the same length of time, from about 1870 to 1900. Each of those ascensions to power altered and even threatened the existing international order, which was then principally under European control.

Transitions Involve Conflict

Previous transitions in the Western world dating back to the sixteenth century had generally involved major conflict, often worldwide. Spain was the dominant power from 1525 to about 1650, France thereafter to about 1750, and then Great Britain. That last transition, certified by the Seven Years' War, had involved a war fought in North America, the Caribbean, and India, as well as in Europe. Early in the twentieth century, leadership passed to the United States without a military conflict with the United Kingdom. That was perhaps because of a shared language, political and cultural similarities. Nevertheless, during the U.S. Civil War, the British government contemplated a "last chance" to suppress a U.S. rise to leadership. Egged on by Napoleon III, who had ambitions in Mexico, the United Kingdom considered joint recognition of, or active intervention on behalf of, the Confederacy.

During the past thirty-two years, China has experienced rapid economic growth. Its GDP is about ten times greater now than in 1980. Its international footprint—political, financial, and trade-related—have grown correspondingly. So have its technological and military capabilities. China's economic performance and mode of governance challenges the Western model. How competition for world primacy will play out during the next few decades is likely to characterize much of the twenty-first century. There are no other contenders; others of the BRIC group (Brazil, Russia, India, China) are not likely to be over the next decades.

The Soviet challenge—and its system—failed. The Soviet Union had a large geographic area, a large population, and an ample natural resource base. But its politico-economic system was dysfunctional and ultimately unsustainable. Although the Japanese economic challenge of the 1980s was thought capable of displacing the United States as the preeminent economy, it did not. Japan was well organized with an educated and disciplined population but was limited by geography, social rigidity, and a population that was less than half that of the United States and was growing much more slowly. In contrast, China now has a much greater population than the Soviet Union, and ten times that of Japan.[31] The future of East Asia lies in the western Pacific and the competition there between China and the United States.

How likely is that competition to become adversarial and even violent? Consider the current and near-term situation. America is used to preeminence after enjoying (or suffering) it for more than sixty years. We haven't always gotten our own way or gone unchallenged (except perhaps in the decade from 1990 to 2000, the shortest period of global supremacy on record). But we have been the principal arranger and often guarantor of the rules of international economic and security relations. China does not overtly challenge that role, but it is serving notice that it does not passively accept our status. China does not feel bound by the existing international institutional arrangements that it had no part in establishing. It does, however, benefit from some of them. For example, loans from the World Bank, its technical assistance, and World Trade Organization rules helped to modernize China.

Despite China's remarkable rise, claims that it is soon to overtake the United States in economic weight are overblown. All international trade and investment are carried out at currency exchange rates. By that measure, China's annual GDP is about 40 percent that of the United States at about $6.5 trillion. Its annual GDP by exchange rate is about $6.5 trillion. As China's economic growth rate slows, probably still exceeding that of the United States by 4 or 5 percent, China would still need twenty more years to catch up with U.S. economic levels. And the gap in prosperity would still be wide.

China's Motivation

China's leadership and public may want to regain a position held for a thousand years as the world's most advanced and prosperous state, dominating East Asia and its surroundings. Chinese leadership seems dedicated to reestablishing that earlier regional status and redressing 150 years of humiliations, disruptions, and impoverishment in the nineteenth and twentieth centuries. Like the heads of other authoritarian (and usually in democratic) states, the Communist Party leadership believes that retaining power is critical to its own and its national well-being. To that end, Chinese leaders prohibit public political dissent and justify suppression by pointing to China's destructive history of internal rebellion. But dealing with domestic fragility in a nation of 1.3 billion is a demanding task.

Chinese leadership truly fears that unrest will ensue from rapid urbanization, economic and social change, ethnic conflicts in outlying provinces, and regional inequality between coastal and interior regions. The leadership relies on economic growth and nationalism to maintain political control. The country's economic growth impresses its neighbors, trading partners, and political interlocutors. Growth also enables China to acquire a massive military capability. China identifies and promotes its economic achievements with nationalism. But because nationalist sentiment has turned on past governments and could do so again, it's a two-edged sword. And the oligarchic political system has its own vulnerabilities: susceptibility to corruption and the lack of accountability to a broad public faction. The Bo Xilai affair, in which a member of the Politboro stands accused of corruption, and connection by marriage to murder, exemplifies these faults and represents an immediate internal threat to Chinese political stability and orderly economic growth. In turn, that would affect Chinese ability to project both its soft and hard power. The allegations mirror widespread dissatisfaction with regional authorities' treatment of the ordinary citizen and lack of a rule of law. The surfacing of the Bo affair also suggests that beneath the smooth exterior of the ruling Communist Party seethe factional, regional, and even ideological conflicts as intense as or more intense than those we see publicly in Western democratic societies. Chinese leadership is transitioning to its 2012 successors in the wake of the Bo "scandal." The new leadership will be the first that Deng Xiaoping did not either designate himself or that has an immediate connection with the founding generation or with the People's Liberation Army. Bo has not made that leadership transition smoother.

Despite its increased economic influence, China has yet to accept responsibility for maintaining the international system. Self-interest dictates its approach to intellectual property rights, currency exchange rates, and international security. China enjoys accumulating financial assets and acquiring title to natural resources across the globe and spends liberally on military and technological strength.

Two States of Being

As China flourishes, the United States fights its way back from financial crisis, slogging through what it hopes is but a bad patch of slow growth. We accumulate massive deficits and use stimulus as a way out. We decry the prospect of crippling public debt, yet fail to face up to the imbalance between entitlements and revenue. We endure a breakdown of governance, political comity, and a sense of government legitimacy. In its favor, America has a long history of recovering from troubled or desperate situations. We benefit from the flexibility of our democratic institutions.

China's internal strains, on the other hand, make it more fragile than is generally understood. China's mercantilist, export-led economic model has its limits, especially for such a large population. The country's transition to domestic-led growth will intensify internal as well as external frictions. Its nationalism sometimes gets out of control. For example, some government-encouraged demonstrations to protest American or Japanese actions had to be restrained before they threatened to severely damage those relations. So far, China has managed widespread unrest through repression combined with minor adjustments. Whether that mode of governance can be sustained remains to be seen.

As for longer-term prospects, changes are sure to take place by 2030 (nearly as far into the future as 2012 was to 1980). Even assuming that global warming does not boil the oceans or upset atmospheric stability, any twenty-year projection can miss important new developments, so five- to seven-year projections are better for identifying issues rather than predicting outcomes. History teaches us that rising powers often engage in conflict—usually war—with leading status quo powers. That should worry us.

There are countervailing factors. The existence of nuclear weapons threatens mutual destruction and inhibits direct military conflict, as it did during the Cold War between the United States and the Soviet Union. Notably, when the United States and China took opposing sides during the Korean War, China lacked nuclear weapons. Political theorists suggest that close economic relations tend to reduce the chances of political and military conflict. (The high level of intra-European trade and investment before World War I is a counterexample.) But the imbalances in trade and related policies have exacerbated U.S.-China tensions and in the short run seem as likely to worsen as to ease. In coming decades such imbalances will have to be balanced either by agreement or through sharp and unpleasant discontinuity.

America's Role in the Pacific

It is not uncommon for the neighbors of a rising power to fear that it will want to dominate them. China's neighbors are no exception, and most of them look to the United States to offset that prospect with a military presence and capabilities. At the same time, they fear that a confrontation between the United States and China could draw them in with inevitable damage. This presents a challenging task for U.S. diplomacy and security.

We need to keep China and its neighbors from confrontation, yet not have those neighbors fall into China's orbit. And we need to avoid conflict with China, yet not accept a Chinese hegemony in East Asia and the western Pacific. Japan, India, South Korea, Vietnam, the Philippines, Thailand, Myanmar—most of these will look to the United States to be the distant balancer to a China that could threaten to exert local domination. Each case is different; we need to be careful in sensitive cases like the China-Vietnam relationship. Some of these countries may conclude that it's safer to steer closer to China than away from it. Political and security concerns about independence exist alongside an economic fact: most of their trade is with China and, unlike U.S.-China trade relations, is fairly well balanced. This situation differs from that of Japan during its economic resurgence after World War II. Japan had almost no economic relations with Western Europeans, who were under military and political threat from the Soviet Union. And Japan's economic relations with its East Asian neighbors did not come with any military threat or significant political influence.

China will inevitably expand its influence beyond East Asia and the western Pacific. As China strong-arms its neighbors, the United States responds to support its own interests, at times seeking some of those neighbors' cooperation in joint military exercises along with the use of their ports and airfields. We did exactly that in 2011 with Australia and the Philippines during our pushback of China in the South China Sea. We need to modulate such actions carefully to limit associated risk. China's leadership may take such actions as evidence of an attempt to contain or suppress its rise and contend that its actions are peaceful. China's neighbors might doubt that assertion.

In turn, Americans are likely to consider China's push for economic and political leadership, and for military dominance in East Asia and the western Pacific (comparable to U.S. dominance in North America and the Caribbean), as potentially aggressive and threatening. The real risk of a self-reinforcing downward cycle, as experienced by Great Britain and Germany in the early twentieth century, could have disastrous results. We might avoid conflict by taking special care to understand China's motives. For example, in January 2012 both Russia and China were the only votes in the United Nations against condemning the Syrian regime's violent suppression of its citizens in an internal uprising. It's important to recognize that Russia and China had very different motives for their negative votes. In China's case, the vote did not indicate support for the existing regime in Syria, but rather China's belief that the international community should not intervene in the internal affairs of another country or protect the American ideals of human rights and self-determination there, even in extreme cases. (I explain, not agree with the Chinese view.) Russia, on the other hand, supports the Syrian regime. Russia has a significant influence in Syria, and Syria provides the only base in the Mediterranean regularly available to Russia's navy. Russia regards the United States as a global adversary, though not on the scale that existed during the Cold War. Russia wants to keep U.S. influence in the Middle East to a minimum.

Looking Ahead to 2030

By 2030 the economies of the United States and China may be roughly equal in size though China's population will be three or more times the U.S. population and China's per capita GDP will amount to a third of U.S. GDP. China's economy has rapidly expanded to second largest in the world; its military budget has grown 10-plus percent or more a year for more than a decade and may well continue through this one.[32] By contrast, the U.S. economic outlook is less optimistic. Owing to the recent financial crisis, our military will see budget limitations and sobering cuts.[33]

Even with that, the United States will remain stronger, wealthier, and likely more influential worldwide than China for the next fifteen to twenty years and probably more. The world still looks to the United States for balance, military strength, and its defense of human rights, even as we Americans become less inclined to try to infuse our democratic ideals into other nations. Meanwhile, China will continue to try to control activities in waters far off its coast and to pursue claims on areas said to be rich in oil (but not proven to be) and rich in seafood. The United States will need to push back.

An opportunity for discussion will surface in 2013, when the United States resettles after its presidential election and China completes a major succession in leadership with Xi Jinping newly at the helm. The Bo Xilai affair has upset the anticipation of a smooth transition of leadership to men of Xi's younger generation. The behind-the-scenes shenanigans by Bo Xilai exposed some of the secret discord among those in power, which was underestimated until the scandal came to light. Despite its internal disharmony, China will continue to develop capabilities that can affect U.S. positions and plans in the western Pacific. For its part, the United States will seek to prevent Chinese domination to the outer limits of the South China Sea.

Unlike the Soviet Union's regime during the Cold War, and Hitler's, the Chinese regime does not claim that its mission is to spread its system over the whole world. And over the past few years, the United States has become less convinced of its own ability to remake the world in its image. Both countries can justify their respective military expenditures and actions to their own ends; the trick will be to do that in ways that promote adequate trust and mutually agreed security postures in Asia.

The military balance is likely to remain in America's favor for at least another fifteen or twenty years. That balance could become problematic within a few hundred or even a thousand miles from the coastline of Asia if China engages in asymmetric warfare. In addition to terminally guided medium-range missiles, China's asymmetric warfare capabilities may include a cyber-attack on infrastructure combined with a malicious attack on the economy of the adversary through various financial instruments, electronic or other attacks on satellite systems, or physical sabotage by surrogates. This could undercut America's overall military advantage.

China's economic, technical, political, and military gains are likely to continue to 2020. Though China just posted its worst economic quarter since 2009, its GDP is expected to continue growing at an annual rate of about 7 to 8 percent through this decade.[34] The Chinese may well prefer to concentrate on their domestic matters and expect better terms from the United States later on. China's leadership has managed the country effectively without much vision, whereas in the last fifteen years American leadership has acted on a variety of visions for its internal management. Thus our biggest challenge is to get the U.S. economy and governance in order. Unless the United States gets its national act together and the Chinese leadership shows more international statesmanship, the histories and characteristics of the two countries suggest trouble ahead.

Getting to 2030 without a frightening confrontation will be a major achievement. By then both countries are likely to face unanticipated mutual challenges. We already share several external threats to our well-being that require cooperation, most notably the proliferation of nuclear weapons, global climate change, and Islamic extremism. Working on these together, difficult as that will be, is one of the best ways to avoid confrontation. Back in 1980, military balance was a major focus of China's leadership, but it was the U.S.-Soviet and China-Soviet balance. Now, China is unwilling to discuss that kind of balance because the present issue is the U.S.-China military balance, and the Chinese probably see their lack of transparency as an advantage. Unfortunately, that lack is a risk for both sides.

A good start now would be to have military participants in diplomatic Track Two (nongovernment) talks or Track One-and-a-Half (nongovernment with government observers) discussions. These could lead to official military-to-military talks, and to agreed rules of the road (that is, rules on the behavior of military and other governmental or commercial maritime and air operations). Eventually, the talks could grow into a discussion and even an agreement on the strategic-military balance. Talks could start with Northeast Asia as a focus, involving four (China, the United States, Japan, and South Korea) of the six parties engaged in the frustrating shell game over North Korea and its nuclear weapons. Then talks could expand to the South China Sea question, too hot to handle now because some elements of the Chinese government have declared the area covering hundreds of miles from shore a "core interest," implying near-sovereignty.

Contrasting Chinese statements about their claims to rights in the South China Sea come from the most senior foreign officials such as Dai Bingguo and from other senior military officials, and from government-run media. The latter groups described the extensive maritime expanse as a core Chinese interest, but later blurred that claim. However, the "nine-dash" line showing Chinese sovereignty very close to its neighbors' coastlines, closer than ever before, still appears on Chinese maps. That, together with the aggressive behavior of some Chinese quasi-military units, understandably worries neighboring countries. Some sort of grand maritime bargain is unrealistic at this stage. Accordingly, U.S. policy should include measures to prevent still more adversarial incidents and actions from setting relations on the wrong track.[35]

The United States needs to find a way to accommodate China's legitimate aspirations and resistance to hegemonic claims in a way that avoids the historic causes of armed conflict, which, as Thucydides noted two-and-a-half millennia ago, are fear, honor, and self-interest. That is, fear of attack or subordination and perceived threats to national honor, self-respect, or vital interests. Americans want others to be like them, which reflects a missionary kind of spirit, whereas the Chinese tend to expect deference from other and lesser countries. These characteristics can easily lead to a clash by exacerbating natural tensions between a leading power and a rising power. A seriously adversarial relationship between the United States and China is not inevitable. Avoiding it will require skill on both sides—perhaps more skill than has been shown in recent years by either side.

If China and the United States Clashed Tomorrow

In a very near-term clash, China has more to worry about in a potential clash with the United States. China imports almost half of its oil from the Gulf region. U.S. naval capacity dominates those sea-lanes. If a conflict occurred with China, we could cut off half its oil supply. That would be a substantial escalation on our part; how the Chinese might react gives one pause.

In terms of pure military force issues, the Chinese force is secondary to the U.S. force, but Chinese scientists are making military advances with antiship ballistic missiles having a 500-mile range. That could alter the balance of power and is important for us to deal with on a military level. We know that China is acquiring and refurbishing a used aircraft carrier, its first. The U.S. fleet has eleven large aircraft carriers, including ten of the Nimitz class; a replacement (Ford class) carrier is under construction for one Essex-class ship that is to be retired, and two other carriers are being planned. Former Secretary of Defense Bob Gates has questioned whether the replacement offers the best use of funds; I share his doubts. The navy also operates nine amphibious assault ships resembling small aircraft carriers. Short or vertical takeoff and landing aircraft, including the F-35, and tilt-rotor aircraft, such as the V-22, and helicopters can operate from their decks.

Acquiring an aircraft carrier is a very expensive proposition. A new one costs about $7 billion, not counting its aircraft, which would entail another $10 billion—and that's just the acquisition cost. A carrier is part of a task force that operates, helps defend, and supports the ship from shore. Total operating costs for those carrier task forces consume about 40 percent of the U. S. Navy's budget, about $50 billion annually. When we learned that China was acquiring an aircraft carrier, some feared that China might immediately overtake the United States in military strength in the western Pacific. That is a complete misreading of the balance.

Rather, the Chinese are developing an "anti-access, area-denial" strategy. Its aim is to counter U.S. military capability with countervailing methods, which include developing such weapons as terminally guided ballistic or cruise missiles that can attack U.S. aircraft carriers. A combination of satellite surveillance and radio-location methods could provide a way for a missile to be fired into a general area. Then some sort of homing device would enable the Chinese missile to hit our aircraft carrier, even though our carrier was at sea and in principle harder to find. It is a sensible Chinese military tactic to try to find a means to do all that. Great powers tend to think in those terms when they see a potential adversarial relationship brewing. It's not a sign that they are going to war, but such thinking can get out of hand.

The Chinese military capability was investigated in a Council on Foreign Relations study under my chairmanship in 2003.[36] Our report's findings led to a conclusion that tried to prevent undue apprehension about China's activities by putting the military balance into proper perspective. Since then, other reports have updated our work and arrived at similar fundamental conclusions. They are these: the continued growth of China's economy, military capabilities, and efforts to produce countervailing strategies against U.S. capabilities could eventually pose serious problems for the United States. But that point has not yet been reached. The United States should remain militarily preeminent over the next two decades if defense funding stays near its pre-Iraq/Afghanistan share of GDP and is wisely spent.

The Left Hand Doesn't Know What the Right Hand Is Doing

During a visit to China in 2011, Secretary of Defense Robert Gates attended the military unveiling of a new weapon that seemed to take the Chinese political leadership by surprise. Such an incident would be unheard of in the United States; an American president would know if a new weapon system was about to be shown in public for the first time during a visit by a senior official of a potential adversary. To me the incident indicated too loose a connection between the Chinese political leadership and its military. I think that Gates himself tried to urge the Chinese leadership, which was then focused on economic growth, to get closer to the military to make sure the leaders of the country knew what their military was doing.

I advise finding a way to produce a dialogue with the Chinese that will push political people into working with the military and thus knowing more about what's going on. That is what we did with the Soviet leadership during the SALT negotiations. When it became clear to us that the Soviet Foreign Office and even the top political leadership had not paid enough attention to what the Soviet strategic forces were doing, the kinds and numbers of weapons they had, and their strategy for using them, the SALT process encouraged, indeed forced us to erect a bridge for dialogue that focused Soviet leadership on the Soviet military endeavors we wished to limit.

JAPAN

During the Carter administration, the Japanese needed reassurance that U.S. normalization of relations with China would not adversely affect our Mutual Defense Treaty with Japan. I stopped off in Tokyo on my way back from Beijing in January 1980 to reassert our commitment. I told Japan that U.S. normalization with China would improve Japanese security by reducing tensions in the area.

Why was I rather than the State Department talking with the Japanese Foreign Ministry? Its Foreign Ministry chose to play the role of interlocutor with the U.S. Defense Department. Japan minimized the salience of its military capability even as it responded to U.S. encouragement of its military's modernization. We urged Japan to devote 1 percent of its GDP to self-defense forces, and it did. It also contributed heavily to the housing and operating costs of U.S. forces on bases in Japan. I made frequent trips to Japan during the Carter administration. The importance that the Japanese attached to the military relationship meant that I would meet with their foreign minister and prime minister, as well as with the director of the Japanese self-defense forces (a position since upgraded to defense minister).

Although Japan's economy has grown slowly over the past two decades, Japan remains a major economic power, only recently passed by China and now in third place. In August 2012 Japan's GDP was valued at about $1.28 trillion for the second quarter of the year, which is slightly below China's $1.33 trillion.[37] Japan's military capability and the coordination of its international security activities with those of the United States have also grown as Japan seeks a balance with China without succumbing to its domination. Joint U.S.-Japanese military exercises are now both more substantive and more publicly acknowledged.

KOREA

During the 1976 presidential campaign, candidate Carter pledged to remove the remaining U.S. ground forces from South Korea. That seemed a reasonable goal. The Korean War had been over for nearly twenty-five years. Formally, it was and still is an armistice. The authoritarian regime of President Park Chung Hee, who came to power in South Korea in a coup in 1961, had put the country on firmer economic footing. By 1977 South Korea's economy was already substantially larger than North Korea's, even though Korea's division at the end of World War II found the North with the bulk of Korean industrial and economic weight.[38]

By 1978 South Korea's armed forces were comparable in size to the North's, with nearly balanced ground forces. U.S. air and naval forces could help compensate for South Korean deficiencies. During the Nixon administration, one of two U.S. Army divisions withdrew from South Korea without destabilizing the situation. President Carter thought that he could remove the remaining division without harm. His campaign pledge to remove nearly all U.S. ground forces from South Korea gave little or no consideration to the broader political and security conditions in Northeast Asia.

Carter was troubled by the South's poor human rights record (North Korea's was incomparably worse, but it was an enemy rather than an ally) and by its meddling into U.S. politics. After his election, President Carter listed the Korean situation among his "highest-priority" issues. He directed an interagency review to come up with a detailed plan for the withdrawal of the remaining U.S. ground force division and all U.S. nuclear weapons in South Korea.

I had been involved in U.S.-Korean security relations since the mid-1960s while I was secretary of the air force. South Korea had sent two divisions to fight alongside the United States in Vietnam and had been rewarded with foreign assistance that helped transform the country's economy. I met then with President Park and knew some of his senior military officials while I was working on the basing and deployment of U.S. Air Force units in South Korea.

When I became secretary of defense, U.S. relations with South Korea had been soured mostly because of an eighteen-month-long "Koreagate" scandal. Elements of the South Korean authoritarian government, through

Washington resident Tongsun Park, gifted certain members of Congress with hundreds of thousands of dollars in an influence-peddling scheme. Park handed off what the *Washington Post* called $20,000 bribes stuffed into white envelopes.[39] "Washington is a marvelous city for someone like me," Tongsun Park told the House Ethics Committee in 1978 after he had exported a million tons of Louisiana rice to South Korea over the previous decade and helped engender still more favorable congressional policy toward the republic. He never went to jail; only one member of Congress, Richard T. Hanna (D-Calif.), did.

Despite that tainted relationship, serious concerns about withdrawing U.S. ground forces from South Korea found voice in interagency meetings I attended. The Joint Chiefs of Staff and the commander of U.S. forces in Korea pointed out that the numerical military balance between North and South Korea failed to tell the whole story. The location of the Republic of Korea's capital, Seoul, was but thirty-five miles from the Demilitarized Zone (DMZ) that separated the two Koreas. Seoul accounted for a third of South Korea's population and economy, which made the country more vulnerable than the arithmetic of force ratios suggested.

Moreover, the North Koreans, who called themselves the Democratic Peoples Republic of Korea, had 50 percent more ground forces than the South. Normally a defense can survive that kind of disparity. But North Korea appeared to have positioned itself for a quick drive into Seoul that could follow a massive artillery strike and an invasion by special forces that would try to infiltrate airfields, logistic depots, lines of communication, and command posts. A surprise attack of that sort would require South Korea to divert forces from their primary mission of repelling an attack through the DMZ to counter other warfare activities of the North. North Korea had devoted 15 percent or more of its GNP to military forces; its army was structured to deliver a massive firepower-and-shock attack on the South.

The Joint Chiefs were convinced that the South Korean forces needed the intelligence, command and control, and logistic capabilities of the U.S. forces there, as well as the support of the stationed U.S. ground combat forces, to resist such an attack. The U.S. State Department, supported by the CIA, was greatly concerned that a U.S. withdrawal of ground forces and nuclear weapons from South Korea could not only endanger that country but also undermine the stability of Northeast Asia. South

Korea, both said, would surely read U.S. withdrawal as abandonment. And the Japanese were likely to wonder if withdrawal would foreshadow a broader relaxation of U.S. commitment to defend Northeast Asia from potential intimidation by the Soviet Union or China.

South Korea–Japan relations had been strained by Japanese occupation of Korea from 1910 to 1945 (though President Park had served as an officer in the Japanese army). Relations between those two countries had stabilized through the presence of U.S. troops in both. That balance was sure to be upset by U.S. withdrawal from South Korea. Even the Chinese might be unsettled by a change in the force balance in Northeast Asia. In 1977 China did not have the confidence in its military balance with the Japanese that exists now.

As a result of these concerns, the U.S. interagency group submitted other options to the president, which were far short of withdrawing the remaining U.S. division from South Korea. Of the president's senior advisers, only Brzezinski supported full withdrawal. Adamant, President Carter decided to go ahead with the troop withdrawal and to plan for the withdrawal of nuclear weapons on a two-year schedule.

My own view is that President Carter was convinced that twenty-odd years after the Korean War armistice was enough time for U.S. deployment in a theater where the South should have been able to take care of the North's military threat. That made a good deal of sense, in principle. Carter was also repelled by the Park regime's authoritarian, military nature (there was widespread concern that his election was rigged) and the sleaziness of "Koreagate." To assuage the repeated concerns of his advisers, Carter approved a plan to retain some U.S. logistic, intelligence, and command-and-control units in South Korea, and to replace them gradually with U.S. funding and training of its capabilities and funding for advanced equipment.

In February 1978 Carter announced that he planned to withdraw U.S. ground forces from Korea within four or five years and in three phases, beginning with a withdrawal of 6,000 ground troops, about half of them combat elements. He made the decision with minimal consultation with the South Koreans, the Japanese, the Chinese, or Congress. Reaction in Northeast Asia was swift: the United States was accused of backing away from its stated security commitments. Three things then happened in rapid succession. Congress erupted in opposition to Carter's plan. I was chosen to defend it. And the National Security Agency (NSA) monitoring North Korean communications was asked to conduct a reassessment of troop mobilization at the DMZ. It returned with a report that stated massive North Korean forces were moving to the border—more than ever before.

On February 20 I returned from Hawaii, where I had reviewed Carter's withdrawal plan with the two senior commanders in the area, General John Vessey and Admiral Maurice Weisner. On February 22 I appeared before the House International Relations Committee and made a statement defending Carter's decision.[40] I said that the Joint Chiefs and I participated fully in the decision processes. I said President Carter's decision had considered South Korea's deficiencies, problems, and advantages. One advantage was that hilly terrain north of Seoul favored defending forces and could help them slow down a North Korean attack. South Korea had constructed extensive fortification within this area, and its army had the benefit of impressive training, high morale, and much combat experience.

Moreover, I told Congress, South Korea retained a security connection with the United States, which changed the dimension of any comparison between North and South Korean force capabilities and vulnerability. In the interest of South Korea's security, and to help address its deficiencies, the United States was prepared to turn over to the South some of our equipment, tanks, radars, and more valued at about $800 million. We planned to train South Koreans in the use of the HAWK missile system and other weapons and to cushion the country from unexpected costs with government-to-government loans and credits as we removed our forces.

I noted that South Korea had greatly increased its own capabilities, manpower, and economic strength. I said that the United States would maintain air force units in the South indefinitely and increase the number of our F-4s there from sixty to seventy-two. That, plus some U.S. Army logistic and communications and intelligence elements on site, could help support the South and be a tripwire for U.S. involvement in case of a North Korean invasion. The pertinent question, I said, was not "Why are we withdrawing our ground forces now?" The question should be: "Why have we maintained ground forces in Korea for so long? And "Were we going to keep them there indefinitely?" The time to remove them was when things were relatively stable, I said. Any transition to a new force posture would produce anxiety until after the new posture was in place for some time.

While those arguments were all factual, my personal view (which I was able to avoid saying) was that the timing was wrong, consultation with South Korea and other countries in the area had been inadequate, and any withdrawals should begin later and be carried out more gradually. As for the NSA's report of massive troop buildup on the border, the agency had conducted a reassessment prompted by the ongoing interagency dialogue. Whether that second look truly found an increase in forces and a great threat was unclear. A former evaluation of a balanced force capability between North and South Korea, whether or not there was an actual change in the North Korean force posture, did not stand up under this intense "second look."

Congress introduced bills to prevent the drawdown. It became clear that if the Carter administration did not change its plans, Congress would. The result was that drawdown was scaled back considerably. The planned first phase of a 6,000-troop withdrawal never happened. The remaining division stayed but was thinned; only some auxiliary units were removed. Plans to gradually withdraw nuclear weapons continued, but the weapons stayed for the time being.

Relations with South Korea never fully recovered during the Carter administration. To provide some reassurance, we set up U.S.-South Korea Security Consultative Meetings beginning in 1978. The location of the meetings alternated between our countries. The first meeting was in San Diego because bad publicity would have been too easy to generate in Washington. We backed South Korea off when it tried to turn surface-to-air-missiles into surface-to-surface-missiles, which would have been able to attack the North. We also forced South Korea to drop a potential nuclear weapons program by threatening to end the security relationship.

President Carter went to South Korea at the end of June 1979, in part to reassure the U.S. military there as well as the South Koreans of our continued security commitment. His lack of rapport with Park was such that the most notable event was a ten-minute wait in the limousine outside the Blue House, the presidential abode. Vance and I persuaded our irritated president to go forward with the meeting. The outcome greatly reduced the scope of force withdrawal and increased U.S. aid to the South's forces. Later, back in Washington, the White House announced the suspension of the original plan, which had been to reduce U.S. forces in Korea by 20,000 personnel.

U.S. relations with South Korea through 1980 largely became part of my portfolio. I suppose that of all of the Carter administration principals I was the least mistrusted by South Korean authorities. The other Carter administration advisers generally stayed away from the unpleasant atmosphere, which remained poisoned. South Korean society was divided except for its dislike of America. Only the reasons varied. The military and right wing–leaning citizens of South Korea doubted our security commitment. The leftists, who gradually came to dominate the educational and intellectual communities, thought that America had engineered and favored their country's military-controlled authoritarian government.

A brief history lesson is in order here that starts before the Carter administration and tells of events that affected our relations later. In 1974 political tensions on the peninsula overall had intensified following an assassination attempt against President Park Chung Lee by an agent trained and aided by North Korea. The president's wife was killed in that attempt. In 1979 Park himself was assassinated by Kim Jae-kyu, the head of his CIA, in what appeared to be a spontaneous reaction to a tirade of criticism Park had just leveled at him. It's been reported that after he shot Park, Kim Jae-kyu went outside the presidential mansion and tried to hail a taxi to get away. The assassination took place only three weeks after I met with Park to complete the implementation of the 1978 agreements. Army General Chun Doo-Hwan wrenched power from a democratically elected new president, declared martial law, and in May 1980 ruthlessly suppressed demonstrations against him in Kwangju, a city in Cholla Province. Most South Koreans incorrectly assumed he did that with U.S. approval.

Toward the end of 1980 Chun's government sentenced a fifty-five-year-old opposition leader, Kim Dae-Jung, to death. I was the government official sent to Seoul with a warning to Chun (with the agreement of the incoming Reagan administration, not yet in office). The *Washington Post* covered my trip in an article on December 14, 1980, quoting some of my words in that hour-and-a half meeting: Kim's execution would have a "very significant effect on U.S.-Korean relations," I said.

The *Post*'s reporter in Seoul, William Chapman, wrote: "By sending Brown to reinforce earlier appeals, the Carter Administration was probably playing its best card. Brown has been regarded in Seoul as a friendly figure on security issues and is thought to have stressed South Korea's military importance in an administration that frequently criticized the country for violation of human rights. Brown also is thought to have been instrumental in turning the Carter administration away from its initial plan to withdraw all American troops from South Korea. Reliable sources said that Brown did not warn Chun specifically of what the American consequences would be if Kim dies and that he did not promise any specific rewards if Kim is saved."[41]

Kim was exiled instead of killed. Chun Doo Hwan served as president of South Korea until 1988. Other Korean army generals followed until, beginning in 1993, opposition civilians (first Kim Young-Sam and then in 1998 Kim Dae-Jung himself) were democratically elected. The alliance with the United States continued, but South Korea's government trended increasingly leftward, skeptical of the United States until in 2008 a center-right candidate, Lee Myung-Bak, was elected. During this thirty-year period, South Korea flourished economically with double the population and thirty times the GDP of North Korea.[42] The North Korean military threat persists and several times has threatened conflict on the peninsula. North Korea also gained its fledgling nuclear weapons capability.[43]

We can extract several lessons from this account. The first lesson is my response to the question, "How firmly can a cabinet member publicly support an administration policy with which he or she disagrees?" My view is that he cannot support it at all, if the policy difference is based on a matter of principle. The Korean decision was not that. It was a mistake of timing and degree, and was badly handled in terms of process and its failure to consult partners and Congress. It was not fundamentally wrong in principle to reduce the U.S. military presence in Korea. I made the best case I could for it, and as I've stated before in this book, I did not want any daylight between the president and myself as his defense secretary concerning his decisions. In any case, the president's decision was overtaken by congressional action and the NSA's "second-look" report.

As the NSA reassessment illustrates, when intelligence attention and surveillance become more intense, one is very likely to find "more" of what one is looking for, in this case more activity from threatening forces. It is still not clear whether North Korean forces on the border had in fact increased, or intelligence collection had just become more intense. (An analogous increase in intelligence on Cuba in 1980 spawned the rediscovery of the "Soviet brigade in the Caribbean," an episode described in chapter 5, which helped sink Senate ratification of SALT II.) More observation will probably show more of what is feared. The lesson learned is that we should not assume that a perception of larger numbers resulting from closer observation means that the actual numbers have increased.

Yet another lesson learned is that failure to consult and hear reaction from relevant, especially allied, governments before we make a major policy change that affects them is almost always a serious mistake, especially in security matters. That failure may very well derail a desirable change and in any event is likely to poison relationships between countries. Distaste for deviations from U.S. norms, let alone from our standards of governance, and a personal dislike of foreign leaders can be understandable and inevitable influences on U.S. policy. But they should rarely if ever be the decisive determinants, especially when a major U.S. interest is at stake. As I told Congress when defending Carter's withdrawal plan, "We must not let the Tongsun Park affair obscure our basic national interests in Korea. To look at Korea solely in terms of this scandal, without regard to our security interests and responsibilities, would endanger not only South Korea and its people, but also the stability of Northeast Asia and the security of this country."[44] As of 2008, we had 28,500 troops in South Korea with no plans to reduce that number.

LOYALTY MUST PREVAIL

In May 1977, after President Carter announced his intention to withdraw ground forces from Korea, the third-ranking U.S. officer in the U.S. Forces Korea Command, Major General John Singlaub, publicly denounced the president's decision. I recalled Singlaub to Washington. After a face-to-face meeting with the president on May 21, he was reassigned. He retired to a lengthy career in right-wing causes. That incident reminded me of a much more famous and consequential one. In 1951 General Douglas MacArthur criticized President Harry Truman's policies in a letter to Republican House minority leader Joe Martin. That led to MacArthur being fired.

That such events are rare is a credit to the disciplined ethic of our senior military officers. While on active duty, and before they retire, the overwhelming majority of officers keep their political views separate and private from their duty of loyalty to their civilian superiors, specifically the president and secretary of defense. After retirement, they have every right, and some feel a professional obligation, to express their views—both informed and otherwise. MacArthur's claim that he owed his loyalty to the Constitution rather than to those he described as temporary civilian leaders suggests that he was unfamiliar with the passage in the Constitution that makes the president the commander-in-chief of the armed forces.

In my experience, most (but not all) military officers identified more closely with, and were less likely to oppose—let alone publicly undermine—their military superiors than they would the civilian leadership in military departments or those in the Office of the Secretary of Defense. This is understandable. The military ethic exalts loyalty, and the time senior officers spend with their colleagues in a military career is longer than the few years shared with individual civilian leaders. That interface must be carefully managed. The deference that military officers give to their civilian superiors, even to those in the chain of command, is not the same as that given to their military superiors. Fortunately, few take the MacArthur approach.

THE SOVIET INVASION OF AFGHANISTAN

On January 9, 1980, four days into my first trip to China, I was asked by the news media how that country and ours viewed the Soviet invasion of Afghanistan, which had happened just before I'd arrived. I answered that both China and the United States had parallel views about the need to strengthen the other nations in the region. I could only speculate about Soviet strategic motives for the invasion, but some factors seemed clear. I told the news media:

> The Soviets must have been concerned about the possibility that the insurgency in Afghanistan would succeed, that the Amin government could not suppress it, and that the USSR might be faced with an independent Islamic regime in a bordering country. They might have had concerns about the spread of those sentiments across the border into the Islamic minorities in the Soviet Union.
>
> Apparently the Soviets concluded it was expedient to invade Afghanistan and murder and replace Amin. In converting Afghanistan from a historic buffer state into a puppet state occupied by

at least 50,000 Soviet troops, the Soviets may have reasoned that they were creating opportunities for themselves, and great risks and potential dangers for the rest of the world. The successful occupation of Afghanistan poses great potential threats to Pakistan and Iran. It could give the Soviets an outlet on the Arabian Sea, an ambition they have long cherished and that goes back to Czarist times. If realized, the Soviets could threaten supply lines in the Indian Ocean that deliver oil to Japan and Europe from the Middle East. The Sovietization of Afghanistan represents a grave threat to Iran, an important key to the Persian Gulf. [45]

By January 13, 1980, John McWethy of ABC News had me as his guest on his *Issues and Answers* television show.[46] I indicated that in all likelihood the Chinese and the United States would separately assist Pakistan economically and militarily as part of a consortium of industrialized nations that believed Soviet action in Afghanistan introduced a new and dangerous element into the world scene. When McWethy asked whether my China trip, if not already planned, would have occurred after the Soviet invasion precisely to send a message to the Soviet Union, my response had to be careful and clear. As I had told Vance and Zbig, I did not want to rub the Soviet Union's nose in our normalization of relations with China any more than I had wanted to avoid normalization in an effort to appease the Soviets. Therefore I said, "I think the message to the Soviets is the same as to everyone else. China and the U.S. have proceeded since the 1970s from enmity to normalization to friendship and potential partnership—not directed against the Soviets. It is directed toward stability and peace and preventing expansionism on the part of others."

McWethy repeated what had become a refrain during the presidential campaign as Carter sought a second term: "Just about everyone running for president this year blames the Carter administration for letting the United States fall behind the Russians in military strength." I responded: "The Soviets have been building up their military power steadily for almost twenty years. When the Carter administration came to office it faced a situation in which U.S. defense spending had been declining over the previous ten years. President Carter reversed that trend. In 1977, 1978, and 1979 defense expenditures increased."[47] So did our military strength.

Thinking back to those events, I have two reactions. First, it is clear in retrospect that the Carter administration did begin the defense buildup that followed the decline after the Vietnam War, and that it deserves credit for successfully resisting Soviet attempts to intimidate Western Europe. We did so by persuading a Congress that was divided on defense matters to support that buildup and by rallying the NATO allies to do the same and to act in concert on AWACS, the Soviets' SS-20 missiles, and other issues.

Our NATO allies represent a democratic political system, an economic resource base comparable to our own, a substantial military capability, and an existing structure of political and military cooperation. Their political support as well as the significant military contribution that NATO allies provide in Afghanistan operations is worth the considerable difficulties they bring. Those are inevitable in multinational operations involving countries with varying degrees of commitment to combat. The value of the NATO alliance and of our ties with the European Union is a lesson not to be forgotten as we approach a difficult strategic and even more difficult fiscal situation.

The United States is no longer as dominant as it was in the 1990s, yet remains the most important global power. To foster global goals of peace, economic growth, and human rights, as well as its own well-being, the United States needs the cooperation of other governments that share our objectives and approach to governance. That will require continued and close political, economic, and security (including military) cooperation with other members of NATO and the European Union. In the western Pacific, Japan and South Korea fill a similar role. Together with the United States, these groups constitute about half of the world's economy and at least two-thirds of its military expenditures. Fortunately, we do not now face a military threat comparable to that of the Cold War. But whatever the security situation may be ten or fifteen years from now, our current funding decisions will greatly affect our ability to deal with them. Compromises on defense budgeting need to take that into account.

Afghanistan remains as intractable for the United States as it was for the Soviet Union, the United Kingdom, and Alexander the Great. A hasty exit may be a mistake, but its situation should not be our concern more than that of its neighbors: Pakistan, India, China, Russia, and Iran. It is past time for an attempt to get them to join us in giving Afghanistan back to its inhabitants to work out their destiny. Each of the outsiders may want to help some faction or some imagined polity. We Americans, indeed all of the outsiders, cannot do the fighting ourselves. Al Qaeda in Afghanistan is less of a threat to the United States than are its devotees in several other places. Weapons and terrorists in Pakistan are a far greater threat. Our actions in Afghanistan should be determined principally by that.

I think it is good that the United States intends to move our combat forces out of Afghanistan by 2014—sooner, I hope. Secretary of Defense Leon Panetta has said we will transfer active fighting to the Afghans though continue training them. Perhaps the United States could build a new country there if we were the Afghan government, but we're not. Should we continue pouring money into Afghanistan after we leave? That is a complicated question with ethical and security implications. From a security point of view, it is more than possible that if the United States does not fund the Afghan government, or even if it does, the Taliban will take over parts of the country. Some worry that action would let al Qaeda mount attacks on the United States from there. But al Qaeda is not in Afghanistan now. If we make it clear that any Taliban host of al Qaeda could expect a devastating attack of the sort that took place in 2002, al Qaeda would be less likely to find haven in Afghanistan than in other places (including Pakistan).

From an ethical point of view, some suggest that because the United States messed up Afghanistan, we owe the country something. In fact, the country was messed up before the United States got in; we messed it up worse. U.S. policy should be geared to working with Afghanistan's neighboring countries, ones that have strategic interest in what happens there. The hope is to find some political and economic settlement all can support. My concern about such a policy is that there is no motivation for other countries to join with us if it looks as though we will be staying in Afghanistan for a long time. We're holding the dirty diaper. Afghanistan is our baby.

Some would espouse the "America, come home" attitude toward all national security challenges. It's one thing to say we need to fix our own problems, quite another to withdraw from the rest of the world. If the United States were to adopt a policy of defending only if attacked, but not to use force or deploy its military anywhere else in the world, the world would become more dangerous—including for us—very fast. It's notable that presidential hopeful Ron Paul's strongest support came from young people who have no way of remembering the world before the early 1990s. They don't know how dangerous that world can be. While advocating caution myself, I am concerned that the United States may pull back too much. Finding the right course between military adventurism and abandonment of the world is the critical issue for American foreign policy and national security now.

British historian Arnold J. Toynbee wrote in *A Study of History,* in a chapter titled "Encounters with Civilizations," that the classic problem of invaders was "an overweening self-confidence bred by the mistaken belief in their own invulnerability . . . [which] leads them on to court disaster by rashly attacking still unbroken peoples whose spirit and capacity for resistance takes them by surprise." I said in 1980 in response to the Soviet invasion of Afghanistan, and I say again now, that there are simple truths we must be wise enough to accept: military force alone cannot solve all the world's problems. Commitment to military force is a very serious business. Such force and our will to use them are necessary and essential to the defense of our vital interests.

America cannot solve all the world's problems and must carefully select where and how to proceed. I would add now, given our fiscal situation and internal problems, we should go forward with a lighter hand.

THE PANAMA CANAL TREATY

From the time of the Monroe Doctrine, the United States has ensured stability and security in the Caribbean. The communist takeover in Cuba eroded that security with what the *New York Times*'s military analyst in the 1960s, Hanson Baldwin, wrote was due to "mistakes and weaknesses that . . . let infiltrators within our outer walls, and what should be our island-speckled ramparts becoming the soft underbelly of North America." That purple prose was an overstatement of the threat. But it was in that broader perspective that any change in the Panama Canal had to be considered. The canal was both a cause and a symbol of American vital interests. The Canal Zone housed U.S. military bases that facilitated operations throughout that region. Free access for the transit of U.S. naval units eased two-ocean planning.

The U.S. Navy depends partly on the canal to provide security in two oceans. But contrary to popular belief, current aircraft carriers are too wide to transit the canal. Passage through it is very important for shipping as well as for exchanging forces from one ocean to another. The issue of how to have access to the canal in war and peace was key to the Panama Canal Treaty of September 7, 1977. I was deeply involved with the contents of the treaty and other statements the United States would need to associate with it. For example, I wanted to make sure that in times of crisis or warfare, as well as in peacetime, we could use the canal after its sovereignty reverted to Panama. Chairman of the Joint Chiefs General George Brown and I came up with a formula for that and advised President Carter to adopt it. We added a key element that persuaded just enough senators to pass it: the United States would retain the right to intervene militarily if the integrity of the canal was threatened.

TURKEY

In 1978, at the time of the looming conflict in Uganda, we needed to move some forces by air over Turkey. Turkey was part of NATO. We had bases there and friendly relations with the government. However, it denied permission for the flyover. The Soviet Union was on the other side of the conflict in East Africa. It moved its forces by flying over Turkey and didn't ask permission. I raised this issue with General Kenan Evren, chief of the Turkish general staff. (In 1980 he led a successful military coup and now, at the age of ninety-four, is on trial for that overthrow.) I said: "What kind of ally are you when you let the Soviets move forces through your airspace, but not us?" He didn't give a very good answer. Perhaps the best one might have been: "You're a friend and friends ask permission. Adversaries don't and we didn't want to get into a war about it." The meeting didn't end badly, but it was a case where I knew I behaved undiplomatically. I could; Turkey depended on us.

I made a similar undiplomatic pronouncement to then French Minister of Defense Yvon Bourges in a meeting he initiated. France had withdrawn from the NATO military structure a dozen years before and sometimes reveled in opposing U.S. political positions. There had been close cooperation between our nations on nuclear matters, as close as possible after Congress limited the sharing of information. However, commercial competition between French and American firms was intense. Bourges pressed me to provide France with some sensitive technology. The French were going to put ballistic missiles on their submarines as part of their deterrent force. Bourges wanted ways to quiet French subs, as we had done on ours, to make it harder for Soviet forces to detect them.

My response was: "France is selling advanced computer capabilities to the Soviets, which enables the Soviets to improve their antisubmarine capabilities. It doesn't make sense for the U.S. to redress the security risks incurred by your sales of computers to our common adversary." He understood what I meant: if you're undermining your security by doing something foolish and adverse to U.S. interests, don't ask the United States to compensate for it.

My behavior in these two instances, as well as my comment to German Chancellor Schmidt, asking him to take care not to alienate the U.S. president, came from a standpoint of U.S. predominance in economics and security. Turkey and France depended on us. We felt we ought to be able to depend on them. The world is very different now, and U.S. underpinning of much of the world's security is less openly valued. So an American secretary of defense might now choose softer, or at least less explicit, language. The United States still has more responsibility for international security than any other country in the world, though our dominance is not what it once was. We have to find new ways to exercise our influence.

THE LEGACY OF CARTER SECURITY POLICIES

The Reagan presidential campaign decried what its managers called the decline and inadequacy of Carter's defense and security policies. I disagreed then and do now. Iran had been a disaster. But overall, the United States at the end of the Carter years was more secure than at the beginning. It's true that the Soviet Union was exerting pressure in various parts of the world. Its forces had invaded Afghanistan. Ethiopia had fallen into unfriendly hands. But we had held off the Soviet attempt to intimidate Western Europe through our reinvigoration and strengthening of the NATO alliance and its successful adoption of the intermediate range nuclear force. The SALT II agreement, even though not ratified, had limited the strategic threat.

The Camp David Peace Accords produced the first peace agreement between Israel and an Arab neighbor. The Panama Canal Treaties ensured that the canal would continue to function in the U.S. interest without a military action and without inflaming our relations with Latin America. Normalization of relations with China had changed the world's strategic situation in favor of the United States. And Carter had emphasized human rights throughout the world, which had not been nearly as prominent in U.S. policy before. That idealism frequently lost out to our strategic interests, as in my opinion it generally should when they compete, but it paid off handsomely in the long run and continues to do so. That many people in the world saw President Carter as a champion for human rights was illustrated on a visit by former U.S. officials (including myself) to the Soviet Union in the mid-1980s. At a U.S. embassy reception there, Jewish and other Soviet dissidents who sought the softening of USSR emigration policy clustered around Cy Vance who embodied the administration's human rights activities. President Carter continues his activities in human rights, just as he championed our military capabilities.

By the end of the president's term, we had begun to turn the post-Vietnam slump into investment in defense. We not only turned around the decline in military capability, we also introduced new technologies. When Soviet military leader Nikolai Ogarkov said, "The Americans are getting ahead of us," he was talking about our new technologies and our turnaround of the post-Vietnam slump into an investment in defense. These, too, were Carter administration accomplishments.

7

That Banner Yet Waves

PREPARING FOR
WHAT LIES AHEAD

In January 1981, at the end of the Carter presidency, White House counsel Lloyd Cutler hosted a dinner at the F Street Club for the president, cabinet, and a few other senior members of the administration. Each person got up and said something about his or her experience. When it was my turn, I made two comments. One was that I had tried to do my best but realized I had sometimes made the president uncomfortable. In particular, I'd pushed for a higher defense budget, as he notes in his book *White House Diary,* when that was politically difficult.

My other comment was that when I came into office I understood in my head that the military capability of the country depended explicitly on its economic strength. After four years as defense secretary, I knew it in my gut. I feel it even more strongly now. Our ability to defend or intervene in conflicts depends on funding and efficiently providing for the specific needs of the various parts of the military, including their equipment, training, and readiness and force structure. Our fiscal constraints ensure that the future push-pull over funding will be harder than in previous decades. Participants in that ongoing tug-of-war will be the military services, current or competing contractors, technology advocates, local interests connected with bases or contractors, and all of their political representatives or supporters.

Our domestic budget and its priorities are one overarching concern. The other, whose resolution should shape the outcome of those debates, is the concept of America's place in the world and the role we want to play.

Too seldom do we ask ourselves how much of a commitment we are willing to make to the internal affairs of other countries or to their defense, how much it will cost, and the probability of various outcomes. The sudden changes in the arc from North Africa to Afghanistan and Pakistan surprised policymakers. This suggests that our state of knowledge is insufficient to inspire confidence about most prospective interventions there.

A cautious and light hand is the logical inference. Recent history provides a lesson: Iraq didn't come out as the George W. Bush administration intended. Whatever problems the U.S. military had in nation building, contractors now under State Department management will have them, too. In fact, contractors have less discipline and fewer skills than the military, or in the case of ex-military contractors, the same skills. And State has less experience dealing with contractors than Defense does.

IMPORTANT CONSIDERATIONS CONCERNING NATION BUILDING

As a nation, we vacillate in our attitude toward nation building. George W. Bush came into office saying "no more nation building." Yet he justified intervention in Iraq partly on the notion that we were going to help build a democratic society there. Nation building has poor prospects of success in a recalcitrant society. Even in Haiti, a nation eager to be tutored by the United States, we're finding it difficult to build a society as a humanitarian gesture. Of course, trying to support local governments and shore up weak ones depends on America having a domestic economy healthy enough to use economic instruments, including foreign aid.

How much money can we afford to spend as a humanitarian peacemaker and nation builder as our own nation climbs out of its current slow growth and long-term fiscal austerity? How many of the world's problems are we going to aspire to solve? How likely are we to succeed? How many American soldiers will we put in harm's way trying to solve the world's problems? Sometimes we should act, but we need to weigh each case carefully.

The United States recently committed to a dozen more years of nation building in Afghanistan. My view is that we're unlikely to succeed, and we need to limit that effort there, partly because its economic cost inflicts pain on the United States and partly because neither our military nor the rest of the U.S. government has that capability. By contrast, after World War II the army was full of people who had been municipal officers and engineers in civilian life. I don't recommend training any substantial segment of our regular military force personnel for nation building. Rather, we could consider using some of the National Guard and Reserve because they are the people with the appropriate civilian skills.

That's not to say we can't give economic assistance to other countries. Economic assistance is always a desirable component of security policy; its cost is far smaller than what the American public believes, and tiny compared with our military budget. I support current Secretary of State Hillary Clinton and former Secretary of Defense Bob Gates in their suggestion to move some Defense Department funds into the kind of humanitarian assistance that will pay off in the long run.[1] But until we get our domestic fiscal house in order, we have to limit our spending on building up other nations. Because of these concerns, a president and secretary of defense, along with the rest of the national security team, need to have clear priorities concerning where and how to allocate money for national security, and where and when to intervene in another nation's problems.

Use A Light Hand Where We Lack Deep Connections

The United States needs to continue what President Barack Obama has done: use a relatively light hand in areas where we don't have deep knowledge or long-term connections. NATO intervention in Libya was not easy though Libya is geographically close to Europe and remote from the Middle East, and Moammar Gaddafi had no sympathizers in NATO after his agents destroyed Pan Am 103. All 270 people aboard that 1988 flight from London en route to the United States died. Gaddafi had no friends among Arab nations, either. Still, intervention in Libya was easier to carry out than it would be now in Syria. Syria's connections with other Arab states are far more complex; so are its internal sectarian divisions.

The Obama administration was divided about how to react to Libya. The president agonized over it and decided that a potential massive killing in Benghazi would be a bad outcome for the reputation of the United States. Nicolas Sarkozy and David Cameron pushed hard from France and Britain. Hillary Clinton, and UN ambassador Susan Rice, as well as Samantha Power, a foreign policy adviser to President Obama, pushed hard from within the administration. The president decided that it wouldn't be in accord with American ideals to let a massacre happen. He decided he didn't want to be held responsible for another Rwanda. The problem was that there was no clear plan or idea as to how military intrusion into Libya would end. All this points to a lack of clear strategy to determine the balance between U.S. interests and humanitarian instincts.

As I write this, no country—including Syria's neighbors—appears ready to consider direct military action to be the right course for stopping Assad's violent suppression of his citizens. Economic sanctions work to some degree. They need to be applied in concert with other nations and take a long time to become effective. Suggestions for a no-fly zone generally ignore the need to begin such an operation with a massive bombing campaign to suppress air defenses. Supplying arms to insurgents within Syria might be a way to go. That may yet happen, and the arms might come largely from Syria's neighbors. That doesn't suggest a good outcome because it would intensify a civil war.

DO OUR INTERESTS AND VALUES ALIGN OR COMPETE?

Except in defending our homeland from direct attack, the United States will find it increasingly difficult to act alone in the world. Depending on the specific situation, we will need to act with others, and not always with the same others, even when we apply economic sanctions. How will we choose when to intervene? How will we know when our interests and values align or compete? Henry Kissinger and James A. Baker III, two of the most effective secretaries of state during the past sixty years, would reconcile "idealism" and "realism" as joint criteria for U.S. military intervention. "Pragmatic idealism," they think, is the appropriate basis for action when American values "impel us to relieve human suffering and our national interest is at stake."[2] Others have described this as a balance between ideals and interests.

I fear that these hinged principles are uneasily yoked. They avoid the real question: how do we strike a balance between our ideals (to relieve or prevent humanitarian catastrophe and advance democracy, human rights, and well-being) and their probable effects on our national interests? Some national interests are vital, others important, still others merely convenient. The appropriate way to balance our values with those interests depends on which category of interests is at stake.

In many cases, idealism and realism conflict, as evidenced by U.S. military interventions in Vietnam, and later in Afghanistan and Iraq by different administrations. Those decisions had short- and long-term consequences, both good and bad. As we ponder potential future interventions, we could divide the issue temporally, noting that our interests are mutable, but our ideals are eternal, and that the two often converge over a long enough timeframe. Indeed, the advancement of our values elsewhere in the world is one of our interests, though hardly our preeminent one, especially where our knowledge of other polities and cultures is modest or worse. Values asserted as universal are usually expressed in terms so general that different cultures can use the same words but mean very different things: justice, freedom, equality, honor are examples. When we get down to specific behaviors, the differences in interpretation greatly influence whether intervention is worth its costs and risks.

About Libya, there was no claim that who prevailed—Gaddafi or the insurgents—was vital or even important to U.S. national interests. British and French leaders apparently considered that intervention in their national interest, including the flow of oil, and despite a potential influx of refugees. They pressed the United States to join and lead the intervention. The likelihood and magnitude of a humanitarian disaster without intervention had to be guessed at and weighed against the probability of a bad outcome. Twenty years earlier, the George H. W. Bush administration had to strike a corresponding balance with respect to Saddam Hussein during the Gulf War. That intervention worked out well, though incompletely, because Saddam remained in power.

Domestically, U.S. interests and values coincide more closely. Our ability to preserve our values at home is our most vital interest. Internationally, we promote our values, which we consider universal. But the people of other countries, let alone their leaders, may not subscribe to our values. In some cases, insistence that others adopt American values conflicts with important U.S. national interests, illustrating John Quincy Adams's admonition that "Americans should not go abroad to slay dragons they do not understand in the name of democracy."[3]

The United States is too deeply involved in and dependent on what happens abroad to avoid interaction with those dragons. But we have something to learn from another nineteenth-century statesman, British Prime Minister Lord Palmerston, who believed values were cloaked by interests: "Nations have no permanent friends or allies, they only have permanent interests."[4]

Of course, nothing is permanent except change. American values have been an essential element in our long-term alliances or friendships with many nations. However, Palmerston's formulation becomes clear if we recast his wisdom in terms of nations rather than regimes. Germany and Japan became allies through the nature of their post–World War II more democratic governments and the convergence of our geostrategic policies with theirs. The shah's regime in Iran was a sort of friend; the current regime is an adversary. China, Russia, India, and Brazil are more complicated cases.

When important U.S. national interests are at stake, we still have to weigh the competing demands on resources, the degree of support by allies and others in the region, and the magnitude and likelihood of potential human suffering if we intervene, or if we do not. It is difficult to judge in advance how these factors will play out over time once interventions take place. Every consideration of intervention will be different and will require balancing differing factors on each side of the decision, whether those factors are motivated by presumed interest or inspired by humanitarian values. In the latter case, the difficulties of dealing with warring or slaughtering factions are likely to be more daunting than the financial cost, but sometimes worth accepting. When major U.S. combat is involved with protecting our interests, financial costs vie with the consequences—unintended, unknown, or likely adverse ones—as weights in the balance.

Do your own Monday-morning quarterbacking of Vietnam, Afghanistan 2002, Afghanistan 2009, Libya 2011, Kuwait 1991, and Iraq 2003. Then, fill out your game card for Syria, Pakistan, and Iran to see what you'd recommend to the president. Making the judgment to intervene is the responsibility and decision of presidents. Congress usually has been satisfied with the right to consult rather than decide, though consultation has not always been afforded in lower-level interventions. In dealing with parts of the western Pacific, Europe, the Middle East, and the Gulf—areas truly vital to U.S. interests—the criteria I have suggested should be followed. When idealism trumps interests, the results are unlikely to be happy.

Our values are permanent; but making them *the* deciding factor is not always in our best interest. Some advocates of humanitarian intervention seem to suggest that a lack of U.S. security interest actually increases the moral justification and urgency of U.S. intervention. In the case of Libya, I advised not going in and published a letter to that effect in the *Washington Post* on April 8, 2011, days after an op-ed by Kissinger and Baker appeared.[5] President Obama's course of action correctly kept the United States in a supporting role, leaving the British and French up front.

Understand the New World Order

America is missionary-like in its eagerness to spread democracy, but it doesn't do empire well. The Romans and the Brits were good at empire, the Romans for hundreds of years and the British for about 150 years. Both of those societies were very different from ours; the Roman Empire maintained an authoritarian state and the British an aristocratic one. As a democracy, America is unruly and (at least we think) not as ruthless as empires that ignored the pain that suppression imposes on others. That's not to say we are innocent of causing pain. U.S. behavior in the Philippines after the Spanish-American War was repressive. We committed some dreadful acts in Vietnam, and we continue to grapple with the results of the atrocious behavior by some of our troops at Abu Ghraib prison in Iraq. As history has demonstrated, beginning with the Athenians in the fifth century B.C., democracies make ineffective imperialists because they are consumed by internal arguments.

That we don't do empire well is another good reason to think through how we want to intervene in the world. Let us be realistic about world threats now. They are localized. They are serious. They are complicated. But they do not put us in immediate existential peril as the Soviet threat did during the Cold War. Even the Pakistani-Indian relationship, which could erupt into a regional nuclear war, does not pose a dire threat to us. We need to rethink how we view the world even as other nations recalibrate their view of us.

The United States is no longer considered the universal defender against an overwhelming global threat. Some countries have started to balance their weight against the United States, disliking its former dominance. What only a few could foresee, however, is that our "sole superpower" status in the world would fade not because of imperial overstretch, but because of our domestic economic behavior and fiscal overreach and the irresponsibility of political leaders and business executives, and the financial institutions that lack transparency. The world may find it misses unchallenged American leadership, and so will many Americans. We are used to thinking we can do anything anywhere the world needs us (or where we think it does). We can't. We must share the new world order or disorder with other powers even as we remain the leading one. That will force us to decide what new form and nature our military should take, at what cost, and how we will organize it, and require a great deal of long-range planning.

VITAL INTERESTS IN THE COMING DECADE

We will be involved with or affected by Afghanistan for a long time. We went into Afghanistan originally to wipe out al Qaeda, which functioned there with impunity. To wipe out al Qaeda, we had to overthrow the Taliban. We did, in a well-planned and well-executed campaign, but we diverted our attention and resources to Iraq. Meanwhile, the Taliban returned to Afghanistan and Pakistan. They are no longer *the* government of Afghanistan. They are one of its conflicting forces, vying for control in the chaos of that fragmented country along with tribal warlords and a weak central government. The hope was to create stability and lessen the risk of a civil war. Now, if order breaks down completely, Afghanistan could become a base from which terrorists could attack the United States.

Can we suppress al Qaeda from a distance? I conclude that we must try. Afghanistan is not the only or principal base, actual or potential, for terrorists. Yemen is going in the same direction as Afghanistan. Would America be willing to wage a ten-year war in Yemen or Somalia or Sudan? What is the future of our relationship with Pakistan, where we've driven the Taliban? They're more dangerous in Pakistan because it has the nuclear bomb and is rife with conflict.

We have clear and vital interests in Europe and East Asia. East Asia views the United States as a defender against overbearing Chinese influence, which doesn't come close to the Soviet threat of post–World War II. There is reason to hope that China will never represent that sort of threat. The sides were clear during the Cold War. Now, there are lots of sides. Therefore we need to adopt a more nuanced tone toward the world and adapt our military capabilities to meet a complicated set of threats and relationships. That will challenge future secretaries of defense and the national security apparatus more generally as the connections among our military, cultural, technical, and economic aims intertwine.

President Carter would place his priorities now on developing nations, human rights, and arms control. His is the list of an idealist deserving of his belated Nobel Peace Prize. My own thinking is less aspirational and more practical. To advance President Carter's list, we have to ensure that the world's major economic regions are not controlled by an adversary. We need to preserve our access to trade and natural resources. We have to reduce our dependence on hydrocarbon energy, especially imports; advance our technological innovation and education; and avoid a protectionist conflict, which would be a threat to our economy and therefore a grave threat to our security. Our values need not conflict with those interests.

How will we grow our economy while reducing our carbon footprint? The United States contributes about 25 percent of the CO_2 emitted into the world's atmosphere, so we Americans can't shoulder the problem of global warming alone.[6] At the same time, we need to consider the potential security problems that global warming could create for our Defense Department as it responds to problems in various parts of the world. Increased incidence of natural disasters and depletion of natural resources can lead to unstable societies, armed conflicts, and human disasters that will require a response.

As for China, I urge less fear over the unfounded prospect that it can overtake us economically or militarily in this decade or the next. China is the new rising power, but unlike the Soviet Union, it doesn't appear to envision a world dominated by its ideology because it doesn't have an ideology. The Chinese want to be rich, powerful, respected, and dominant in their region. The United States and China are locked in an uncomfortable economic embrace. Although China can buy up a modest fraction of America, the assets remain here. The U.S. debt that the Chinese hold is as big a problem for them as for us.

STABILIZE DEFENSE FUNDING TO 4 PERCENT OF GDP

My reading of U.S. security needs, based on what I see as our foreign policy objectives and the likely future threats, suggests that our military capability will require something under, but near 4 percent of GDP in the defense budget over the next decade. That figure would be the top line of the defense budget. Of course, the exact amount would emerge from a detailed look at specific needs and programs. We can fight about the details of how to efficiently apportion it. But wild swings in the total over a few years at a time surely are not efficient. So let's eliminate as much as we can of wasteful argument and noise and heat that goes around that top-line number.

The world situation appears to change every few months. Our programs and procurement policies can't. It takes up to twenty years to formulate, express, procure, and deploy a new weapons system. To be ready for what the world throws at us, we need to create continuity in our procurement and defense programs. The executive branch, and especially Congress, change many parts of the five-year program every year, even if they leave the top-line total of the defense budget the same, which they often don't. The analogy is a family in a home with a household budget that fluctuates yearly. The family responds by selling its house and moving into a bigger one during a good year, then selling again and moving into a smaller house the following not-so-good year. Those wild swings are what we do to the defense program—to the detriment of long-range planning. It makes little sense to operate that way.

SET GOALS AND PRIORITIES
FOR DEFENSE PROCUREMENT

When they fund procurement, the executive branch and Congress are often faced with a hard choice: stretch out the purchase of weapons, which raises unit costs, or spend more rapidly and then close production lines completely, which could leave us without an operating line for restocking in the future. Though wasteful in the short run, I tend to favor the flexibility of "warm" production lines, operating at a low level but able to be ramped up to a higher rate if and when needed.

This is one small example of a more general issue: consensus on defense spending in this country will not be restored without a national strategy.[7] That means political decisions on national security priorities that lead to defined requirements for military capabilities, and then to programs and their funding. Absent agreement on these issues, it is not surprising to see funding and programs driven by narrow, often parochial concerns associated with particular proposals for deficit reduction or for helping some contractor, constituent, or contributor. Setting priorities for defense calls for leadership in the most fundamental sense. The vague, misleading, and sometimes mendacious generalities characteristic of political campaigns are no substitute.

Massive cuts in outlays for defense and international affairs, no matter how they are defined and quantified, would produce a dramatic and dangerous change in American foreign policy and our role in the world. Significant cuts from the defense budget already set in motion for the years immediately after 2012 will likely be implemented. Those cuts are fiscally prudent and politically necessary as part of what should be a domestic economic plan to increase revenue and lower expenditures (especially entitlements). These can be phased in gradually as recovery increases our GDP. But cuts deeper than that would be severely deleterious, especially the sequestration embodied in current law. It cuts $50 billion a year for the next ten years from defense, and also from non-defense discretionary programs including food stamps and Medicaid. Sequestration would leave entitlement programs untouched. Entitlement programs are those expended automatically without congressional actions, such as Social Security and Medicare.

Solving our budget problem in a way that shares burdens and sacrifices equitably across our nation's domestic and international priorities has not been and will not be easy. Budget problems, if protracted, will lead to an explosion of debt and another financial crisis. We must phase in fiscal tightening, arranging for it to be triggered by an acceleration to a higher rate of economic growth. As an example of increasing revenue, I favor a progressive consumption tax. This would be appropriate only after the economy has recovered. Until then, consumption should be encouraged rather than increasingly taxed. A progressive consumption tax would be managed in the present IRS system, not at the point of sale. It would be at a much higher rate on the millionth dollar spent than on the fifty thousandth dollar. A CSIS commission explored this approach thoroughly.[8]

This approach gets wide support from serious tax reformers. Recipients of special tax treatment, who together constitute a majority of voters, are more vigorous in defending their privileges than the advocates of overall reform. That makes reform close to impossible, barring a disaster that forces a completely new start. The choices we have to make are painful but are the burden of leadership. Leadership must surmount partisanship and parochialism to clearly and honestly explain the choices to the American people.

Most economists believe that Franklin D. Roosevelt improved the economy with a Keynesian approach when the nation fell into the Great Depression of the 1930s. His administration increased expenditures. So has the Obama administration, though not enough. By 1937 Roosevelt decided that he was increasing the debt by too much and stopped spending. The country fell back into recession in 1938. Unemployment, which had peaked at 24.9 percent at the depth of the Depression, had improved to 14 percent when government spending increased, but climbed again to 19 percent in 1938 when spending stopped. That recession didn't end until war started in Europe and the United States spent on armaments for our own and our allies' defense.[9] In 1941 the unemployment rate dropped to 10 percent and by 1942 to 4.4 percent.[10]

Defense spending—both in preparation for that war and during it—pulled us out of recession. We could have stimulated the economy as well by government domestic investment. That is what the first phase of the New Deal did. The lesson learned is that in the short run, when unemployment is high and production well below capacity, having the government spend money on almost anything helps pull the country out of recession or depression. The extreme of that is loading up helicopters with cash and dropping it. During the Roosevelt administration, political cartoonists lampooned jobs created by the New Deal, portraying them as a matter of digging holes and filling them up again, or raking leaves and letting them blow back. There are better and more productive ways of spending to stimulate the economy. Sensible investment in infrastructure is one.

COORDINATE ECONOMIC AND FOREIGN POLICY

As we go forward, the Defense Department and State Department will need to work together far more closely. As military personnel and the State Department's private contractors work with various government agencies, the many levels of human interaction will make for a complicated universe. The executive branch will need to align our foreign policy strategy with our economic interests to deal with embargoes, trade sanctions, and technology transfer. To that end, there needs to be an economic voice at the level of the National Security Council (NSC).

It could be the voice of a cabinet member, the director of the Office of Management and Budget, the director of the National Economic Council, or the chair of the Council of Economic Advisers. While recognizing that few if any of them will be up to Alexander Hamilton's standard, I recommend making the secretary of the treasury, as the senior cabinet member dealing with economic affairs, part of the NSC that advises the president on foreign policy, military, and other security matters. Economic advice increasingly infuses foreign policy decisions. At present, such advice is not sufficiently or formally organized. Instead, staffers deal with other staffers in an ad hoc way to get things done, while the principals participate less than they should. We need to protect our country's economic base and health as part of our diplomatic and military strategy. We also need to use our economic and financial strength as national security tools. Both functions would be served by having a powerful and sophisticated economic voice at the table.

THE COMPLEX ISSUES OF DUAL-USE TECHNOLOGY

A complex issue is how to control the sales and other transfers of dual-use technologies, which can be used in both civilian and military systems. In comparison, weapons systems transfers are relatively simple, although they involve both diplomatic and military issues. They are covered in a munitions list maintained by the State Department but in practice are handled in top-level negotiations between governments. The militaries of both the United States and the purchaser deal with the specifics. The president decides which foreign countries can buy U.S. technology, weighing such factors as considerations of regional security and balance, the risk of a change in the strategic orientation of the recipient, and the effect on the relations with other regional powers. Selling advanced fighter aircraft to Taiwan or Saudi Arabia illustrates the complexities in deciding to whom we sell weapons systems.

The dual-use issue is further complicated by the various ways that specific technologies can be used once in hand. For example, advanced computers and sensors, and satellites and their launchers, have very clear civilian uses, but ones that can be adapted for military purposes we neither endorse nor intend. An important question to ask here is: how likely is the sale of a technology for civilian use to boomerang against us if an ally turns hostile with a regime change, or an ally transfers our technology to a U.S. adversary? The Commerce Department's Bureau of Industry and Security, which has license authority over a long list of dual-use technologies, considers the economic benefits of sales and whether embedded intellectual property will remain protected. Commerce's primary responsibility is to advance U.S. economic interests. Hard sales equal hard cash. Often, Commerce tries to ease policies for transfer while Defense argues to tighten them. Debates rage in an effort to reconcile these disparate interests. Major cases reach the White House with the Economic Council and the NSC staff involved.

Overreaching is common on both sides of the policy disagreements. During the 1980s and 1990s, opponents of the transfer of high-tech information systems prevented U.S. manufacturers from exporting computers to certain nations. Meanwhile, European and Japanese manufacturers were freely exporting their equivalent equipment to those same nations. In a contrary example experienced during the Carter administration, Senate objections, especially by the hot-tempered Senator John Culver (D-Iowa), fortunately helped prevent the planned sale of E-3 AWACS aircraft to the shah's Iran just before the Iranian Revolution would have turned that capability against us. Whom we can and should sell arms to will become more complicated as the Islamic world roils.

It's a hornet's nest dealing with the disparate and often conflicting elements of economic risk and benefit, military danger, and diplomatic leverage. Despite my aversion to having more policy decisions centralized at the White House staff level, this policy area justifies setting up a new (small) office there to adjudicate these matters.

FORGE MORE FOREIGN POLICY CONSENSUS IN CONGRESS

As a practical matter, the lack of consensus in Congress now (compared with past decades) needs to be overcome. I suggest that the members of Congress identify a small group in each chamber that is willing to commit the time necessary to master the substance and details of foreign policy matters. These Senate and House members need to possess enough political stature with colleagues to deliver on agreements made with the administration. To be an effective partner in foreign policymaking, Congress needs to be able to make lasting decisions rather than fight every issue endlessly.

SELECT CABINET OFFICIALS WITH EXPERIENCE

Presidents need to select their cabinet officials and their deputies wisely and draw them from a wider field. In recent decades it has been the almost universal practice to assign top jobs (and those at a level or two below that) only to people from the party in power, excluding others even if they are highly qualified. In the Clinton administration, the last two deputy secretaries of defense, both very able, had been congressional staffers who took that route to senior subcabinet level. In contrast to the 1970s, the number of staffers taking that route has become a torrent, especially so lately. The good thing about former congressional staffers is that they know how Congress works in terms of horse-trading and mollifying special interests. That's not absent in the executive branch, but the lack of public accountability and the great partisanship that now describes congressional staffers' work differs from the responsibility that the executive branch owes to the nation as a whole. Issues need to be debated in the executive branch from a national point of view.

ALLOW PRACTICAL COMPROMISE

Experience shows that policies formed through consultation between Congress and the executive branch are better and more effective than those formed without it. The goal is a creative tension in the context of the division of powers. Instead, we struggle with deadlocked factions, continuing resolutions, and antagonistic attitudes that at times seem intractable. Political polarization studies show that you can't predict how members of Congress will vote on foreign policy by how they vote on domestic issues. For example, both Republicans and Democrats are worried about China, but for different reasons. The Republicans worry about China as a potential military threat; the Democrats worry China is a job stealer. That both parties worry about China is a starting point for formulating U.S. strategy.

ELIMINATE THE EXTRA LAYER
IN THE INTELLIGENCE COMMUNITY

In September 1994 the Commission on the Roles and Capabilities of the U.S. Intelligence Community was formed to assess the future direction, priorities, and structure of the intelligence community in the post–Cold

War era. Originally headed by Les Aspin, it subsequently came under my chairmanship. The president appointed nine members; eight were nominated by congressional leadership. We produced a report in March 1996 after more than a year of work. We recommended strengthening the hand of the director of national intelligence (the CIA director in his role as head of the entire intelligence community). We suggested rationalizing the inevitably dispersed intelligence activities of the various parts of the government, establishing closer ties between producers and users of intelligence, and simplifying congressional oversight. Our report was comprehensive and thoughtful. The Clinton administration accepted the recommendations that could be adopted through presidential action. The Congress did nothing, especially about itself. [11]

Later, after the 9/11 attacks, another commission spent a year and a half looking at that specific event and produced a careful analysis of what had gone wrong. But then the same panel conducted a hurried two-week examination of the structure of the intelligence community. It properly cited the failure of FBI-CIA cooperation as a major reason for the tragedy. The commission then concluded, strangely, that an important part of any solution would be to create another layer on top of the existing structure and to give its head authority over the CIA and more influence over the Defense Department's intelligence agencies that report to the secretary of defense. The panel was less specific about the FBI. [12] Congress enacted legislation that followed that recommendation, creating a director of national intelligence (DNI). The resulting layer consists of 1,500 personnel, including the usual panoply of principal deputy directors, deputy directors, associate directors, and assistant deputy directors.

Inevitably there has been conflict between the DNI and the CIA director and some friction between the DNI and the Defense Department. But if the DNI layer continues to exist (Congress finds it even harder than the executive branch to admit mistakes), that added layer needs to be drastically thinned.

THE NATIONAL SECURITY HORIZON

The existential threat to our country would be a nuclear attack by a major nation, which the end of the Cold War has rightly removed from the daily thinking of U.S. national security officials. Second-tier attackers with considerably less capability to deliver attacks, such as the North Koreans or potentially the Iranians or an unstable Pakistan, know our capability for devastating retaliation. That deterrence can be enhanced with a low level of ballistic-missile and other active defense; border controls are even more relevant to preventing nuclear attack on the United States.

An Iranian nuclear weapons capability would be very dangerous, and I would not rule out an attack on their nuclear facilities if negotiations fail. While such a response would delay an Iranian nuclear weapons capability, it would increase their determination for one and thus its likelihood. In any event, I am confident that Iran would not risk a nuclear attack on the United States. It could, however, try to advance its drive toward regional hegemony by deterring U.S. interference. An Iranian threat to use nuclear weapons on regional U.S. allies might cause those allies to ask the United States to back off. But a U.S. policy of nuclear retaliation against such an action should deal with it. I don't think Iran would risk launching a nuclear attack on Israel because Israel would retaliate by destroying Iran. Israel believes that a nuclear-armed Iran is going to feel more enabled to launch nonnuclear attacks. Iran might do that with or without a nuclear capability.

Given the Russian emphasis on its tactical nuclear weapons, we should not remove the remaining U.S. tactical nuclear weapons in Europe. Those weapons act largely as a symbol of U.S. commitment and therefore should continue to be available to sustain the security of Europe, including that of allies in Eastern Europe, unless and until the Russian tactical nuclear forces also stand down. As the focus of U.S. military attention turns to the western Pacific, and as the European members of NATO further reduce their own defense budgets, it becomes even more important to rationalize their defense industry, reduce duplication of costly high-tech items, and increase force efficiency through specialization and task sharing.

America must keep an adversarial power from gaining control of the world's major regions—Western and Central Europe and East Asia, which are half of the world's economy, and the Middle East and Persian Gulf, which are the source of much of the world's oil. Though Africa is potentially important as a fount of natural resources, its strategic weight is less important than that of other regions. The Western Hemisphere south of the U.S. border is growing more important economically and politically. But countries south of Mexico do not pose a serious security problem for the United States, despite the nuisance behavior of populist or dictatorial anti-U.S. leaders. Elsewhere, India is rising and important as a potential associate of the United States; India would not use the word "ally." South and East Asia are politically and economically closer together than they were twenty-five years ago, when the subcontinent was considered a kind of byway. It no longer is. East Asia and Europe are central to our interests. The United States and China will be the key players for the next fifty years.

NO PROTRACTED GROUND WARS
IN THE COMING DECADE

When I look at the defense horizon, I do not see our ground forces engaging in a major land battle with another major power. How can I say that when we have 150,000 troops fighting in Southwest Asia? They're not engaging with a major land power; they are doing counterinsurgency work and nation building.

There is no major adversary to involve us in a major ground war in the coming decade. No nation in Europe; all there are allies. I see no extended engagement in land wars in Asia using large forces. No adversarial force can compete with us in the Middle East. We're not going to invade Iran. If we were to use military force there, it would be by other means. Russia has a substantial ground force, but it's not going to invade Europe. If its ground force deploys to Caucasian Georgia, there's no point in our trying to intervene. Russia will not invade the Baltic states and risk reigniting the Cold War. Russian nuclear forces are potentially world destroying, but with the end of the Cold War, their potential does not translate into practical power. The Russians have substituted their nuclear force for their diminished conventional military capability.

The Chinese have major ground forces, but we surely will not engage in a land war in China. We need to find a way to avoid getting into the action-reaction scenario with China that exemplified our competition with the Soviet Union during the Cold War. There is reason to believe that avoidance of military conflict with China is possible. If the North Koreans are crazy enough to attack South Korea with artillery or try to invade with ground forces, it's up to the South Koreans to defend themselves. We have 28,600 troops there to provide needed airpower and as a tripwire to assure that we would engage. We would help South Korea with command and control, intelligence and communications, and air and maritime support.

We should not build a force capability for major land battles in Asia, even though parts of Asia will be the principal superpower arena. Any ground combat in which we engage should be carried out principally by indigenous forces in terms of the number of troops and in the fighting. I believe we can count on that from our South Korean allies; elsewhere I'm not so sure.

World Turbulence Not an Existential Threat

The area of most active and worrisome turbulence extends from Morocco through the subcontinent. Although several distasteful authoritarian allied leaders have been displaced there, their successors may be harder to deal with and still other leaders are at risk. We need to pay attention to ongoing events, but the turbulence does not present an existential threat to America. There is some reason to believe that new domestic (as well as neighboring country) sources of energy, mostly in the form of hydrocarbons and eventually renewables, will allow us to reduce our imports to half their present level. Though oil prices would still be set globally, we would reduce (but far from eliminate) direct U.S. exposure to Middle East events. The developing countries vary more widely in their economies and polities but will have growing influence, especially regionally. Brazil, India, Indonesia, and South Africa are in this category.

Overcome Geography with Technology

A proponent of the influence of geography on politics was Sir Halford John Mackinder (1861–1947). He viewed the heartland of Eurasia as the driving force of world history.[13] While mountains and rivers and coastlines continue to influence world politics, that thesis is harder to sustain today. Defense strategy, modern transportation, and universal telecommunication have shrunk borders. Today, major powers operate globally. That is why China is rapidly growing its naval capability. China recently acquired a thirty-year-old Soviet aircraft carrier and is building one of its own (the United States has eleven) and is developing weapons with which it could attack U.S. forces on land, sea, or in space.

China's ambitions—and new weapons systems—could alter the balance of power. Our military planning must deal with that future balance and ensure that it supports America's strategic position. China is still far from able to challenge the United States militarily in most of the world, including the Indian Ocean, chokepoints in the Persian Gulf and the Strait of Hormuz, and the Strait of Malacca. The United States will remain the strongest power militarily and the weightiest power economically for decades. The future stability of international security depends on how China and the United States deal with China's rise, how China will be integrated into the way the world is run, and how China will influence the rules.

PLAN FOR A LONG-RANGE BOMBER

How the United States and China see the other's military capabilities, and the blend of pugnacious, adversarial, and cooperative elements at play at any given time, will influence their relationship. For example, the United States needs to be ready to deal with China's ongoing development and deployment of a conventionally armed missile that could strike a target as far as 1,500 miles away. For twenty-five years I've argued that America needs a bomber able to penetrate sophisticated defenses and deliver great force over very long ranges. The advantage of this aircraft over a standoff bomber with cruise missiles is one of cost-effectiveness. The long-range penetrating bomber that I advocate could travel almost the entire range of a sortie and therefore could launch shorter-range missiles, which are less expensive than longer-range ones.

As our security interests turn to the Pacific, we must recognize that the use of our forward land bases rely on tactical aircraft with a radius (except for the force-stressing option of repeated air-refueling) there and back of 300 to 500 miles. We have few aircraft (less than a score of B-2s) that can penetrate sophisticated defense systems. Tactical aircraft payloads are smaller and less efficient for delivering ordnance on target. When facing an adversary that can attack our forward bases and threaten our naval forces out to long distances, a big, long-range bomber will be required. The point is that the United States will, in some cases, need to launch interventions from very far away.

Defense Secretary Leon Panetta plans to rebalance forces so that 60 percent of the navy's assets are assigned to the Pacific Ocean. That would involve six aircraft carriers and a majority of the navy's cruisers, destroyers, combat ships, and submarines. These would be fortified by more military exercises in the Pacific and more port visits. Secretary Panetta has stated that these preparations are in response to projections by the International Institute for Strategic Studies showing that for the first time total military spending by all countries in Asia would surpass all military expenditures in Europe.[14] Some of these U.S. plans could come under the knife if sequestration takes place—that is, the proposed additional $500 billion in defense cuts over the next decade beyond the $500 billion already ordered to occur beginning in 2013 and extending through the next ten years.

AFRICA AND SOUTH AMERICA

The biggest players in sub-Saharan Africa are South Africa and Nigeria. The United States has no strategic issues or alliance with either of them. Nigerian oil is important but not a geostrategic or military issue. The Caribbean, despite Cuba, is an "American lake." The United States has not been as dominant a force in South America as in the Caribbean since separating Panama from Colombia to enable our construction of the Panama Canal. The Monroe Doctrine still applies, and we would not want South America to be dominated by any outsider or, for that matter, by a hostile insider. We've had a touchy history with Brazil, but no strategic issues. Sales of strategic jets to Latin America were deeply discouraged during the Carter administration for two reasons: Latin America included unsavory regimes, many of them dictatorships, and we did not want our sales of military equipment to fuel an arms race in Latin America. So they bought their aircraft from Europe and Russia. As a result, we lost whatever influence we might have gained, but felt morally superior while Europe and Russia gained favor.

MIDDLE EAST ALLIANCES

I expect the U.S. commitment to Israel to stand. Sympathy and empathy for Israel in the United States extend far beyond the Jewish community. Some say Israel may disappear given the repeated instability and violence in the Middle East. I've heard that forecast since 1966. If an "expert" says something long enough and it comes true, he can claim to be right and forget that he also said "soon." I don't think Israel will disappear in the foreseeable future. There are reasons for concern that come more from internal threats than external ones. Half of those entering Israel's elementary schools are children of ultra-Orthodox Jews or of Arabs. Fifteen years from now half the adult population will be from one of those two groups; both have uncertain loyalties to the state. There is currently turbulence around trying to mandate army or national service for the ultra-Orthodox. It remains to be seen if that proposed policy will survive.

I believe that the United States should continue to press the Israelis and Palestinians for a two-state solution. The nature that solution might take is well known. The timing of reaching it is not. Israel feels safe from its immediate neighbors (though not from non-state actors in some of them). It fears Iran, which would probably not be assuaged by a two-state solution. Mahmoud Abbas, elected leader of the Palestinian National Authority, can't agree to a settlement until the struggle with Hamas, the more intransigent of the Palestinian factions, is resolved. The Arab Spring has greatly reduced U.S. influence in parts of the region. Arab leaders and publics point to injustice in the Israeli treatment of Palestinians, but also project some of their own deficiencies onto that external cause.

The United States needs to remain on good terms with Saudi Arabia because it is the world's swing producer of oil. The Arab Spring hasn't reached there—yet. Some experts have been predicting the demise of the Saudi royal family for as long as predictions of the demise of Israel, and with similar inaccuracy. But the next decade may be different. In fact, in some ways it surely will be.

RUSSIAN OIL AND GAS

What remains of the former Soviet Union's world power is the economic influence that Russia can wield through its oil and gas and the status conferred by its nuclear weapons. Europe's dependence on Russian oil and gas gives Russia some leverage, as illustrated a few years ago when it intimidated Ukraine into paying more by cutting off Ukraine's gas supply. Ukraine countered by shutting off pipelines running from Russia through Ukraine to other Western European countries. As other sources of gas become available, Russian economic influence will decline. For now, its energy sources will continue to be important for China as well as for Europe. Russia's demographic decline and failure to develop its economy beyond the natural resource sector suggest that its economic and political influence will eventually wither further. As of now, Russia could seek to dominate nearby neighbors in Europe. It will be important for the United States, NATO, and the European Union to continue to prevent that.

POLAND, HUNGARY, AND LATVIA

Poland is gradually industrializing as international companies locate there for its trained, hardworking people. Hungary is drifting to the right politically. Both countries are in the European Union though not on the euro, which is lucky for them. There is a danger that Russia may try to intimidate Eastern European countries to gain more influence over their internal policies and obtain economic concessions from them. In an extreme case, which I doubt would happen, Russia might attempt to move into Latvia or encourage a coup there since a third of Latvia's population are ethnic Russians.

A STANDARD FOR STARTING A LAND WAR

Combat during U.S. interventions in Kuwait in 1991 and Afghanistan in 2001 lasted only weeks and ended favorably. Subsequent actions in Iraq and Afghanistan have lasted for years with unfavorable results. The history of the past fifty years suggests that when we can't accomplish a mission on the Eurasian landmass with ground forces of two or three U.S. divisions, we shouldn't attempt it. Another lesson learned is that the major ground force in any large-scale land war should be indigenous. If you can't count on them plus two or three U.S. divisions to do the job, then the job probably can't be done. In the Iraq War, we deployed about 150,000 troops before the surge, and things haven't turned out well. We deployed 400,000 in the Gulf War, but that was not an exception to my rule of thumb because the main fighting involved three U.S. ground force divisions plus air and naval forces.

A good standard is not to begin an intervention without a reasonable belief that it would require no more than three U.S. divisions for no longer than three months. Our forces for major combat should be weighted toward air and naval power, including long-range bombers and arsenal ships that have a variety of missile and other ordnance capabilities. Such ships could also carry irregular forces into different places. Some of that fleet could be submersible if its vulnerability becomes a concern.

Realistic expectations dictate that we should be able to quickly deploy a few divisions for overseas fighting. A U.S. division involves 9,000 troops and up to 15,000 if you include a share of corps organizational support—intelligence, communications, artillery units, and combat support forces. For every division in protracted action, you need two or more at home training or regrouping.

In terms of force structure, we may not need all eleven of our aircraft carriers, but it doesn't make sense to try to reduce that number by more than one. The plan now is to trim air force squadrons and navy ships and to reduce ground forces substantially. The cuts will take place over several years and will make it more difficult to sustain the level of forces we have had in Southwest Asia over the past decade, which is probably not a bad thing.

CREATE A SEPARATE CAPABILITY FOR QUICK REACTION

We need a way to react to immediate needs, as former Secretary of Defense Robert Gates found when an urgent need for specially armored vehicles in Iraq wasn't being met. The army and marines had something coming along in five years, but their thinking was: why upset the program? The conflict between short-term and long-term planning could be solved through a separate organization, preferably Defense Department–wide, or with an organization that can react to sudden needs within each of the service branches. That kind of quick-reaction organization, with its own timelines and programming, will not be easy to sustain within the framework currently in place. In past wars, the urgency of short-term needs was overriding when people were getting killed in large numbers. In peacetime, or quasi-peacetime, quick reaction tends to be suppressed, though Gates ordered things done quickly in a few instances. As air force secretary I managed to push through a quick-reaction capability during the Vietnam War in the form of the AC-47, a DC-3 equipped with a heavy machine gun usable in areas that had little antiaircraft opposition. Its descendant, the AC-130 with one or more cannon of up to 105 millimeter caliber, is in active combat use.

The same problem showed up in Donald Rumsfeld's time, when it became clear that unmanned drones were going to be very important. The services, for institutional reasons, resisted buying more of them partly because the drones didn't fit into their plans. Automation in the military puts people out of work, just as it does in the civilian sector. Every drone that replaces a manned aircraft removes a pilot's job in the air force and navy. You still need some people to operate drones, but not as many and not with as much training as given to our pilots. We have to be able to override the inertia of bureaucracy with a quick reaction organization empowered to meet urgent needs, from procurement through deployment. The senior executive in charge should be able to override the senior military officer who pounds the table and says: "But we always do it this way."

COUNTERING TERRORISM

Countering terrorist organizations like al Qaeda depends on intelligence capabilities. That applies especially to gaining and using cooperation from countries in which terrorist organizations are based, and using local experts in the United States. Outside our country, we can best apply force against terrorists through precision delivery systems like drones acting from a distance. Though some would argue that drones lack the "eyes" to distinguish operatives from innocent civilians, that's not so. Drones, with their precision delivery systems, cause far fewer civilian casualties than tanks, guns, bombs, hidden landmines, and other weapons of war.

THE MILITARY OF THE FUTURE

The uniformed military are drawn unevenly from the U.S. population. Those who do the fighting, training, acquisition, community relations, and humanitarian work with people from other countries do not come, as many think, from the lowest socioeconomic class. Rather, most military people are from the middle class, many from rural environments and small towns. A few come from military families, some of which have produced generations of senior officers. Fewer still come from the highly educated economic elite that dominates the upper echelons of government and of society. That disjunction is troubling because the elite can find it too easy to get into wars their children aren't fighting.

Many opinion leaders and the population as a whole compartmentalize national security. They applaud the military without having much to do with it. More to the point, as wars are fought in Iraq and Afghanistan, much of the American population is not touched by what happens there. This unevenness has caused some to advocate a revival of the draft. They suggest that had the troops been conscripted, more Americans would have objected to the Iraq and Afghanistan wars. They say those wars would have wound down faster, with fewer tragedies for the families who lost loved ones or hardships for the injured. With a draft, they argue, we would have had a bigger fighting pool, which would have shortened the long and multiple tours of duty.

A draft is not the solution. Two million young men and two million young women reach age 18 each year. If all went into universal service for two years, we would be dealing with 8 million new recruits. The size of our armed forces is such that only a small fraction of people eligible to be drafted—fewer than 10 percent if only men are counted, 5 percent if women are included after the contentious debate that would involve—would serve on active duty in a maximum tour of two years. But two years are not enough to make today's members of the military fully effective. For the kinds of wars we fight now and are likely to face in the future, our troops need to be experienced. They need to be in the military for at least five or six years to learn how to best deal with the particular dangers of either antiterrorist combat or more conventional warfare. A draft lottery can't produce that kind of experience; lacking experience a force would be both ineffective and doomed to massive casualties.

We cannot maintain nor do we need the far larger force that a draft for a useful term of service would entail. In terms of cost, training, and equipment, the economics are daunting. Added to that, as we saw in Vietnam, are the challenges of morale and efficiency that accompany conscripted troops. A draft does not give us unlimited man- (and woman-) power. It only produces that illusion, a dangerous illusion because what seems to be an abundance of manpower could tempt us into escalation without justification. Let's remember the history of the draft. Conscription was first instituted during the Civil War; some bought their way out with substitutions. The tsarist Russia policy of "kidnapping" men into the army for twenty-five years is an obvious nonstarter. Neither of those approaches is a good model.

Jettison the Idea of a National Service Alternative

Some people advocate a "national service" with alternative kinds of work. Universal or "national" service is attractive at first glance. But it is nearly impossible to make it a fair part of a general conscription policy that requires service in the military. Who should do service tours as an orderly in a retirement home rather than fight? Should different lengths of obligation compensate for the disparity? Are women subject to the service requirement under alternative service? Alternative service might do lots of good, but it's not clear how it helps the military. Carrying bedpans is not the same as being a soldier, nor does it lead to a military career. France, which founded mass conscription at the end of the eighteenth century, gave it up in the twenty-first century for the reasons described.

The U.S. military is well served with volunteers who tend to stay longer and learn the skills that benefit security. Many choose the military as a career path that pays increasingly well. On the other end of service, we need to find better ways to transition military personnel back into civilian life if and when they choose to return; I discuss this later in this chapter under "Military Transition Education." What we mustn't do is funnel troops into wars we cannot win or put them in harm's way in countries that don't want to be rebuilt in our image, or that are too corrupt for us to try. An all-volunteer military works. It needs to be maintained at a size no less, and no more, than what we decide we can support.

Change Retirement Policies That Mitigate against Military Careers

A military personnel matter in need of attention is the policy of retirement. When I was secretary of defense, the military rules dictated that after you served twenty years you earned a pension. If you served nineteen years and eleven months, you got no pension. Your pension didn't increase by much if you served longer than twenty years. Most of our services operate this way, though you can now retire after fifteen years with a smaller pension and enjoy a bonus if you sign up for the last five years. Still, this policy works against an ideal pattern for a military career. Not everyone wishes to stay in the military for fifteen years, or should. For people you'd like to encourage to stay longer than a few years but not fifteen, the pension rules interfere. And incentives should be available for those who are valued and want to keep working beyond twenty years.

I tried to change the pension policy when it required twenty years of service; it proved impervious. Some senior officers, especially those near retirement, saw twenty years as a good goal line. They had mixed feelings about changing a policy that rewarded what they had invested so much time in achieving. Even the four-star officers who served with enthusiasm for thirty years said the prospect of a good pension after only twenty years was one attraction that made them enlist as young men. In some cases, the need to serve a full twenty years to get any pension was what had kept them in the military. At age fifty-five or sixty, these people thought that eighteen-year-old recruits would feel the same way.

However, at the other end of the spectrum, few new recruits said that they signed on thinking about retirement pay. I realized that my best audience was not new recruits or near-retirees; it was personnel in mid-career who had much to gain. I campaigned hard with personnel officers for more flexibility in the retirement policy. And I was successful, with all the services signed on until the last minute, when the navy fell off. The secretary of the navy couldn't persuade his senior officers to support the new policy.

Old habits are deeply ingrained in an institution. It takes a lot of spade-work to change them. Perhaps if I'd started earlier to try to make changes and worked to educate personnel people sooner about the advantages I saw, the initiative would have succeeded. (The RAND Corporation has undertaken a new study in 2012 that explores various ways to modern-ize military retirement policy and pay, and in particular for reservists).[15]

There have been some changes since I tried my hand at flexing benefits, but not in all services. Pay levels have risen substantially, to the point that overall personnel costs may be out of balance with other defense costs. For example, a lieutenant colonel with ten years of experience deployed in a combat zone makes about $106,000 a year, untaxed, and with twenty years of experience about $120,000. Both figures represent a 16 percent increase from 2001.[16] With inflation so low, there is no need to keep rais-ing military pay at the rates we've raised it in the past. Of course, anyone being shot at deserves bonus pay, and gets it. But not everybody is being shot at. Those not in combat zones earn taxed income, but enjoy subsi-dized health and pharmacy benefits and potential pension benefit contri-butions. At least some of the benefits (for example, the health insurance contribution levels for families) will probably have to be reconsidered.

Talking about Don't Ask, Don't Tell

An initiative lately pushed on the military is the new policy that replaces Don't Ask, Don't Tell with full acceptance of homosexuality, explicit or suspected, which had previously led to discharge. The final change came last year with the full support of Mike Mullin, chairman of the Joint Chiefs of Staff, and with various degrees of acceptance by the other chiefs.

Before the policy changed, the military was surveyed as to how it felt about the proposed new policy of acceptance. Resistance surfaced mostly in the marines, in particular among older, senior officers. The most reluctant of the Joint Chiefs was the marine commandant, who expressed concern about its possible effect on enlistment rates. So far there has been no sign of any effect, and the military are as usual carrying out their orders. The senior officers' objection was that implementing new policies during a war was too disruptive, but lately we're almost always engaged in a war of some sort. We've had some military operation going for almost all of the past twenty years. My guess as to why some senior officers really objected may be uncharitable. I suspect they find a new policy too much trouble. They would prefer to postpone it until they retire and let someone else implement it.

When I was secretary of defense, Representative Barney Frank, who is openly gay, wrote me a letter asking my view of homosexuality in the military. I said that the close quarters of military life made homosexuality a problem of discipline and good order. Of course, all senior military people knew there were homosexuals in the ranks. Absent overt activity, it was tacitly accepted as long as people performed their duties well. Given societal attitudes in 1979, an overt acceptance probably would not have worked.

Looking back, I'm sorry I wrote that letter to Barney Frank. Over time I have come to believe, along with much of the country, that homosexuality in the military does not create a problem. Younger people have fewer problems with the new policy than senior military who, being older, might reflect the attitudes of years past. Attitudes have changed drastically over the past dozen years. To be fair to the military, it has often done what was right despite prevailing attitudes. For example, despite American prejudice against African Americans in the late 1940s, Harry Truman ordered the military to integrate. He didn't expect that prejudiced people would change their minds. He did expect the military to follow orders.

There were probably some whose prejudice was so strong that they resisted orders and military discipline, but most troops, even if prejudiced, would not. What Truman did was unpopular. The military pioneered integration because it could. Beginning then, and long after, the military was the only U.S. institution in which black people commonly gave orders to white people. That is still more the case in the military than in the rest of society, though the disparity is not as great as it once was. The military is also a place where upward mobility is more possible than elsewhere in society. You're more likely to find people from families in modest circumstances rising to the top. True, some of the officers have gone to the military academies; many have graduate degrees, but many went to state universities and not Ivy League schools. The military is not threaded with elitism in that sense.

Chaplains Should Wear Military Uniforms

We talk about the separation of church and state, but what the Constitution says is there should be no establishment of a single religion in public life, which is not the same thing. Certainly the framers of the American republic did not exclude religion from their daily lives. The separation that Jefferson had in mind was intended to protect religion as much as to protect the state from religion. Chaplains wear military uniforms so they can better identify with the people they serve in the military.

Military Transition Education

As we transition troops from the battlefield to the civilian sector, we rely on colleges to train them for jobs. I propose that instead of relying solely on the G.I. Bill and various for-profit and public colleges to do that work, the military undertake more of this task itself, or work directly with the Veterans Administration in this endeavor. Training for the job market could be a standard part of military discharge and an advantage afforded to any person who served. This would eliminate unevenness in current educational opportunities depending on where a person lived and what college they got into and would immediately impart skills useful in the workplace. Our troops are well schooled in discipline, a prerequisite for the job market. They have basic educational skills, or they would not have been accepted into an all-volunteer military. It stands to reason that they would be able students for military-based education programs.

The reverse of this idea did not work in an experiment begun in 1968 when Bob McNamara, then defense secretary, started a program called Project 100,000.[17] It aimed to take underprivileged youth who had failed the Armed Forces Qualification Test, an admission test, by scoring under

IQ 80, and upgrade their basic education so they could pass and become useful in the military. The Vietnam War saw the program begin; it was curtailed in 1971 still in an experimental phase and under controversy. What did take place didn't work. The reason seemed to be that if by the age of eighteen a youth lacked the educational skills to meet basic military educational requirements, it was too late and too hard to teach reading and writing as a catch-up course.

Women in the Military

Women are underrepresented in the military in key and joint roles. When I was air force secretary and the proud father of two young daughters, I was keenly aware of the neglected talent of women, and I expanded the role of women in the air force, who were then under a separate branch of the air force. The branch director, Colonel Jeanne Holm, later became the first female two-star officer—a major general—in any of the services. When I left my air force position to become president of Caltech, that institution admitted its first women undergraduates after a delicate process of negotiation with its trustees.

I wanted to continue opportunities for women as a matter of policy and good sense when I was defense secretary. I chose Deanne Siemer to be general counsel of the Department of Defense. She was the first woman to hold that position. The only woman of similar rank had been Anna Rosenberg, who served as assistant secretary of defense to George Marshall in 1950. I also selected Antonia Chayes as assistant secretary and later under secretary of the air force. And I appointed women to positions of deputy assistant secretaries of defense and of the military departments. Some of these women deservedly achieved even more senior positions as time went on. It wasn't until 1980 that the service academies graduated and commissioned their first women graduates. I vividly recall handing diplomas to the top ten West Point cadets at their graduation and noting that several of them were women. In that post-Vietnam era, the proportion of women in the armed forces began to grow toward and past 15 percent. Since then, women have made enormous strides toward full participation; that was the start.

8

Land of the Free

STIMULATING THE
NATIONAL ECONOMY FOR
INTERNATIONAL SECURITY

I write this book on the brink of the 2012 presidential election. A highly polarized House of Representatives has been debating whether, on the assumption that no increase in taxes can be allowed, to cut another $50 billion next year from military spending and as much from various domestic programs that provide Medicaid, food stamps, and other benefits for poor Americans. If so, the cut next year would be the first installment of a ten-year sequestration. Whether that outcome proceeds is unclear, but the issues remain: what, if any, tax revenues will be increased; what, if any, entitlements will be cut; what discretionary (nonentitlement) expenditures, including defense, will be cut; and when and how will all or any of this be phased in? (Keep in mind that defense spending apart from war costs accounts for about 4 percent of GDP while health care approaches 20 percent.) Meanwhile we citizens are barraged with advice urging us to advance technology innovation, enable a smoother flow from battlefields to stateside jobs, and improve science and math education. How can we act on all that when some of our political leaders run on platforms of "no compromise" and legislators vehemently disagree on principles and details or how to implement them?

Decrying putative U.S. decline is not enough. Exhortations are not enough either. And practically all road maps for action, including my own, lack credible political strategies to accomplish all those goals. Meanwhile, domestic and international challenges mount, interact, and reinforce one another. Obviously we cannot deal with international challenges if our

214

polity is dysfunctional, uneducated, or in economic depression. As unemployment persists, corporate CEOs blame uncertain taxes and regulations as the reasons why they aren't investing in more workers. Those are not the main reasons. Companies need to know there will be a demand for their goods or why invest or hire to produce more or new products? Will people spend their money, and if so, on what?

That is why stimulating demand is the right thing to do. Government can stimulate demand by extending unemployment benefits and reducing withholding taxes so people have more money to spend. If done in the near term, we'd increase the market demand so that firms that do the investing and hiring can have a reasonable expectation of selling their goods and services. Without market demand or its expectation, more hiring won't happen. To argue that a demand isn't there because people are worried about their incomes amounts to circular reasoning. If nobody else provides market demand, the government has to do it.

Stimulus is not a substitute for drastically revising the tax code and the entitlement structure. Government also has to reduce future deficits to an acceptable level. A reasonable measure is a deficit, excluding interest on the debt, that is a percentage of the GDP roughly equivalent to the rate of real GDP growth. The challenge, not an easy one, is to time the stimulus and the deficit reduction in the right way. The sensible approach is to slowly phase in the fiscal squeeze so that market recovery, aided by the stimulus, would add jobs and accelerate GDP growth to more than 3 percent a year. That squeeze includes slowly phasing in entitlement reductions and reducing the rate of government spending as the recovery gains strength.

Getting the timing right will be difficult and requires wise action by the executive branch and Congress, as well as by the Federal Reserve. By writing that sentence, I've already exposed the flaw in my suggestion. But it is nevertheless the best, or least bad, approach because if we avoid deepening the pain now (which stringency would cause by slowing economic growth), we'll be better able to weather that stringency later. If we do the opposite—crack down hard now as Britain and much of the euro bloc are doing—there's a real danger of creating national disaster.

Let's look at what we ask for when we call for reducing entitlements or raising taxes or eliminating loopholes. Most Americans benefit from government social programs like Medicare and Social Security or "tax expenditures"—that is, tax deductions or special treatment of some income, the most notable being mortgage interest and tax-free employer-paid health care. But few of us think (or want to think) of ourselves as among those who rely on the government. We prefer to think of "other people" as the recipients of entitlement programs and "tax loopholes," and we consider *them* the proper targets of deficit reduction.

We mistakenly believe that our taxes disproportionately support the undeserving or "slothful" poor when it's the middle class that is the principal beneficiary. As of 2011, fully 18 percent of Americans relied on Medicare or Social Security, and millions more soon will as baby boomers increasingly cross the threshold of the current normal retirement age of sixty-five for Medicare and Social Security. Both Medicare and Social Security benefits amount to about $12,000 per person using the programs, and make up an increasing share of federal and state government spending, outgrowing tax revenues.[1] According to the Social Security Board of Trustees, the Social Security trust fund will cover the cost of Social Security benefits until 2037, though more stresses on the system may put the year at 2036. After that Social Security taxes are expected to fund only about about 78 percent of the benefits promised by current law.[2]

Medicare is much worse off. On average, lifetime Medicare costs, which most people think their individual Medicare taxes will pay for, will be about two and a half times more than what beneficiaries will have paid. That means the rise in Medicare costs will have to be curbed, or taxes will have to be raised to a crushing degree to pay for the program.

After reviewing OMB data, Nobel Prize–winning economist and *New York Times* columnist Paul Krugman concluded that "older people get most of the benefits, primarily through Social Security and Medicare, but aid for the rest of the population, though of a smaller size, has increased at about the same rate through programs for the disabled, the unemployed, veterans, and children."[3] Yet any attempt to change benefits will draw opposition from the people affected by them. People sixty-five and older, with the support of those aged fifty-five who are contemplating their retirement prospects, constitute a powerful interest group. So a solution affecting Medicare solvency is easier said than done. An even more difficult task lies in dealing with health care and its delivery overall. Some issues such as juvenile diabetes and obesity require changes in people's behavior. European publics fare better than Americans. Their governments spend less on health care and derive superior results, leaving more money to spend on other parts of their social safety net.[4] The United States has hit on a health care system uniquely inefficient and perverse compared with those of France, Switzerland, and Germany, which are not purely government systems. The United States simply doesn't do health care rationally. On the other hand, U.S. national defense does have a more rational framework.

The good news is that our country is not divided on everything. In the past it took a major depression or a war to make Americans pull together. I hope that Congress and the president will not wait until a crisis of that magnitude erupts before agreeing on a phased but sustainable fiscal path. As demonstrated in Europe, when the noose of austerity is too tight, the pain proves too intense for the public to bear. Voters in most European countries are showing that they are not willing to go along with fiscal strangulation. In France, voters sent Nicolas Sarkozy packing, opting instead for the (proposed) more gradual fiscal cuts endorsed by newly elected French President François Hollande. The Dutch government fell over a similar issue. Greece's severe budget cuts portend an even harsher fate for its citizens.

It's become clear that the struggling economies of Europe cannot budget-cut their way back to growth. Rigid austerity has made their debts harder, not easier to pay off. For example, the ratio of debt to annual GDP in Portugal was 107 percent when the country received a bailout last year. Since cutting pensions, slashing public spending, and raising taxes, Portugal has seen the ratio rise to 118 percent, and it will continue to rise as Portugal's economy shrinks. As most European economists crunch the numbers, they conclude that severe austerity is a mistaken way to relieve debt. Instead, Europe's central bank is beginning to inject liquidity by loaning money into the continent's banking system and adding money to underfinanced bailout programs. The banks are using much of that money to buy government bonds, which they consider safe and which pay a higher interest rate than the European Central Bank charges the banks. Should the bonds default or fall in value as interest rates spike, the banking systems could collapse. Here at home, I would have the federal government borrow money (at near zero interest rates) to begin rebuilding the national infrastructure. This would provide added economic stimulus over the next few years during which the economy will almost surely operate below its potential and unemployment will remain high.[5]

DEFENSE INNOVATION
CAN STIMULATE THE ECONOMY

Technological innovation, often motivated by defense needs, substantially benefits not only our nation's security but also its domestic economy. Innovations in military technology have spun into profitable civilian industries that boost our economy. Civilian products from military spin-offs include sensors, telecommunication equipment, microelectronics, semiconductors, GPS, and even Velcro. A prime example of the power of military innovation is the civilian jet aircraft industry, essentially spun off from defense. The first American jet airliner, the 707, was a modification of the C-135 air force transport plane designed in the 1950s. And the loser in a competition won by the C-5 transport (developed when I was secretary of the air force) became the 747 passenger plane. A more recent military innovation, the fly-by-wire control, has found its way into new passenger airliners. Military "spin-off" products, as they are called, contribute directly to our standard of living, our global competitiveness, jobs, and family incomes.

Products that begin in the civilian sector and become usable by the military are called "spin-ons." Computers are but one example. Some spin-ons spawn further military contributions to the civil sector. For example, the DEW line control center developed in the 1950s to intercept possible Soviet bomber attacks on the United States used electronics originating in the civilian sector. The large-scale purchases that it required built up the scale of the civilian computer industry. Then that industry used technology seeded by the thermonuclear weapons program.

Some military innovations are developed with the idea that their cost can be justified by their eventual commercial application. But unless market-driven, a commercial project simply won't spin off from a military program successfully. Take the case of the V-22, an aircraft that can take off and land vertically. Because its propellers can be rotated from the vertical plane, as on a fixed-wing aircraft, to a horizontal plane, as on a helicopter, the V-22 takes off and lands much like a helicopter, yet can fly at about 360 miles an hour over a long range, about 500 miles. It works, but it's very complicated.

The commercial forecast for the V-22 was that big-city use would partly justify its cost. The aircraft needed but a 50-by-50-foot "runway."

The Department of Defense spent close to $60 billion on developing and procuring the plane, including fixing its safety problems. The air force eventually dropped out of the program. Members of Congress from Texas (representing Bell Helicopter) and from Pennsylvania (representing Boeing Vertol) pushed hard to keep the tilt-rotor technology despite then Secretary of Defense Dick Cheney's repeated attempts to swing the ax. In 2007 the V-22 represented 70 percent of the marines' procurement budget with no civilian spin-offs yet in sight.[6]

The aircraft never lived up to its commercial promise because high operating costs and its daunting downdraft eclipsed its advantages. Though a strong selling point had been that the plane needed little stand-alone runway, any airport requires acres of maintenance equipment. Metropolitan airports don't have that extra acreage, which is one reason why helicopter service has shrunk in major cities, including midtown New York.

SOMETIMES THE GOVERNMENT GETS IT RIGHT

A major weapons system can evolve quickly and efficiently when we omit the many layers that erode responsibility and impede progress—in effect when we shoot around bureaucratic encumbrance. As mentioned in chapter 3, it seemed the Polaris program, the submarine-launched ballistic missile program established in the 1950s, was not going to work because warheads were so heavy you needed a missile bigger than one you could fit into a submarine. The original plan was to have it carried outside the submarine. At Livermore Lab we came up with a warhead small enough for a solid-propellant missile to be included inside the submarine hull. We could do that because the navy established a special Polaris program, headed by a three-star admiral. I wound up on the steering committee. Given complete autonomy, we developed the system in about three years by avoiding external nitpicking and sniping, constant reviews, and program revisions. The project succeeded in half the normal time. Many subsequent highly classified (top-secret) programs handled this way have also achieved their objectives in better than usual delivery times, cost, and performance. You can only do this with a limited number of programs because too many would overload the system. Eisenhower himself designated that Polaris be handled this way. The moral of the story is that too many levels of review delay, confuse, and drive costs up.

WHY MILITARY PRODUCTS ARE SO EXPENSIVE

Critics correctly argue that the military pays far too much for civilian products. One reason is that all products used by the military must adhere to the specific rules of the Armed Forces Specification Procurement Regulations (ASPR) System. It requires rigorous testing under extreme conditions that go far beyond what is normally needed. Therefore many civilian products of potential military use are not sturdy enough to be allowed "as is." The military must undertake parallel development and procurement at ten times the cost.

Military devices that emerge under those extreme requirements often result in low levels of production at higher costs per item. And there are other problems. Whether products are adapted from civilian use or developed exclusively for the military, costs usually run higher than original estimates. Sometimes the cost overruns result from changes in requirements or design in the development process. The process and production can take longer than originally scheduled, or come up short on promised attributes, or deliver equipment that is difficult to maintain or sustain. Past secretaries of defense, especially Bill Perry who had pushed the "off-the-shelf" idea while he was undersecretary, have tried to solve these problems with limited success. We should keep trying.

There's another mismatch to contend with, too. While product specifications can be overly stringent, the qualifications required of military procurement officers may not be stringent enough. It takes someone technically proficient and managerially capable to see products through the current military procurement system. Few personnel in that system get a long enough run at their jobs to become proficient. Frequently a procurement officer will be moved between operational or logistic or development jobs every few years. Although many procurement officers have considerable technical ability, purely technical careers often have limited promotion opportunities. The result is short assignments that prove inadequate for developing and procuring major programs that last many years.

ESTABLISH A SEPARATE UNIFORMED PROCUREMENT SERVICE

How do you give a procurement officer enough technical experience to be able to choose from competing proposals the solution that best fulfills performance, maintenance, and operating objectives at most benefit for the cost? How do you make sure that a technical expert isn't drawn to technically clever but not operationally useful ideas? And how do you trust a person who can crunch numbers in a cost-benefit analysis, but hasn't seen combat, to visualize how a weapons system would work in the field—in desert or jungle or still other terrain?

Only a fair amount of time at the job enables a development and procurement specialist to identify and mitigate risks and trouble-shoot unforeseen problems that pop up during the development process. That individual must also have the management skills to align disparate parts of a new system developed by various contractors and subcontractors to ensure the project is delivered on time and within budget. Instilling technical, analytical, operational, and managerial know-how in a procurement officer's repertoire is nearly impossible when procurement duties do not produce a career path. Add in complex procurement rules and the muddy process of how programming and budgeting trickles through the executive branch and Congress and we have a system badly bent and nearly broken.

The French seem to have found an antidote to these deficiencies in a military acquisition service. The French General Directorate of Armaments is a corps of officers and civilians dedicated only to developing and procuring military equipment. The corps reports to the French minister of defense. (The Soviet military procurement system had some similar characteristics.) The procurement officers within the corps become experienced enough to take charge of specific long-range programs. They can be promoted within the procurement service and have a full career in it. That distinct career path does not fully exist in the United States, and to the degree that it does, it is available only within one's single military service. That insularity inhibits equipment from being compatible and interoperable across services, thereby encouraging duplication and extra cost.

It's time to form a separate uniformed service to supervise procurement and the development of weapons systems and other materiel. A separate military procurement service is not without its risks, however, even if structured so that its officers maintain a formal connection with their own branch of service (though promotion and assignment would fall under the procurement service). For example, if procurement officers never saw combat or held other operational responsibilities, they could fail to recognize how new systems would work when put to physical and tactical use. The present procurement process presents opposite risks: officers whose careers have been in combat roles are prone to being sold infeasible solutions because they like a certain weapon design no matter its cost, maintainability, or production timeline.

The new procurement service would need to bridge the chasm between technological experience and operational knowledge. In one respect, the current system attempts this by moving procurement officers from operations to acquisition and back again. But the present system usually calls for performance requirements at a given cost before one knows the optimum balance among various performance metrics, training needs, and maintenance features. That leaves little room for creative technical or operational thinking.

I believe that the right approach is to arrive at a cost and schedule based on a careful plan that balances all the necessary characteristics during the design process. One component in this balance should ensure that military products are developed to be compatible across services if their use is meant to be similar. All this could best be done under a separate development and procurement organization. I recommend that it begin, though the process to establish it will not be easy. Current law puts development and procurement in the military departments' Title 10 responsibilities. Change would require congressional action.

CHALLENGES TO INNOVATION

In past decades, some of the largest and most innovative private corporations funded central research labs. Like the rest of the economy, the Defense Department tapped into these "idea factories" for both basic and advanced research.[7] The corporate labs included Bell Labs owned by AT&T and its affiliated equipment maker, Western Electric, and labs dedicated to research and development in General Electric, IBM, Westinghouse, RCA, and a few others. Of those that still exist, few are more than remnants and much narrower in scope.

Deregulation and competition ended AT&T's monopoly and eroded the market dominance of IBM and GE. Some technological advances entailed much larger capital costs, as in the case of computer chip fabrication facilities. Increasingly complex projects incorporated the work of scientists across disciplines; that also made research more expensive. Firms answerable to their shareholders could no longer afford to invest in research that *might* produce profit far in the future. So the labs shut down or downsized.[8] Research people were farmed out to operating divisions to do short-term projects.

Universities picked up some of the research burden. Some faculty members started up businesses, especially in biomedicine, chemistry, and engineering sciences. That was a good step toward keeping innovation alive. It is not enough. New industries and major new products require large-scale prototypes, which can't be funded by small businesses and universities.

NARROWING OF THE CONTRACTOR AND SUBCONTRACTOR BASE

Yet another challenge for government-led technological programs has been the narrowing of the general contractor and subcontractor base that does defense work. These companies were staffed with specialized technical experts whose high security clearances allowed them to work on new, secret military capabilities. The boom-and-bust fluctuations in funding discouraged and consolidated subcontractors. Civilian technology markets grew and were more attractive customers to contractors. What the Defense Department had in mind for the major contractors was mergers; what they encountered were buyouts. Senior people in the consolidating companies vested their options and left with big payouts. The debt-to-equity ratios of the consolidated companies rose, which made them less financially secure. They had to worry more about recovering higher overhead and making more profit. As the number of major new weapons systems programs fell, the overhead had to be spread over a smaller base.

Some firms that remain capable of taking on sizable defense contracts are diversified enterprises that can afford to separate their defense business from their civilian business, if they have it. But the profit margin is far lower for defense business. And government procurement is carefully watched by congressional staffers with parochial loyalties. To ensure congressional support, contractors spread their subcontractors out geographically. Smaller companies found defense procurement processes too bureaucratic and unreliable to handle and exited the defense business. The base for defense contracting continues to erode.

For its part, the government needs to control the projects it contracts out and decisions affecting them, but also needs to allow good contractors some creative leeway in projects. So far, that balance has been poorly struck. For example, some space programs kept "in the black" (in extreme secrecy) and given creative freedom turned out to be expensive disappointments. On the other hand, the Lockheed "skunk works" operated in secrecy with fewer levels of review and produced good products: the U-2, the SR-71, and the F-117 aircraft.

I've had a long history with contractors from multiple perspectives. In running Livermore Laboratory as a nonprofit contractor, and later the Jet Propulsion Laboratory, my concern was to outperform other government labs and keep our contractual promises. The future of the lab depended on it, though not immediately. As director of Defense Research and Engineering (DDRE), however, my focus shifted to seeing that contractors' promises, performance specs, and schedules met strategic objectives and conformed to the overall balance of all projects under way.

As air force, and later defense, secretary, I learned about various schemes for inducing contractors to be efficient, meet schedules, and limit overruns. I also learned that none of the schemes work. You're setting up a game, and the more detail you put in, the more you encourage a contractor concerned about its own financial interest to game the system. We've tried best and final price contracts, but the contractor who gives you the best price doesn't always provide the optimum product. Attempts to encourage competition by splitting a production run even after one competitor's version has been chosen (a suggestion advanced by members of Congress who like to spread the wealth among their constituents) doesn't usually work either. When military procurement officers, even those with a keen understanding of technical trade-offs and manufacturing capabilities, are pushed into setting difficult and expensive goals for performance, the contractor obliges with promises that can't be met.

We should try a different approach and tell contractors: here's the schedule and the money, and that's all there is, period. You tell us how you would balance and meet various performance characteristics, committing contractually and financially to what you propose. The winning contractor would be the one whose innovative design was judged likely to produce the best cost-benefit balance. The difficulty in that approach, one followed in the 1950s, is that it allows the government decisionmaker to judge the design subjectively. In this era of suspected political influence, Congress and the public demand a formulaic, numerical basis for decisionmaking allowing little to no subjective assessment. Even with purely numerical scores that decide the winner of a contract competition, the losers still challenge the winner with lawsuits that can cost millions of dollars to defend and hold up the government's project in court for months if not years. The Government Accountability Office, or worse, a federal court, ends up making a military-technical decision based on its judgment of the fairness of the competition.

Officials in the Department of Defense have put a range of incentives into their contracts: for example, more money if you finish before deadline or even on it, and penalties if you don't. The government still gets stuck with "change orders," which allow contractors to request more money to solve problems as they develop or legitimately to pay for government-demanded changes as unforeseen needs arise. One problem is that the contractor's proposal team isn't always its execution team.

We've run pre-competition competitions and fund contractors to gear up so they can offer a knowledgeable and more specific proposal. Keeping that kind of competition rigorously fair is tricky when contractors ask intelligent questions about what you mean in certain specifications. You are obliged to show all contractors any answers to a specific contractor's questions or face lawsuits by losers claiming "unfair advantage." The questions that competitors raise during the question-and-answer period could target risks early except that contractors use opaque phrasing to prevent competitors from sniffing out the approach they may be taking. If the questions are vague, the answers can't be of service to anyone. All in all, even that process blocks dialogue meant to encourage creativity.

In principle, we could do more technological innovation in government-operated organizations (arsenals, naval shipyards) as we did for some things through World War II. Even then there were no arsenals for aircraft. Shipyards are still quasi-governmental entities. Over subsequent decades, the kind of talent we've needed for technological innovation has been more difficult to find within government. One obvious reason is that the government can't offer the salaries that corporations pay. People at the middle and upper levels of private industry make much more than those at the top of government. The higher up you go, the greater the salary disparity between industry and government. So, and this is appropriate, other satisfactions motivate government service.

SMACKED BY THE REVOLVING DOOR SYNDROME

The issue of the revolving door further discourages people with talent and ambition from entering government because after they've worked in government at a high level, or on a specific program, for example, making key decisions about a combat aircraft program, they can't use that experience on the same program for a government contractor upon leaving government, ever. And there is a general proscription against dealing with a former government agency on any matter for two years. That puts in limbo a former government employee who wants to climb a corporate ladder.

For that reason, many people with talent and ambition don't come into government. Instead the government substitutes additional layers for competence. If people working on a project aren't as good as you wish, then you'd better have other people watching them. That governmental layering of responsibility and accountability encourages contractors to do unnecessary things and creates unnecessary activities that cost time and money. There is no solution for this short of a revolutionary change.

Fortunately, the civilian sector is less subject to these problems. But on the government side what suffers most from these challenges is technological innovation, and not only in defense. We rely on innovation to compete in a global marketplace. We depend on it to help boost our slowed economy and get us out of debt. Our ability to be innovative affects the attitudes of other countries toward the United States. For example, as Japan and Korea think about their relations with the United States as compared with their relations with China, our economic and technological strength matters as much to them as our commitment to their security.

How will we cope? With the private sector lacking the kind of central research labs we used to depend on, with the talent for technological innovation not sparkling through government halls, and with universities making up only a portion of the deficiency, it is time for a new federal role in facilitating technological development. However, that innovative thrust needs to be insulated from politics, parochialism, and impatient stockholders in the private sector. Those defects are now present in most government-funded civilian technology programs. This may be the right time to try something new.

BLUEPRINT FOR AN INNOVATION CORPORATION

I credit the original suggestion for something new to John Deutch, who offered it when I chaired a panel in 1992 called The Government Role in Civilian Technology: Building a New Alliance. The panel was sponsored by the Committee on Science, Engineering, and Public Policy of the National Academy of Sciences.[9] We recommended a new strategy to facilitate government support of technology, noting that a higher rate of technological performance could come from capitalizing on private sector strength with federal support.

Building on that idea, I now propose that an innovation corporation be established and funded through federal appropriations for the purpose of producing and demonstrating prototypes of technological processes, products, or installations at full scale. These demonstrations would embody technological advances after doing the corresponding research, development, and design. The private sector would share in the work of the innovation corporation in a public-private cooperative funding arrangement, then pick up and deploy the demonstrated technology commercially. This arrangement would provide the new technology with a strong component of market-driven demand. The corporation would enable the government to encourage projects and at the same time insulate them from political polarization, parochial interests, or excessive layers of review, to which most government-funded civilian technology programs are currently subjected. (The V-22 tilt-rotor aircraft project illustrates why the innovation corporation would need to operate independently from political influences and why the market will do a more objective job of determining the viability of selected programs.)

The public-private venture I recommend would focus only on technologies that the private sector could not develop on its own or would not because the payoff is too unsure, too far off, or not sufficiently appropriable by the first innovator. The goal of the innovation corporation would be to stimulate private sector development and investment where market forces are inadequate. We would aim for technology that could strengthen U.S. advantages in both the domestic and global markets.

Typical federal financial support for research and development and technology is not coordinated, nor does it allow selection of investments in areas of high risk and high potential payback that would support U.S. advantages. The innovation corporation would support demonstrations of various technologies rather than subsidize particular industries. It would have a clear framework and rationale for organizing federal investments and financial support. Guidelines as suggested in the National Academies study would include the following:

—*Costs Would Be Shared.* Private sector firms or institutions would bear about 50 percent of the total program costs of any pre-commercial R&D or technology development project. That would stretch resources, provide incentive, and ensure that projects would be able to become commercially relevant.

—*Industry Would Participate in Project Initiation and Design.* The long-term objective is to enhance U.S. productivity. Private sector proposals and federal needs have to be explored and aligned to spark success. Industry is in closer contact with private markets, though the government as a customer for some technologies would stimulate their adoption.

—*Projects Would Be Insulated from Political Concerns.* Projects would be selected on their merits as decided by experts in scientific, technological, and economic disciplines, and insulated as far as possible from special interests and pressures from the political spectrum.

—*Project Investments Would Be Diversified.* The innovation corporation would fund projects that do not compete with activities elsewhere in the federal government. The goal is not duplication but diversification.

—*Foreign Countries Could Participate.* If it is decided that some components of the project could be developed outside the United States to reduce time and costs, decisions allowing foreign participation should reflect clear recognition of the benefits and risks of collaboration between the U.S. and foreign firms.

—*Program Evaluation Should Be Rigorous.* Objective and knowledgeable experts should conduct an independent review for the president of the United States at appropriate intervals.

The innovation corporation is not about "saving" any particular industry. It is not about which industries or companies have the most influence. It is about a government-financed entity making decisions for funding without government direction or political influence. That is why a large appropriation up front is in order. It could be tens of billions of dollars in addition to private sector contributions and leveraged modestly by borrowing. Large amounts are appropriate because individual technology demonstrations could cost hundreds of millions of dollars. You don't want small annual appropriations because then a member of Congress could say, "I didn't like what you did because it gave no direct help to my constituents so you get no money from me from now on." We also would not want the corporation to float stock and go public because then all the influences of the financial markets would predominate.

Projects that the corporation might fund could include clean energy on a large scale, for example, producing butynol from trash crops that would supply a far cheaper alcohol more akin to fuel than is currently produced by making ethanol from corn, which is expensive and requires better land on which to grow.

I emphasize that the corporation would *not* be a for-profit business; rather, its purpose would be to demonstrate applications of technology to benefit the U.S. economy. One reason not to make the corporation into a business lies in the failing record of profit-making government-sponsored enterprises. The Comsat Corporation, a spin-off from the space program to produce communication satellites, wound up being acquired by a defense contractor. Fannie Mae and Freddie Mac morphed into essentially private corporations that could turn to the government if they got into trouble. Once in a conversation with Tim Geithner when he was head of the Federal Reserve Bank of New York and before he became secretary of the treasury, I remarked, "Look, if Fannie and Freddie [GSEs, or government-sponsored enterprises] get into trouble, the government will have to bail them out."

He said, "No, we're definitely not going to do that." And I said, "You have to say you won't so as to keep from increasing moral hazard, but you will do it." Geithner expressed the government's position. It had to be the government's position. But nobody believed it, including the financial markets, which is why the GSEs were able to get low interest rates. Yet Freddie Mac and Fannie Mae acted like private institutions. Because they were private financial corporations, their executives wanted to be paid like executives in the private financial sector. They floated stock and got options, wanted to get bigger, and gave more loans. They went along with what banks suggested, which was to securitize the loans, sell them off, and forget about them. Being able to afford a housing loan was no longer the criterion for getting one. At the urging of successive administrations and Congresses, the executives reduced the requirements for credit worthiness and down payments to the extent that default was inevitable when housing prices stopped soaring and fell.

One lesson in this for the innovation corporation is that just as there was a near-universal belief that everybody ought to own a house, so will special interests try to shape public opinion by suggesting that everybody ought to have a solar-heated house or an electric car. It is essential to prevent that kind of influence from becoming decisive for the innovation corporation (and thereby creating another Solyndra, a failed solar energy firm subsidized by the federal government).[10] At the same time, the innovation corporation must be accountable to the political system that funds it, so devising its structure is critical. Its board of directors needs to include experts in finance, technology, economics, and management.

A corporation of this nature is not without precedent. During the 1930s and 1940s, the Reconstruction Finance Corporation did something similar, although it focused on industrial facilities in the existing economy rather than on innovation, except in the case of synthetic rubber. It spent almost $10 billion over two decades, an equivalent of $200 billion now.[11]

Another example of government funding for research and development began in 1987. The U.S. government, judging Japanese semiconductor manufacturers to have surpassed U.S. competitors, funded a consortium of semiconductor manufacturers named Sematech to advance U.S semiconductor technology. The Defense Advanced Projects Agency provided $500 million. Seven years later, the U.S. industry had caught up and Sematech completed a transition to an industry-sponsored, advanced technology organization.[12] In retrospect, my own judgment is that it was not a great success. The industry was already highly competitive. That inhibited the sharing of technologies that might have become decisively advantageous. Payoffs on the very large investments needed for fabrication facilities were risky, but relatively fast (years, not decades), and the successive generations of chip technology were short-lived, lasting only a few years. That said, the proposed innovation corporation is totally different from these enterprises. It would focus on technologies with much longer development times and operating life spans, such as energy plants and transportation systems. It would build much larger demonstration projects. And it would work in areas where the private sector should be more willing to take all of the post-demonstration risk with payoffs that are far more stretched out than in the case of semiconductors.

Yet another type of investment experiment and one currently in operation can be found at In-Q-Tel, a CIA-funded program begun in 1999.[13] Its approach was initially modeled on venture capital investments in young firms that worked on technologies potentially relevant to intelligence needs. Unlike the proposed innovation corporation, In-Q-Tel averaged about $1.5 million per investment, so was clearly not going to do much to establish new industries. It was more of a window into technology for the CIA. Though not a bad idea, and perhaps a profitable investment, In-Q-Tel is no model for renewing the nation's infrastructure with massive injections of advanced technology. The innovation corporation would build demonstration projects to convince the private sector that the innovations it developed would merit the private sector's continuing investment—in the tens or hundreds of billions of dollars.

STIMULATE EDUCATION FOR JOBS
THAT NOW GO BEGGING

Globalization of production has introduced a huge influx of low-cost labor into the world markets that squeeze U.S. wages, especially at low skill levels. The automotive industry is an example. Factory floor jobs pay half of what they used to; offshoring to developing countries provides cheaper wages and benefits, though American productivity in some industries is hard to beat. However, some jobs in the United States go begging—jobs for skilled machinists are one example—because we're not training enough people to fill them. If trained, they would be employed.

This suggests a need for a post-secondary education path for non-college youth. The president was recently engaged in a debate with some Republicans who think subsidizing a college education with low-cost student loans is an example of the government doing more than it needs to do. I don't think that's the right criticism. A more relevant one is that the government needs to encourage another career path—a vocational one. This would not preclude having academic components in its curriculum. They could be offered too, with vocation the primary focus.

Some community colleges are training high school graduates, and they are retraining the newly unemployed for well-paying jobs that require technical skills. The colleges also offer a pastiche of liberal arts courses that encourage lifelong learning. The nature of jobs will keep changing; without continuing education, some people are going to be left behind. That is part of the problem of the long-term unemployed. Many of the jobs they know how to do are gone forever, often to countries where the pay is lower.

A related concern is the high education costs being shouldered by college students. It is not good for the country when students enter the workforce already carrying substantial debt. Higher education and vocational training will exert a large effect on the growth of GDP and personal income levels, and in turn on tax revenues. Those revenues have to support programs for retirement and medical care; one way or another federal dollars will be involved. Federal support for education is thus fully justified. I doubt that we have the optimum mix of grants and loans.

Yet another policy prescription, apart from educational paths, concerns immigrants. Those who arrive with technical skills, or develop them through U.S. higher education, are a valuable resource. We should encourage them to stay and become Americans. They have the potential to contribute a great deal to our economy and our culture just as immigrants have done in the past. They also will contribute to our tax base. In fact, Americans now in their forties and older will have to rely on the tax contributions of present and future immigrants and native-born Americans with productive educations. They will be paying the taxes needed to keep solvent the trust funds for Medicare and retirement benefits. Those taxes will be needed because the older group will collect in benefits (mostly medical) several times what they paid in.

9

Home of the Brave

AMERICA AT A TIPPING POINT

Perhaps when people of my age and Brzezinski's express concern about possible national decline, our views are influenced by identifying our own physical decline with national decline. The truth is that America is still second to none. Our military power, coupled with that of our allies, is unmatched by any combination of nations on earth. Our allies are allies by choice.

Those who hold high positions have a solemn obligation to tell the American people the truth about national security. Sometimes the truth is palatable; sometimes it is not. It has been my experience in government that when confronted not with a myth or a promise, but with the truth, the American people recognize and accept it. The truth now is that our military capability over the next decades, and with that much of our ability to affect the international environment, hinges on choices we must make without delay. Even without the much more drastic cuts embodied in the sequester schedule beginning in 2013, the 2011 Budget Control Act (BCA) passed by bipartisan majorities in both houses will reduce army and marine corps end-strength by 72,000 and 20,000, respectively.

With BCA, the navy will probably lose some seventeen ships; the air force will cut 10 percent of its fighter squadrons. There will be another round of base closures.[1] The armed services will have to compete in the perennial fight for resources. Many different interests are involved, even within the military, and not all of them relate to interservice rivalry. When it comes to closing bases, for example, senior military personnel will understandably fight to keep a base near their prospective retirement home open because it houses the medical services they will need.

One of the most politically fraught competitions within the defense budget mirrors what is happening in the civilian world: an intergenerational struggle between funding current and post-service compensation. Over the previous decade, total military personnel costs have soared, growing at an annual inflation-adjusted rate of 4.2 percent, partly because of TRICARE for Life health care benefits, which did not exist before 2001, but now cost $11 billion a year. The Department of Defense spends 33 cents for every dollar of basic pay to fund the military pension system. If military personnel costs continue growing at the same rate as they did in the past decade while the overall budget remains flat, which is the most favorable budget prospect, personnel costs will increasingly consume the entire defense budget by fiscal 2039.[2]

That growth means ever less money for research and development, procurement of weapons and supporting systems, readiness, training, and other priorities. It also means tough choices are in order, starting now. Top civilian and military leaders in the defense department should discuss what health and pension benefits can be reined in. The pension benefit, for example, is a noncontributory one.[3]

CHOICES AFTER ABU GHRAIB

Other choices have to do with keeping and enforcing military rules that reaffirm the nation's values. In 2004 I served on an independent panel convened by Secretary of Defense Donald Rumsfeld to review Department of Defense detention operations following the scandal at Abu Ghraib, a military prison in Iraq. That is where U.S. forces humiliated captives in part by making them pose naked. The panel was chaired by former Secretary of Defense James Schlesinger and included Representative Tillie Fowler (R-Fla.) and General Charles A. Horner of the U.S. Air Force. We testified before Congress on August 24, 2004, and I issued a statement of my own about the 300 cases of alleged prisoner abuse I helped to investigate. Much, but far from all, of that abuse occurred at Abu Ghraib prison in Iraq.[4]

To put it bluntly, we found atrocious behavior by uniformed military, and it was not limited to a few. There was *no* evidence of a policy issued by senior civilian or military authorities that countenanced, let alone encouraged or directed abuse. Secretary Rumsfeld had authorized an order, but then rescinded it, for only two cases of severe methods of interrogation. That order referred to al Qaeda members held at the Guantanamo Bay detention camp and thought to be knowledgeable about plans for 9/11 and future terrorist attacks. Those interrogation methods departed from the principles of the Geneva Conventions and those in Army Field Manual 34-52. Authorization to use those aberrant methods of interrogation on any prisoner required specific approval of Secretary Rumsfeld. Apparently, that condition was widely misunderstood or ignored.

I stated that the responsibility for deficient oversight at Abu Ghraib should fall on commanders on the scene and should proceed right up through the chain of command to the Joint Staff of the Joint Chiefs and to the Office of Secretary of Defense. My view when I was secretary of defense, and now decades after, is that there is a difference between discomfort and torture. What torture does to the victim is horrible. But what it does to the society that permits it is even worse. Torture should be forbidden, as is specified in the Army Field Manual (FM 34-52 and successors) and in President Obama's Executive Order 13491. I can conceive of urgent situations, especially on the battlefield, in which an interrogator believes that vital information must be obtained within hours and decides to use torture, even though it is forbidden. This may be justified despite the considerable weight of the argument that torture does not always elicit the truth.

For example, in the early 2000s, Lieutenant Colonel Allen West of the army had forces under fire and needed information from a captive quickly. He fired a gun near the head of a captive (not at it) and got his information. He knew this was against the rules. He turned himself in and was reprimanded and later resigned. Though he knew that his method of getting information was wrong, he felt he had to do it to save his troops. I applaud that kind of behavior, whatever one may think about West's subsequent political career in Florida.

On the other hand, waterboarding crosses a well-defined line. There are those who say waterboarding is routinely administered to some of our U.S. special forces to train them how to resist torture if captured. This misses the point. Our people have a choice. They volunteer for the waterboarding and can ask that it be stopped. That's not the same thing as administering it to captives.

The armed forces regulations clearly forbid torture. A secretary of defense should have control over how his troops conduct themselves. Though Secretary Rumsfeld was careful about the treatment of prisoners during interrogation and instituted stringent rules, he does bear some responsibility. The uniformed military bear most of the immediate responsibility. During the press conference following the findings of our Abu Ghraib panel, I was asked if Rumsfeld should resign. I answered that if the head of a department had to resign every time anyone down below did something wrong, the cabinet table would be very empty. Don Rumsfeld writes in his memoir that he did offer his resignation, which President George W. Bush did not accept.

The Abu Ghraib panel did find specific derelictions of duty. People were punished and a few careers were ruined. The choice going forward is do we keep to the rules or not? In my view, the Geneva Conventions rules, codified in the U.S. Army Manual, are right. They never should have been broken, nor should they be broken in the future. The people in charge need to enforce them.

As for prosecuting prisoners of war who are deemed terrorists, in principle you can detain prisoners of war until the war is over. It's not clear when, if ever, the "war on terrorism" will be over. Should terrorism be defined as war or as criminal behavior? It's hard to arrive at general principles, and each case may need to be treated separately. I do believe that military justice can be just, so it is not off the table to use military trials, which don't provide as full a spectrum of defendants' rights as civilian trials, but nevertheless do provide fair trials.

CHOICES ABOUT WHAT WE TEACH IN SCHOOLS

Education, health care, and defense make up nearly a third of the U.S. economy. Of the three, education has the smallest budget, yet the most influence on future productivity. We need more youth to become highly educated scientists, engineers, and technicians. So we need to find a way to interest children in these fields early on. Our schools don't do enough of that. Moreover, many elementary and high schools are ineffective in education overall. Some charter schools offer a good alternative as competitors to public education, but are too small a fraction of the country's schools to meet America's educational challenges. In fact, the lack of substantial teaching of history and civics, as well as science, denies youth the tools necessary for informed public discourse.

According to public surveys, most people think the state of elementary and high school education in this country is poor, but the education their own children get is good. Both those judgments can't be right. I believe the latter is wrong. Quality in education varies enormously. There is a layer of education at elementary and high schools that serves a small fraction of the public well, indeed the fraction of elites who think they run the country. However, the general level of education of high school graduates is not good, a condition that spills into colleges then forced to teach high school–level classes to compensate for poorly performing secondary schools.

To some extent, this problem stems from a lack of central direction from the federal government. For example, to get a good textbook written and into broad circulation, big states must adopt it. But some state legislatures don't believe in evolution, which causes problems for science textbook writers and for teaching science. Solid information about evolution and much else could be disseminated by using the Internet and teaching by telecommunication, but technology alone generally lacks the personal touch often necessary in education.

A more successful approach to teaching science using the personal touch may be one we tried while I was president of Caltech—which was to persuade universities, apart from schools of education (about which I don't have a high opinion), to reach out to elementary and high school students and interest them in math and science, important subjects for technological innovation. Many of our faculty encouraged local students to participate in research projects at Caltech. I think that many of our best universities have not lived up to their potential in this regard. If universities take responsibility for reaching out to young students, both the universities and the students may reap benefits at the college level.

Newt Gingrich, often in trouble for his provocative turn of phrase, famously opined that the way to solve the problem of "underclass kids" is to take them out of the milieu they face in rough neighborhoods and put them in an orphanage. Taking children away from their parents—even if the word "orphanage" is changed to "camp" or, in another context, "communal rearing"—generally goes against the grain and is an uncomfortable if not cruel suggestion. Still, there is a good deal to be said for taking children out of a crushing environment. It would be a different matter if parents volunteered their children for an educational program, but giving up children, even for a weekend "camp," could mean some Temporary Assistance for Needy Families (TANF) money would be lost to parents who rely on it. This is not an approach that parents would be prone to adopt.

Another problem is the lack of specially targeted alternatives to the standard four-year college curricula. Some states, notably Indiana, are adapting the two-year community college model to meet workforce needs by training technicians. This is one example of how decentralizing our educational system can offset some of its faults. An essential component here, as elsewhere, is teacher quality, which cannot be measured only by credentials and long tenure.

As for the student body, an interesting aside is that when I was Caltech president, fewer than 10 percent of the undergraduates were women. So for the sake of undergraduate social life I toyed with the idea of letting the nuns who operated a nearby school, Marymount in Los Angeles, buy land that Caltech owned and set up near us. Caltech's trustees and faculty were outraged with the idea. At a faculty meeting one member got up and said, "Have we forgotten Galileo so soon?" I could barely restrain myself from laughing out loud. My idea went nowhere. Fortunately, another solution gradually emerged over the subsequent forty years. Now, of Caltech's entering undergraduates, almost 40 percent are women.

AVOID AVENUES ALREADY WELL EXPLORED

Technology has sparked many of the world's revolutionary changes. Yet many subsequent improvements on those breakthroughs have been only marginal. It is important to guard against the imagined hope that continued work on the same technology will yield further developments that will themselves be revolutionary. Edward Teller, for example, was convinced that he could come up with something better than his original design for the hydrogen bomb. He didn't know how it would be better; he avidly wanted to seek a new technology or different application that would make the bomb a more efficient weapon. But our nuclear weapons technology was no longer the driving factor in our security.

The trick is to recognize when you've reached a point of relatively unrewarding return on yet further investment of resources in the same technology. Every new technology has its day and then you move on. The next big leap may take place in a very different arena. That's as true in biology as in defense matters. As our elected leaders make choices of what programs to pursue, they need to remember the law of diminishing returns.

That law was impressed upon me when I took flying lessons. I began them before I became air force secretary, in fact while I was still director of Defense Research and Engineering (DDRE). I learned to fly a single-engine plane but never got a pilot's license, partly because of what Curtis LeMay, air force chief of staff, said when he sat next to me at a dinner. When I mentioned taking the lessons, he said: "I'll give you one piece of advice. You're not going to be an experienced pilot. If the weather isn't perfect, keep your ass on the ground."

CHOICES ABOUT PROTOCOL

A small point, but perhaps interesting to those who follow the protocols of social events, is that during the Carter administration's White House dinners, I was troubled that senior military people were not invited. OK, I thought at the first dinner and even the third, but by the fifth I passed word to the White House protocol staff that no member of the Joint Chiefs of Staff had attended. I thought it very important they not be left off the list. I was quite willing, indeed happy, to let the chairman of the Joint Chiefs or a service chief be invited instead of me. The Carter protocol people never did that and never responded to my note. I doubt that it was a presidential decision to de-emphasize the military. Perhaps people at State had drawn up the guest list. There was always a bit of tension about protocol among officials at State, Defense, and on the National Security Council. I never did find out the reason for excluding the military, but it affected the relationship between the military and the president.

Another incident that affected that relationship concerns a letter President Carter hand-wrote to me after some military association publications ran articles that demanded higher pay for military personnel. (The military associations are private bodies, usually run by retired military.) Carter's letter said, in effect: "When I was in the navy, pay was not what was important. Why don't you do something about this [criticism]?" I knew his letter reflected his personal attitude that military service was not just another job. I was concerned about the possible reaction of those who might not understand the president's intent. What I did was put the letter in a safe and locked it. "Don't show this to anybody," I said to my staff. The next week the full text of the letter appeared in the *Army Times*, the *Navy Review*, and the *Air Force Journal*. To this day I believe that someone in the White House leaked the letter thinking he was doing the president a favor. Well, he wasn't. Some in the senior military felt the president was accusing them of being wrongly motivated. I sold my home in Georgetown recently and turned over classified information contained in my personal safe to the Defense Department. The letter was there, still in its envelope.

PROTECT THOUGHTFUL INPUTS TO THE NATIONAL SECURITY AGENDA

We will need to paint a clear picture of America's security interests over the next years so that a president and secretary of defense can deal with a Congress and a public beset with deep political divisions. As the executive branch and Congress make choices that affect long-range strategic thinking, they must find ways to separate careful thinking from the pressures of media noise. Media headlines create avenues for politically opportunistic rather than thoughtfully strategic solutions to the nation's problems. It will be important to retain and use expert research available from federally funded think tanks (and those privately funded, including some with whose views I strongly disagree) and to avoid the tendency to cut funds from research institutions during times of fiscal austerity.

The State Department is especially subject to media pressure and, in turn, to even more pressure from Congress, which accords it less kindness than it does Defense. Congressional overseers of the Defense Department regard it symbiotically as both a recipient of their funding, and as an organization on which they depend because almost all members of Congress have defense contractors in their districts. A few legislators have more of a parasitic attitude: little support for Defense but great demands for expenditures in their districts. There is nothing analogous about congressional oversight of State, which has few if any businesses in the districts of its congressional overseers. The State Department's embassies can provide help to members of Congress on overseas visits, but it's the Defense Department that gets them there.

During my tenure at Defense in the 1960s and 1970s, whenever the United States had a quarrel with another country, the State Department argued loudest to reduce U.S. military connections to it. This serves a dual purpose for State. First, it can be a useful lever against the offending country. Second, it gives the State Department a unique line of communication by cutting the Defense Department out of the intercountry relationship. That's an ancillary motivation, but a tempting one. The State Department has its own legitimate complaints. In recent decades the State Department has found itself host to, but not controller of, a number of contingents from other government departments within its embassies. For example, an ambassador may find himself dealing with FBI agents, Commerce Department personnel, Defense Department people, and others. In principle, the ambassador is the U.S. official in charge of all U.S. personnel operating in his host country. In reality, it doesn't work that way because people from other agencies take their orders from their superiors in Washington.

SEWN TOGETHER AT THE DIVIDE

My father was a soldier in World War I, an AEF (American Expeditionary Force) artilleryman in combat in France. He was a modest man. In 1940, when I was twelve, he took me along on a trip to Washington. He was a lawyer with a case that brought him to the office of our local congressman. I remember the deference he showed to the congressman's staffer. I remember touring the monuments and memorials: Washington's, Lincoln's, and Jefferson's recently dedicated one. I remember watching from the Senate gallery as Happy Chandler, then a Kentucky senator, later the baseball commissioner, declaimed on the Senate floor.

When I became secretary of defense and visited our military bases, I was reminded of a singularity that had occurred to me when I first took office in the Pentagon as director of Defense Research and Engineering in 1961. As far as I know, the United States is the only country in the world that has named some of its bases for generals who fought unsuc-cessfully in a rebellion, that is to say, the Civil War, formally known in army records as the War of the Rebellion. Naming those bases for leaders of the losing side may be seen as a purposeful attempt to heal the rift in our country after the Civil War. But there are few if any southern bases named for northern generals, or vice versa. So the singularity may also be seen as a sign that the war's scars had not healed when those bases were named. The more profound divisions between Red and Blue states, and our deep schism regarding what we want, and don't want, from our government all remain.

As a secretary of defense, I have stood at the Tomb of the Unknown Soldier at Arlington National Cemetery. Seeing a soldier's final resting place both saddens and reminds me that our country needs a quiet and firm strength based on adequate armed forces, solid and determined lead-ership, and cohesion among our people. The inscription on the tomb reads: "Here rests in honored glory an American soldier known but to God." He is a World War I soldier. This way of honoring those who have died in the nation's wars can be traced back to Lincoln's words at Gettysburg in 1863: "That we here highly resolve that these dead shall not have died in vain."

In 1876 the women of Columbus, Mississippi, which had been a Con-federate state, visited a local cemetery to decorate the graves of their hus-bands, brothers, and sons. Their sadness, already great, deepened when they saw the bare graves of the Union soldiers, far from their homes and loved ones. So these women of Mississippi decorated those graves, too. Newspapers across the nation recounted that act of kindness. (Similar gestures were made in Alabama and other southern states.) The North and the South responded with an annual observance of Decoration Day. In 1882 Decoration Day became Memorial Day.

So perhaps the divisions between Americans now can be overcome, or at least managed. If some women of the South could look beyond their strongly held beliefs and grief only a decade after the Civil War to deco-rate Northern men's graves, surely we and our elected representatives can see across our differences, and can look across the aisle as Republicans and Democrats, as minority and majority points of view in the chambers of Congress, to find ways to come together for our one precious nation. Our cohesion, more than anything else, will protect us into the future.

AFTERWORD

When my years of full-time government service ended in 1981, I embarked on a thirty-year career in the corporate and educational sectors. I've been a corporate director of more than a dozen businesses, including Mattel, IBM, and Cummins Engine, and an outside consultant to about as many. I've also been a trustee of about ten nonprofit organizations. The firms of which I've been a corporate director have included high-tech, consumer, industrial, biotech, and financial establishments. My consulting has served U.S. and European industrial and financial firms, and I've been a partner at the private equity firm Warburg Pincus, where I led reviews and forecasts by outside economic advisers.

When I left the Defense Department in January 1981, I joined the Johns Hopkins University School of International Studies on a part-time basis, first as a visiting professor and later, until 1992, as chairman of its Foreign Policy Institute. Since the 1980s I've served as a trustee (now trustee emeritus) of the RAND Corporation, a nonprofit institution that helps improve policy and decisionmaking through research and analysis. I am a trustee of the Center for Strategic and International Studies (CSIS) in Washington, D.C., and participate in its work. Since leaving government office, I've been chair or a member of various U.S. government commissions on strategic forces, intelligence organization, innovation, and government reactions to terrorism. And I've written many tracts and another book called *Thinking about National Security*, published by Westview Press in 1993.

I served as chair of the Defense Policy Board for five years during the 1990s and since then—and still—serve as a member. The Defense Policy Board advises the secretary of defense and his staff on strategic, military, and international political issues. Brent Scowcroft was chair after me for about a year at the end of the Clinton administration. Currently, John Hamre, the chief executive officer of CSIS, chairs the Defense Policy Board, which has about fifteen members and meets quarterly at the Pentagon. All of this activity—both advising government and working in the for-profit and nonprofit private sectors—affords me a wide view of how our country copes with its internal and external challenges and provides more lessons learned.

The first lesson learned—actually relearned from my service on government boards and commissions since leaving office—is the difference between being a senior government official and advising from the outside. I had known as secretary of defense and in my earlier government jobs that it's a lot harder to make decisions and take responsibility than to cheer, boo, or shout directions from the sidelines. I found myself empathizing with secretaries of defense I advised as some took careful notes and used the group as a sounding board, and others merely listened or deflected suggestions. The insiders, with much more information, are immersed in decisions about the nation's security, whether about resource allocation, the effects of which last for decades, or immediate operational life-and-death matters. Knowledgeable outsiders can offer the insiders a long-range perspective that insiders may not have considered or given adequate weight because they are preoccupied with short-term decisions as well as the pressures and crises that fill their in-boxes. We "outsiders" can offer views on long-term consequences of those decisions based on our cumulative experience.

In the business world, I have seen firsthand how CEOs function in their roles as corporate leaders and as they prepare to leave their positions. I offer my insights about that because all sectors of America—including its government and educational system—rely on the strength of its economy. The economy is driven in large part by business, which in terms of profitability and efficiency is one of America's more effective activities. (America's performance in dealing with the inequality of economic benefit is less impressive.) There is a natural tendency for a CEO thinking about a successor (which many leaders prefer not to do at all) to favor a version of him- or herself. That often means somebody almost but not as good, and seldom better. Therefore, I think a board of directors needs to actively make the choice rather than rubber-stamping the departing CEO's choice. That's not easy because the board usually won't know candidates as well as the CEO. One way to fix this problem is to separate the chair of the board from the CEO and allow the chair to spend more time on the inside of the corporation. That would provide some balance. The downside of that approach is the possible conflict over who's in charge.

Executive pay has become outlandish. Prospective CEOs from outside the corporation demand large guaranteed pay packages on joining. That escalates the compensation of senior executives overall, especially as compared with average worker incomes. That difference has ballooned even as CEO pay often separates reward from performance or personal risk. For example, if you do well in the financial sector and don't bring down the economy, you get an enormous amount of money. If you fail, or even if you help precipitate a crash, you get paid almost as much. That undermines the basis for societal solidarity. Herb Stein, chair of the Council of Economic Advisers in the Nixon administration, described the disparity in compensation (even before it reached its current height) as "unlovely." I think he was right. The argument that a company is dependent on an individual star (who would go elsewhere if not paid a lot) is almost always unconvincing. But CEOs will continue to compare their compensation for running corporations owned by others with the often even bigger compensation earned by financiers who manage money owned by others, and who take a share of the profits but hardly of the losses.

There are exceptions. In addition to some who are still active CEOs, I name three: the late Steve Jobs of Apple; Lou Gerstner, chair of the board of IBM from 1993 to 2002; and Henry Schacht, for two decades CEO of Cummins Engine Company, who became a close personal friend. They were worth everything they were paid because of their contributions to their companies. How you walk back exorbitant CEO compensation I don't know. The people who are exceptions to the rule tend to be motivated by things other than money—which, Gerstner and the others would probably agree, also motivated them. I suggest that if the government taxed away 90 percent of the compensation paid to CEOs over $10 million or $20 million annually, and everyone knew that would happen, it would satisfy the ego requirement of being in the top tier, that is to say, one of the highest-paid people at the pretax level. It would make sense for company founders, like Jobs, to retain most of their capital gains. Creating a tax system like that would illustrate that the devil is indeed in the details.

Capping pay for CEOs won't change the huge payouts to movie stars or sports stars whose contributions are unique. But the even larger payouts for hedge fund managers and CEOs of some financial institutions are poisoning society. The distribution of income and assets in the United States is more skewed than it is in other advanced democratic societies, and more skewed than it used to be. That's not a healthy situation because it undermines the sense of shared interest, shared values, and of family in the broadest sense—of being part of a larger family essential to a stable democratic society.

It is our domestic issues that chiefly mark whether our society is attractive and healthy, or not. Many of these indicators, improving until two or three decades ago, have slowed, stalled, or fallen back. These include the disparities in education, societal wellbeing, life expectancy, and health among different segments of our population. That is a matter of real concern. So is the deterioration of the family and its responsibilities for its children. Whether or not you think illegitimate birth is a sin, it is socially dysfunctional for fully 41 percent of our births to be in that category, which in legal terms means a child whose parents were not married at the time of his or her birth.

According to the Centers for Disease Control and Prevention, nearly 1.7 million unmarried women aged fifteen to forty-four gave birth in 2009, the most recent year for which data are available.[1] Similar statistics have been reported for some Scandinavian countries, but their statistics do not reflect societal effects as damaging as in the United States, partly because their incidence correlates less with socioeconomic status. I am not disparaging single-parent families; rather, I draw attention to a need to address the great challenges for the parent who was single at the birth of the child and must work and raise children, not to mention the challenges for the children.

There is also inequality between the old and the young in America, such that the old have a social safety net whereas many of the young do not. Now that we live longer, we've created a twenty- or twenty-five-year gap between retirement and death. As the entire baby boom generation crosses the threshold of sixty-five, the average age of American citizens will rise and create more pressure on public health care funding. The cost of caring for an aging population is further magnified by the use of more expensive treatment. We will almost certainly have to raise taxes to cover those prospects, despite best efforts to rein in costs.

Another challenge is our aging and crumbling infrastructure—sewers, bridges, airports. Aging infrastructure damages growth in productivity. We're going to need to choose what to fix and fix it. All those decisions are hard to come by: we've become two nations, divided economically and politically. The division is illustrated by the lack of socializing among members of Congress, even to the trivial point of getting a member of one party to sit next to a member of the other party at a presidential address. These days many elected representatives don't socialize in Washington because many of them don't live there; they fly home on weekends. When I was in office the socializing we did (and I was not notably sociable) enabled trust or at least provided the opportunity to hear another point of view expressed one-on-one.

Many of America's problems—blighted neighborhoods, unemployment, lack of education and community—are interconnected and show up in frightening fiscal terms. The ratio of national debt to annual GDP is rising toward 100 percent. The primary deficit (excluding interest on the national debt) is more than 5 percent of GDP and is projected to balloon after 2016 unless there are major changes in tax rates and entitlements. This is a Gordian Knot. The analogue of Alexander's solution to the Gordian Knot is revolution, which history tells us makes things worse for an extended period of time. (We can see it unfolding in the aftermath of the Arab Spring.)

All these ills admitted, the United States also has favorable features. America still has by far the largest economy in the world, though other nations are gaining. The U.S. per capita GDP is the highest of any large nation. (Those of Norway, Luxembourg, and Qatar are higher.) That combination is unique. The United States has the highest-quality centers of university education and of basic and applied research in the world. Other nations have tried to hitch their academic institutions to innovation in their economies, but no nation has been as successful as ours. Our economy can grow and make more jobs; there's not a fixed amount of labor to be done. Our relative decline as other nations grow from a lower base may be uncomfortable for us, but can be managed. Over the long run, if we can last it out, the growth of economies elsewhere will help grow our own. In the short run, we need fiscal and monetary stimulus to provide jobs and encourage economic growth. In the medium and long term, we need the opposite, fiscal tightening to limit or reduce public debt and encourage private investment. That is to say, the proper choices differ for the different time scales, and we need to make the right choices for each.

If all this seems overwhelming, consider this. When I began my work in Washington, first in 1956 as a member of the Polaris Steering Committee, then as a senior Department of Defense official in 1961, many stalwarts of previous generations were still active. I saw and spoke with them. Alice Longworth, Theodore Roosevelt's daughter and the widow of a Speaker of the House, delighted in mischievous gossip. Eddie Rickenbacker, then chairman of Eastern Airlines, had been a World War I air corps ace.

I worked with heroes of World War II: Jimmy Doolittle, Curtis LeMay, Maxwell Taylor, Arleigh Burke. Prominent New Dealers from FDR's White House—Tom Corcoran and Ben Cohen, Jim Rowe and Abe Fortas—were still active in politics. Some leading legislators of the 1930s and 1940s were in office or still in Washington into the 1960s: Wright Patman, Carl Hayden, Burton Wheeler, Everett Dirksen, Sam Rayburn, Joe Martin, and Charles Halleck. Lyndon Johnson had been a junior member of Congress in New Deal days.

That's not just a list of names. The presence of those figures on various sides of the issues from times of earlier challenge and danger, from times of severe domestic depression and social disruption—of world wars—made a deep impression on me and can remind all of us that America has come through very difficult times successfully. We tend to forget that at the time of those difficulties no one could have full confidence of a successful outcome. The same holds true now. We have no guarantees. Our anxiety fuels contentious political rivalry. The same arguments about the role of government and the role of the United States in the world that ricocheted on radios in the 1930s echo now—amplified by new media and more cash.

The United States has no heavenly mandate to exercise world leadership. In fact, we are stumbling. But we have not fallen. We have a combination of assets unique among the populous nations—a favorable geographic position, natural resources, the ability to attract talented immigrants and to integrate them into a diverse but fundamentally unified and growing population. Above all, we have a flexible political system that despite its current dysfunction has the proven ability to adjust. Compared with America eighty years ago, we are more open, more fair, and a richer and stronger country. We have the ability to address what we must to remain strong and prosperous. It is no small assignment, no small challenge, but we are not a nation of small aspirations. We are a nation of people who get things done. We have brought our flag through perilous fights. Now, it falls on each of us to join in protecting our interests abroad while guarding values that embody the rights and duties of each of us at home.

Let's do it.

NOTES

CHAPTER I

1. Natural Resources Defense Council (NRDC), "Table of Global Nuclear Weapons Stockpiles, 1945–2002," NRDC Nuclear Program, November 25, 2002 (www.nrdc.org/nuclear/nudb/datab19.asp); Department of Defense, "Fact Sheet: U.S. Nuclear Transparency," May 3, 2010 (www.defense.gov/npr/docs/10-05-03_fact_sheet_us_nuclear_transparency__final_w_date.pdf).

CHAPTER 2

1. Todd Harrison, *Analysis of the FY 2012 Defense Budget* (Washington: Center for Strategic and Budgetary Assessment, 2012), p. 12.

2. *2011 Economic Report of the President* (Washington: Government Printing Office (GPO), 2011), p. 90.

3. Amy Belasco, "The Cost of Iraq, Afghanistan, and Other Global War on Terror Operations Since 9/11," Congressional Research Service Report for Congress, RL33110, p. CRS9 (www.infoplease.com/ipa/A0933935.html#ixzz1wTNkOZe4).

4. Harrison, *Analysis of the FY 2012 Defense Budget,* pp. 1–86. See also table at "Estimated War-Related Costs, Iraq and Afghanistan," Info please, 2012 (www.infoplease.com/ipa/A0933935.html#ixzz1wTNkOZe4).

5. See "Andrew Marshall, Who Runs Gov?" *Washington Post* (www.washingtonpost.com/politics/andrew-marshall/gIQAyeVSKP_topic.html). Also see www.sourcewatch.org/index.php?title=Andrew_Marshall.

6. Dwight D. Eisenhower, "Defense Reorganization Bill," letter to Chairman Carl Vinson, House Armed Services Committee, May 16, 1958 (www.presidency.ucsb.edu/ws/print.php?pid=11061).

7. See Dwight D. Eisenhower, "Transmitting Draft Bill on Defense Reorganization," letter to the President of the Senate and to the Speaker of the House of Representatives, April 16, 1958 (www.presidency.ucsb.edu/ws/print.php?pid=11351).

8. See Dwight D. Eisenhower, letter to the United States Congress on Reorganization of the Defense Establishment, April 3, 1958 (www.presidency.ucsb.edu/ws/?pid=11340#axzz1vtkUjsZ0).

9. Charles Johnston Hitch and Roland N. McKean, *The Economics of Defense in the Nuclear Age* (Santa Monica, Calif.: RAND, 1960).

10. Harrison, *Analysis of the FY 2012 Defense Budget,* p. v. Information on the GDP in 2011 is available at www.politifact.com/virginia/statements/2011/aug/05/randy-forbes/forbes-says-us-defense-spending-measured-against-g/.

11. "NATO Standardization, Interoperability and Readiness," Hearing before the House Committee on Armed Services, September 21, 1978, p. 2.

12. Harold Brown, Statement before the House Committee on Armed Services, September 13, 1978.

13. See OECD Stat Extracts, iLibrary.

14. Harrison, *Analysis of the Fiscal Year 2012 Defense Budget,* pp. v–vii.

15. Quoted in Ruchir Sharma, "China Slows Down and Grows Up," *New York Times,* April 25, 2012, p. A23.

16. Alan Sager and Deborah Scholar, "Health Costs: Behind the Numbers," Letter to the Editor, *New York Times,* May 6, 2012 (nytimes.com/2012/05/07/opinion/health-costs-behind-the-numbers.html).

17. See USgovernmentspending.com, U.S. GDP history.

18. Congressional Budget Office (CBO), "Long-Term Implications of the 2012 Future Years Defense Program" (GPO, June 2011), pp. 17–20.

19. U.S. Department of Defense, "Function 150 & Other International Programs," Executive Budget Summary, Fiscal Year 2012.

20. CBO, "Long-Term Implications of the 2012 Future Years Defense Program," p. 1.

21. "How Does U.S. Health Care Compare to the Rest of the World?" *The Guardian* (Manchester), March 22, 2010 (www.guardian.co.uk/news/datablog/2010/mar/22/us-healthcare-bill-rest-of-world-obama).

22. Jane Perlez, "Panetta Outlines New Weaponry for Pacific," *New York Times,* June 2, 2012, p. A7.

23. Harold Brown, "Annual Defense Department Report: Fiscal Year 1979," Office of the Secretary of Defense (http://history.defense.gov/resources/1979_DoD_AR.pdf).

24. See also Frank Camm, *The Development of the FIO00-PW-220 and FII-GE-100 Engines: A Case Study of Risk Assessment and Risk Management* (Santa Monica, Calif.: RAND, 1993). For more on the F-16 engine, see Federation of American Scientists, "F-16 Fighting Falcon" (www.fas.org/programs/ssp/man/uswpns/air/fighter/f16.html).

25. Christopher Drew, "House Votes to End Alternate Jet Engine Program," *New York Times,* February 16, 2011, p. B1 (www.nytimes.com/2011/02/17/us/politics/17-f-35-engine.html?_r=1&pagewanted=print).

26. Ibid.

27. Armed Forces History Museum, "Harrier—The Jump Jet Aircraft" (www.armedforcesmuseum.com/harrier-%E2%80%93-the-jump-jet-aircraft/); "The Harrier Jump Jet: 45 Years," Defense Media Network (www.defensemedianetwork.com/photos/the-harrier-jump-jet-45-years-photos/); "Harrier," Discovery Chanel (www.yourdiscovery.

com/machines_and_engineering/industrialrevelation/planes/harrier/index.shtml); see also www.harrier.org.uk/history/index.htm.

CHAPTER 3

1. Ruben F. Mettler, Interview with Carol Butler, Redondo Beach, Calif., *NASA Oral History,* April 7, 1999, p. 1.

2. Thom Shanker and Eric Schmitt, "More Satellites Will Act as Eyes for Troops," *New York Times,* February 23, 2010 (www.nytimes.com/2010/02/24/world/asia/24satellites.html), p. A6.

3. "Robert William Komer," Arlington National Cemetery Archives, August 12, 2000 (www.arlingtoncemetery.net/rwkomer.htm).

4. Harold Brown, Statement before the House Subcommittee on Investigations, Committee on Armed Services, October 3, 1978.

5. Harold Brown, Interview by Erin Mahan and Edward Keefer, Office of the Secretary of Defense Historical Office, Oral History Interview, February 11, 2001.

6. See biography of David Jones at InsideAF.mil.

7. Paul M. Besson, "The Goldwater-Nichols Act: A Ten Year Report Card," Program on Information Resources Policy (Harvard University, 1998), p. 66.

8. Pat Jacoby, "York Remembered as Scientist, Humanitarian, Leader," This Week at UCSD, October 12, 2009, with photo of Harold Brown delivering a eulogy.

9. Remarks at a service for Eugene Ghiron Fubini. See Harold Brown and Bert Fowler, "Eugene Ghiron Fubini," *Physics Today,* December 1997, p. 91.

10. C. Northcote Parkinson, *Parkinson's Law: The Pursuit of Progress* (London: John Murray, 1958).

CHAPTER 4

1. "Mohammed Reza Pahlavi," *New World Encyclopedia* (www.newworldencyclopedia.org/entry/Mohammad_Reza_Pahlavi).

2. Jimmy Carter Library and Museum, "The Hostage Crisis in Iran," November 2009 (www.jimmycarterlibrary.gov/documents/hostages.phtml).

3. Jimmy Carter, *White House Diary* (New York: Farrar, Stauss, Giroux, 2010), p. 367.

4. Secretary of Defense Harold Brown and General David C. Jones, News Conference at the Pentagon, Washington, April 25, 1980.

CHAPTER 5

1. Viktor Adamsky and Yuri Smirnov, "Moscow's Biggest Bomb: The 50-Megaton Test of October 1961," *Cold War International History Project Bulletin* 4 (Fall 1994): 19–21.

2. For more information, see Vitaly I. Khalturin and others, "A Review of Nuclear Testing by the Soviet Union at Novaya Zemlya, 1955–1990," *Science and Global Security* 13 (2004): 1–42.

3. "The Years of Atmospheric Testing: 1945–1963" (www.cddc.vt.edu/host/atomic/atmosphr/index.html).

4. "Summary of U.S. Nuclear Test Series," Trinity Atomic website (www.cddc.vt.edu/host/atomic/atmosphr/ustable.html).

5. For more on Paul "Red" Fay, see Keith Thursby, "Paul Fay Dies at 91; Friend of JFK, Former Navy Official," *Los Angeles Times,* September 30, 2009.

6. "From a Position of Strength," *Newsweek,* December 4, 1961.

7. "President Kennedy Inspects Ballistic Missile Early Warning System in the United States," *Critical Past,* Vandenberg Air Force Base, California, March 23, 1962 (www.criticalpast.com/video/65675025276_President-Kennedy-inspects-Ballistic-Missile-Early-Warning-System_RVX-II_Mark-IV).

8. Glenn T. Seaborg, *Kennedy, Khrushchev, and the Test Ban* (University of California Press, 1981).

9. For a history of the Eisenhower moratorium on nuclear testing up to Kennedy, see William Burr and Hector L. Montford, eds., *The Making of the Limited Test Ban Treaty, 1958–1963,* National Security Archives, August 8, 2003 (www.gwu.edu/~nsarchiv/NSAEBB/NSAEBB94).

10. Harold Brown, Testimony before the Senate Armed Services Committee, January 11, 1977.

11. See www.af.mil/news/story.asp?storyID=123020473.

12. A video of this event is at www.youtube.com/watch?v=yOz-c3yU1Nk ; it contains factual errors by its photographer/narrator, but shows guests, the plane, and the U.S. Air Force secretary.

13. On August 1, 1977, President Jimmy Carter approved Public Law 95-82 that required the Department of Defense to notify Congress when a base was a candidate for reduction or closure—and to wait sixty days for a congressional response. That legislation permitted Congress to thwart any Defense Department proposal to initiate base realignment and closure studies unilaterally by refusing to approve them and gave it an integral role in the process.

14. For more on MAD, read Harold Brown interview by John G. Hines, Johns Hopkins Foreign Policy Institute, Washington, November 8, 1991.

15. For a detailed history, see Burr and Montford, *The Making of the Limited Test Ban Treaty, 1958–1963.*

16. Glenn A. Kent, *Thinking about America's Defense: An Analytical Memoir* (Santa Monica, Calif.: RAND, 2008), p. 3.

17. See www.answers.com/topic/precision-guided-munition.

18. See 2004.12.01-Revolution-in-War.pdf

19. See www.af.mil/information/factsheets/factsheet_print.asp?fsID=108.

20. Harold Brown, "The Need for MX," Statement to the Senate Armed Services Committee, June 5, 1980.

21. Harold Brown, Testimony before the Senate Armed Services Committee, June 5, 1980.

22. Harold Brown, News Conference, Office of Assistant Secretary of Defense Public Affairs, August 22, 1980.

23. Ibid.

24. Cold War Museum, "*SALT I & II*" (www.coldwar.org/articles/70s/SALTIandII. asp); Federation of Amerian Scientists, "Anti-Ballistic Missile Treaty" (www.fas.org/ nuke/control/abmt/); Notburga K. Calvo-Goller and Michel A. Calvo, *The SALT Agreements: Content-Application-Verification* (Hingham, Mass: Martinus Nijhoff, 1987), pp. 29–48.

25. Harold Brown, Statement to the Committee on Foreign Relations, July 9, 1979.

26. For more on SALT I, see Gerard C. Smith, *Doubletalk: The Story of SALT I by the Chief American Negotiator* (New York: Doubleday, 1980).

27. Secretary of Defense Harold Brown, Q and A session, following remarks to overseas writers, Washington, October 20, 1980; Calvo-Goller and Calvo, *The Salt Agreements*, pp. 29–39, 348–51; Department of Defense, "Fact Sheet: U.S. Nuclear Transparency," May 3, 2010 (www.defense.gov/npr/docs/10-05-03_fact_sheet_us_ nuclear_transparency__final_w_date.pdf [April 20, 2012]), table 1.2, "Nuclear Weapons, 1972."

28. Calvo-Goller and Calvo, *The Salt Agreements*, pp. 29–39, 348–51.

29. Bureau of Arms Control, Verification and Compliance, U.S. Department of State, New Start Treaty Aggregate Numbers of Strategic Offensive Arms, June 1, 2012 (www. state.gov/t/avc/rls/191580.htm).

30. Harold Brown, "New Nuclear Realities," *Washington Quarterly* 31 (Winter 2007–08): 7–22.

31. See www.jfklibrary.org/Asset-Viewer/ZgLsd8Qx0kefPPeR3VK-7w.aspx#.UB mRb5yRL0E.email.

CHAPTER 6

1. Harold Brown, Statement on NATO Standardization and Interoperability and Readiness, House Committee on Armed Services, September 21, 1978.

2. Harold Brown, Statement before the House Committee on Armed Services, September 13, 1978.

3. Harold Brown, Department of Defense transcript of interview with Lothar Ruehl, Bonn, Germany, following NATO Nuclear Planning Group Meeting, Bodo, Norway, June 4, 1980.

4. Harold Brown, Statement before the NATO Defense Planning Committee Ministerial Session, Brussels, Belgium, May 17, 1977, followed by a news conference there on May 18.

5. Brown, Statement, September 13, 1978.

6. Dennis M. Drummond, "Getting Traffic Moving on NATO's Two-Way Street," *Air University Review*, September-October 1979 (www.airpower.au.af.mil/air chronicles/aureview/1979/sep-oct/drummond.html); "Department of the Army Historical Summary, 1979: Development," chap. 11, sec, 187 (www.history.army.mil/books/ DAHSUM/1979/ch11.htm).

7. Harold Brown, Statement before the Budget Committees of Congress and the Senate, March 1, 1978.

8. Harold Brown, Testimony Regarding CX, MX, and Chemical Weapons before the Senate Armed Services Committee, Washington, DC, June 5, 1980.

9. NATO, "NATO OTAN, NATO E-3A Component, NATO's Flagship Fleet" (www.e3a.nato.int/eng/html/organizations/history.htm).

10. NATO, "AWACS: NATO's 'Eye in the Sky,'" May 11, 2012 (www.nato.int/cps/en/natolive/topics_48904.htm).

11. Harold Brown, Interview by Erin Mahan and Edward Keefer, Office of the Secretary of Defense Historical Office, February 11, 2001.

12. Amy F. Woolf, "Nonstrategic Nuclear Weapons" (Washington: Congressional Research Service, January 28, 2009), p. 16.

13. Harold Brown, Interview by Thierry de Scitivaux of TF-1, Paris, France, July 1, 1980.

14. Nikolai V. Ogarkov, "Military Science and the Defense of the Socialist Fatherland," *Kommunist* 7 (May 1978), pp. 110–21.

15. Federation of American Scientists, "Intermediate Range Nuclear Forces" (www.fas.org/nuke/control/inf/).

16. F. Stephen Larrabee and Peter A. Wilson, "NATO's Shrinking Resources," op-ed, *International Herald Tribune,* May 17, 2012 (www.nytimes.com/2012/05/17/opinion/natos-shrinking-resources.html).

17. American-Israeli Cooperative Enterprise, "McDonald Douglas F-4 Phantom II" (www.jewishvirtuallibrary.org/jsource/History/phantom.html).

18. Jimmy Carter, *White House Diary* (New York: Farrar, Stauss, Giroux, 2010), pp. 216–26.

19. Ibid.

20. U.S. Department of State, "U.S. Egyptian Relations, Defense" (www.state.gov/r/pa/ei/bgn/5309.htm).

21. See www.state.gov/r/pa/ei/bgn/3581.htm.

22. Harold Brown, "Remarks by Secretary of Defense upon First Visit," King Faisal Academy, Riyadh, Saudi Arabia, February 10, 1979.

23. Harold Brown, Statement, Amman, Jordan, February 13, 1979.

24. Harold Brown, Statement, Cairo, Egypt, February 16, 1979.

25. Harold Brown, Remarks at dinner hosted by Mod Kamal, Cairo, Egypt, February 16, 1979.

26. Harold Brown, Statement, Tel Aviv, Israel, February 16, 1979.

27. Jimmy Carter, *White House Diary,* pp. 344–45.

28. "Mutual Defense Treaty between the United States of America and the Republic of China," Taiwan Documents Project (www.taiwandocuments.org/mutual01.htm).

29. U.S. Embassy Beijing, "High-Level Visits and Speeches" (http://beijing.usembassy-china.org.cn/highlevel.html); Jimmy Carter, *White House Diary,* p. 354.

30. News conference with the Secretary of Defense, May 29, 1980.

31. "Population," *CIA World Fact Book, 2012* (www.cia.gov/library/publications/the-world-factbook/rankorder/2119rank.html).

32. Ruchir Sharma, "China Slows Down, and Grows Up," op-ed, *New York Times,* April 25, 2012, p. A23.

33. Harold Brown, "The U.S. and China: 1980, 2012 and 2030," address at Brigham Young University, Provo, Utah, January 19, 2012.

34. Sharma, "China Slows Down, and Grows Up," p. A23.

35. Kenneth Lieberthal and J. Stapleton Roy, "The U.S. and China Need to Show a Little Mutual Restraint," *Washington Post,* February 10, 2012.

36. Harold Brown and others, "Chinese Military Power," Task Force Report, Council on Foreign Relations, May 2003 (www.cfr.org/china/chinese-military-power/p5985).

37. Quoted in David Barboza, "China Passes Japan as Second Largest Economy," *New York Times,* August 15, 2012 (www.nytimes.com/2010/08/16/business/global/16yuan.html?pagewanted=all), p. B1.

38. "South Korea," *CIA World Fact Book, 2011* (www.cia.gov/library/publications/the-world-factbook/geos/ks.html).

39. Michael Dobbs, "Koreagate Figure Tied to Oil-For-Food Scandal," *Washington Post,* April 15, 2005, p. A19.

40. Harold Brown, Statement before the House International Relations Committee, February 22, 1978.

41. William Chapman, "Brown Presses South Korea Not to Execute Dae-Jung," *Washington Post,* December14, 1980, p. 18.

42. "South Korea," *CIA World Fact Book, 2011.*

43. For a more detailed history of North Korea, see Victor Cha, "The Impossible State: North Korea, Past and Future," *Ecco,* April 2012.

44. Brown, Statement, February 22, 1978.

45. Harold Brown, News Conference, Beijing, January 9, 1980. Also see later remarks by Harold Brown to the Council on Foreign Relations at the Harold Pratt House, New York City, March 6, 1980, for further explanation of ramifications of Soviet invasion of Afghanistan.

46. Harold Brown, Interview by John McWethy and Bob Clark, *Issues and Answers,* Beijing, China, January 13, 1980.

47. "Defense Spending in the 20th Century," *U.S. Government Spending* (Office of Management and Budget, 2011) (www.usgovernmentspending.com/spending_chart_19 02_2015USp_13s1li011mcn_30f_Defense_Spending_in the20th_Century).

CHAPTER 7

1. U.S. Department of State, *Function 150 & Other International Programs,* Budget of the United States Government (Washington: Government Printing Office, 2012).

2. Henry A. Kissinger and James A. Baker III, "Grounds for U.S. Intervention," Opinion Editorial, *Washington Post,* April 8, 2011.

3. John Quincy Adams, Speech to the U.S. House of Representatives on Foreign Policy (July 4, 1821), Miller Center of Public Affairs, University of Virginia (http://millercenter.org/scripps/archive/speeches/detail/3383).

4. David Brown, *Palmerston and the Politics of Foreign Policy, 1846–55* (Manchester University Press, 2002), pp. 82–83. Palmerston made his statement in a speech to the House of Commons, *Hansard* (House of Commons Official Report), March 1, 1948.

5. See www.rand.org/commentary/2011/04/30/WP.html.

6. For more information, see Sarah Ladislaw and others, "A Roadmap for a Secure, Low-Carbon Energy Economy" (Washington: Center for Strategic and International Studies and World Resources Institute, January 2009). See also U.S. Energy Administration,

International Energy Statistics, June 2012 (www.eia.gov/cfapps/ipdbproject/IEDIn-dex3.cfm?tid=90&pid=44&aid=8); World Resources Institute, "Carbon Dioxide Emissions," CAIT International Data Set, June 15, 2011 (www.google.com/publicdata/explore?ds=cjsdgb406s3np_#!ctype=l&strail=false&bcs=d&nselm=h&met_y=per_capita_emissions&scale_y=lin&ind_y=false&rdim=country&idim=country:185&ifdim=country&tdim=true&hl=en_US&dl=en_US&ind=false).

7. Harold Brown, *Toward Consensus in Foreign and Defense Policy* (Washington: Johns Hopkins Foreign Policy Institute, 1989).

8. Senators Sam Nunn and Pete Domenici, *The CSIS Strengthening of America Commission, First Report* (Washington, D.C.: CSIS Books, 1992).

9. Robert VanGiezen and Albert E. Schwenk, "The Great Depression and the Federal Role in the Economy," Bureau of Labor Statistics, January 30, 2003 (www.bls.gov/opub/cwc/cm20030124ar03p1.htm).

10. Ibid.

11. Institute on Armaments Service for Major System Developments, "Preparing for the 21st Century: An Appraisal of U.S. Intelligence," Commission on the Roles and Capabilities of the United States Intelligence Community, chaired by Harold Brown, Executive Agency Publications, March 1, 1996, Featured Commission Publications (www.virtualref.com/govdocs/258.htm).

12. Ibid.; Loch K. Johnson, "The Aspin-Brown Intelligence Inquiry: Behind the Closed Doors of a Blue Ribbon Commission" (Central Intelligence Agency) (www.cia.gov/library/center-for-the-study-of-intelligence/csi-publications/csi-studies/studies/vol48no3/article01.html).

13. See Halford John Mackinder, *Democratic Ideals and Reality* (New York: W. W. Norton, 1962, originally published 1919), p. 150.

14. Jane Perlez, "Panetta Outlines New Weaponry for Pacific," *New York Times,* June 2, 2012, p. A7.

15. James Hosek and Beth Asch, "Reserve Participation and Cost under a New Approach to Reserve Compensation," RAND National Defense Research Institute, sponsored by the Office of the Secretary of Defense, 2012 (www.rand.org).

16. See 2012 Military Pay Charts at www.military.com/benefits/military-pay/charts/2011-military-pay-charts.html. The 2012 pay reflects a 1.6 percent pay increase for all service members. This raise was .2 percent more than the 2011 military pay increase.

17. Assistant Secretary of Defense (Manpower and Reserve Affairs), "Project One Hundred Thousand; Characteristics and Performance of 'New Standards' Men. Description of Project One Hundred Thousand," September 1968.

CHAPTER 8

1. "Reliance on Safety Net Rises," *New York Times,* February 11, 2012 (www.nytimes.com/interactive/2012/02/12/us/relying-on-government-benefits.html).

2. Treasury Secretary Timothy Geithner is quoted in the *National Journal* as saying that "the combined Social Security retirement and disability programs have dedicated funds sufficient to cover benefits for the next 20 years, but in 2033,

incoming revenues and trust fund resources will be insufficient to maintain payment of full benefits." Geithner—who opened his remarks with an affirmation that the program would be able to fill its commitments to current beneficiaries for "years to come"—said the projections were more pessimistic this year in large part due to an assumption of lower real wages over the next seventy-five years. Quoted in Katy O'Donnell, "Social Security Can Sustain Benefits for Only 20 More Years, Geithner Says," *National Journal*, April 23, 2012 (www.nationaljournal.com/budget/ social-security-can-sustain-benefits-for-only-20-more-years-geithner-says-20120423).

3. Paul Krugman, "Moochers against Welfare," *New York Times*, February 16, 2012, p. A23. See also Selena Caldera, "Social Security Is a Critical Income Source for Older Americans: State-Level Estimates, 2007–2009," AARP Public Policy Institute, Washington, D.C.

4. "How Does U.S. Health Care Compare to the Rest of the World?" World Health Organization Statistics, 2012, *Guardian* Data Blog, March 22, 2010 (www.guardian. co.uk/news/datablog/2010/mar/22/us-healthcare-bill-rest-of-world-a).

5. "On the whole, the pace of real GDP growth so far during this recovery has been almost as fast as was the case at a similar stage of the recoveries following the 1991 and 2001 recessions, which is noteworthy progress given that the earlier recoveries received a strong boost from residential home building and State and local government spending. Because of the excess home and office construction during the housing bubble, construction of structures has been notably weak so far in this recovery. In addition, once Recovery Act funds began to phase out, State and local governments cut spending and laid off workers at a faster pace. Both of these developments are unprecedented headwinds that were not present during other postwar recoveries." Quoted from *The Economic Report of the President 2012* (Washington: Government Printing Office, 2012) (www.nber.org/ erp/ERP_2012_Complete.pdf).

6. Jeremiah Gertler, "V-22 Osprey Tilt-Rotor Aircraft: Background and Issues for Congress," Congressional Research Service, March 10, 2011 (www.fas.org/sgp/crs/ weapons/RL31384.pdf), pp. 1–3.

7. Walter Isaacson, "Inventing the Future, The Idea Factory by Jon Gertner," *New York Times Sunday Book Review*, April 6, 2012.

8. Ibid.

9. Harold Brown, *The Government Role in Civilian Technology: Building a New Alliance* (Washington: National Academies Press, 1992). See also John Deutch's *What Should the Government Do to Encourage Technical Change in the Energy Sector*, MIT Joint Program on the Science and Policy of Global Change, Report 120 (May 2005).

10. Eric Lipton and John M. Broder, "In Rush to Assist a Solar Company, U.S. Missed Signs," *New York Times*, September 22, 2011 (www.nytimes.com/2011/09/23/ us/politics/in-rush-to-assist-solyndra-united-states-missed-warning-signs.html? pagewanted=all), p. A1.

11. Reconstruction Finance Corporation—Infoplease.com (www.infoplease.com/ ce6/history/A0841310.html).

12. "Sematech History," Sematech (www.sematech.org/corporate/history.htm).

13. Rick E. Yannuzi, "In-Q-Tel: A New Partnership between the CIA and the Private Sector," *Defense Intelligence Journal*, May 4, 2007 (www.cia.gov).

CHAPTER 9

1. Todd Harrison, "Strategy in a Year of Fiscal Uncertainty" (Washington: Center for Strategic and Budgetary Assessments, February 2012), pp. 1–10 (www.csbaonline. org/wp.../strategy-in-a-Year-of-Fiscal-Uncertainty.pdf).

2. "Long-Term Implications of the 2012 Future Years Defense Program," Congressional Budget Office, June 2011, pp. 16–19.

3. Charles A. Henning, "Military Retirement Reform: A Review of Proposals and Options for Congress," CRS Report for Congress (Washington: Congressional Research Service, November 17, 2011), p. 3

4. Harold Brown, Statement on *Final Report of the Independent Panel to Review Department of Defense Detention Operations* before the Senate Committee on Armed Services, September 9, 2004. See also Press Conference with Members of the Independent Panel to Review Department of Defense Detention Operations, Federal News Service, Washington, August 24, 2004 (www.c-spanvideo.org/program/SDet&start=333); James R. Schlesinger and others, *Final Report of the Independent Panel to Review Department of Defense Detention Operations,* August 2004 (www.defense.gov/news/ Aug2004/d20040824finalreport.pdf); Independent Panel to Review the Department of Defense Detention Operations, "Military Detention Operations," Senate Committee on Armed Services, September 9, 2004 (www.c-spanvideo.org/program/MilitaryDet).

AFTERWORD

1. Joyce A. Martin and others, "Births: Final Data for 2009," *National Vital Statistics Report,* vol. 60, no. 1 (November 2011), p. 2.

INDEX

A-7 tactical aircraft, 101
A-10 Thunderbolt, 124
Aaron, David, 79, 139
Abbas, Mahmoud, 204
Abu Ghraib, 189, 234–36
AC-47 aircraft, 206
AC-130 aircraft, 206
Adams, Brook, 149
Adams, John, 41
Adams, John Quincy, 187
Afghanistan, 10, 98–99, 186–87, 205;
    future prospects, 177–78, 184–85,
    190; Soviet invasion of, 119, 152,
    175–76
Africa, 203
Agnew, Spiro, 41
AIM 9-L program, 137
Airborne Alert system, 107–08
Airborne Warning and Control System
    aircraft, 52, 61, 138–39, 177, 196
Aircraft carriers, 164, 205
Air force, U.S., 55, 56, 60–61
Air force secretary, Brown's service
    as, 4, 66, 67, 104; aircraft deci-
    sions, 101–2; base closing decisions,

102–03; nuclear strategy and,
    104–05; opportunities for women
    in military during, 213; Vietnam
    War and, 95–100, 206
Akhromeyev, Sergei, 3
Al Qaeda, 178, 190, 207
Anderson, George, 55
Andropov, Yuri, 125
Andrus, Cecil, 149
Apel, Hans, 140
Arab Spring, 204
Argentina, 127
Armed Forces Specification Procure-
    ment Regulations, 220
Army, U.S., 55, 233
Army Field Manual, 235, 236
Aspin, Les, 20, 198
Assad, Bashar al-, 186
Assad, Hafez al-, 144
Assistant secretary for public affairs, 49
Assistant secretary of defense for inter-
    national security affairs, 40, 49
Atmospheric Test Ban Treaty, 128
AWACS. *See* Airborne Warning and
    Control System aircraft

B-1 bomber, 111, 114

B-2 bomber, 114–15

B-52 bomber, 61, 114, 115

B-70 bomber, 55

Baker, James, 44, 186

Bakhtiar, Shapour, 76

Baldwin, Hanson, 179

Ballistic missile early warning system, 21–22

BAMBI program, 34

Baroque weapons systems, 33–34

Barrow, Bob, 151

Bazargan, Mehdi, 77

Bechtel, Steve, 45

Bechtel Group of Companies, 44–45

Begin, Menachem, 144, 145–46

Belarus, 127

Bell Laboratories, 92, 222

Bergland, Bob, 149

Bermuda Summit (1961), 93–95

Bikini atoll nuclear tests, 1

Bin Laden, Osama, 59, 82, 134

Bleak House, 5

Blumenthal, Michael, 149

Boehner, John, 33

Boeing, 101

Bohlen, Chip, 88

Bourges, Yvon, 180–81

Bo Xilai, 157–58, 161

Brademas, John, 34, 53

Branches of military. *See* Military departments of army, navy, and air force

Brandt, Willy, 142

Brazil, 127, 156, 203

Brezhnev, Leonid, 115, 116, 124–25

Brown, Colene, 39, 67–68, 152, 154

Brown, Deborah, 68, 152, 154

Brown, Ellen, 68

Brown, George, 15, 55, 58, 180

Brown, Pat, 102

Brzezinski, Zbigniew, 74, 75, 83, 123, 144, 169, 233; Brown and, 14,

43, 46; Carter and, 45–46; China policy, 150, 151, 152; Iran hostage crisis and, 76, 77–78, 80; Vance and, 15, 42, 43, 45

Buchanan, John, 21

Budget, Defense Department: Carter administration, 176–77; competition among military branches for share of, 12–13; conceptual approaches to decisionmaking, 18–19; congressional role in, 9, 20–22, 25, 34–35; cost-benefit analysis of weapons systems, 93; current, 29; decisionmaking factors, 18, 23–24, 25–26; demands on secretary of defense's attention, 17; effect on national economy, 29–32; executive branch involvement, 20; five-year plans, 19; as function of U.S. national economy, 9–10; future prospects, 10, 214–15, 233–34; health care portion, 27–28, 234; international comparison, 26, 27, 29; jointness goals and, 60; line items, 20; percent of gross domestic product, 9, 10, 22, 27; political environment, 10, 20, 25, 32–33; recommendations for, 191–94; sequestration threat, 193, 203, 214; size of, 22–23, 26–27, 28*f*; strategic significance, 17. *See also* Procurement

Budget Control Act, 233

Bureaucracy, 5, 50–51, 72–73, 103–04

Bureau of Industry and Security, 195–96

Burke, Arleigh, 248

Bush (G. H. W.) administration, 21, 44, 115, 187

Bush (G. W.) administration, 26, 33, 34, 45, 184, 236

Butynol, 229

C-5 aircraft, 101–02
C-47 aircraft, 97
C-130 aircraft, 97
Califano, Joe, 149
Caltech, 4, 47, 115, 117, 122, 153, 213, 237, 238
Cameron, David, 185
Camp David Peace Accords, 144, 145–47, 148, 181
Canada, 60
Carlucci, Frank, 44
Carter administration: appointment of Joint Chiefs chairman, 55–56; arms control negotiations, 43; Brown's personal relationships in, 14–15; budgeting philosophy, 19; cabinet appointments, 39, 40–41, 42–43; China policy, 150–55; Cold War policies, 3; conflicts among advisers, 42–44, 45–46; Defense Department budget, 22–23, 24, 25, 34–35; Defense Department's policy alignment with, 50–51; efforts to curtail nuclear proliferation, 126–27; foreign policy and security challenges, 3; Israeli-Egyptian peace talks, 144, 145–47, 148, 181; legacy of security policies of, 181–82; national security advisers, 8, 15, 45–46; Panama Canal Treaty, 3, 9, 43, 179–80; relationship with military, 239–40; relations with Japan, 166; relations with South Korea, 166–74; request for cabinet resignations, 148–49; White House staff, 42. *See also* Iran hostage crisis; Secretary of defense, Brown's tenure as; Strategic Arms Limitation Talks (SALT I, SALT II)
Center for Strategic and International Studies, 243
Central Command, 58
Central Intelligence Agency, 66, 69, 96, 198, 231

Chain of command, 10–11
Chairman of the Joint Chiefs: Carter administration appointment, 55–56; in chain of command, 10; responsibilities and authorities, 8, 57, 59; vice-chair position, 15–16
Chandler, Happy, 241
Chaplains, 212
Chapman, William, 172
Chayes, Antonia, 213
Cheney, Dick, 44, 219
Chernenko, Konstantin, 125
Chief of staff, military departments, 12–13, 57, 58
China: Afghanistan and, 177; autonomy of military leadership, 165; Carter administration and, 3, 9, 150–55, 181; defense spending, 27; economic growth, 154–55, 156–57, 161, 162; future prospects, 19, 156–65, 190, 191, 200; military capability, 164–65, 201–02; nuclear capability, 105, 113, 127, 129, 132; political environment, 157–58, 161, 165; regional relations, 159–60; risk of international conflict, 159; South China Sea claims, 163; Soviet invasion of Afghanistan and, 175, 176; Soviet proposal for attack on, 118; Vietnam War and, 97, 98–99
Christopher, Warren, 41, 83
Chun Doo-Hwan, 172, 173
Churchill, Winston, II, 141
Civil aviation, 218
Civil War, U.S., 155–56, 241–42
Claytor, Graham, 48, 68–69
Clifford, Clark, 25, 98
Clinton, Hillary, 185
Clinton administration, 41, 49, 83, 114, 130, 147, 197
Cohen, Ben, 248
Cold War: Carter administration accomplishments, 181–82; Defense

Department budget, 22–23, 24; lessons from, 132–33, 142; Middle East in, 75; nuclear capability and policy, 2, 4, 24, 36, 37, 69, 70, 86–95, 104–15, 139–41; strategic considerations in Europe, 135; Turkish airspace issues, 180–81; U.S.-China relations, 150, 151–52; U.S.-Soviet military capability, 2–3, 37, 86–93, 177. *See also* Strategic Arms Limitation Talks (SALT I, SALT II)
Combat commanders, 10, 12, 13, 51–52, 59–60
Commanders-in-chief. *See* Combat commanders
Commission on the Roles and Capabilities of the U.S. Intelligence Community, 197
Congress, U.S.: Brown's office and, 49, 52–53; competition among military branches for appropriations from, 12–13; Defense Department budget authority, 9, 20–22, 25, 34–35, 240; foreign policy capacity, 196; in Iran hostage crisis, 80; NATO budget allocation, 136–37; proposed U.S. military withdrawal from South Korea, 170–71; ratification of SALT II treaty, 118–20; staffers, 21, 73, 196–97; State Department and, 240–41
Conscription, 207–09
Constitution, U.S., 6
Cooperative Threat Reduction program, 130
Corcoran, Tom, 248
Council of Economic Advisers, 195
Cruise missile program, 110, 117–18, 139–40
Cuban missile crisis, 107, 119, 133
Culver, John, 196
Cutler, Lloyd, 183
Cybersecurity, 162

Dai Bingguo, 163
Davis, Lynn, 49
Defense Advanced Research Project Agency, 31, 63, 230
Defense Department: constitutional basis, 6; global security responsibility, 27; growth in bureaucracy, 72–73; humanitarian interventions, 185; State Department and, 241. *See also* Budget, Defense Department; Defense research and engineering; Secretary of defense, generally
Defense Policy Board, 244
Defense Research and Engineering, 3–4, 7, 50, 63, 65, 88, 89–90, 107, 108, 224
Defense Science Board, 52, 64
Delta team, 82
Deng Xiaoping, 151, 153
Dense Pack strategy, 112–13
Deputy director of operations, 15
Deputy secretary of defense, 39–40, 47, 50
Desert Storm, 59
Deutch, John, 68, 227
DEW line control system, 218
Dickens, Charles, 4–5
Dineen, Gerald, 152
Director of national intelligence, 8, 198
Dirksen, Everett, 248
Distribution of wealth, 246
Dobrynin, Anatoly, 120
Don't Ask, Don't Tell, 210–11
Doolittle, Jimmy, 248
Douglas-Home, Alec, 94
Draft, military, 207–09
Drone aircraft, 206, 207
Dual-use technologies, 195
Duck and cover defense program, 92
Dulles, John Foster, 106
Duncan, Charles W., Jr., 40, 47, 50, 68, 74

Economic performance: benefits of immigration, 232; China's growth, 154–55, 156–57, 161, 162; coordination of foreign and economic policies, 194–95; current challenges, 193–94, 214–15; determinants of, in U.S., 9–10; distribution of wealth, 246; effect of defense budget on, 29–32; future challenges, 246–48; global warming and, 191; gross domestic product, 29; innovation in defense technology as stimulus to, 218–19; law of diminishing returns on technology investment, 238–39; national security and, 183; recommendations for strengthening, 215–17, 244–45; South Korea's growth, 167; tax policy, 193; U.S. share of global economy, 9. *See also* Budget, Defense Department; Procurement

Education: of military recruits, 212–13; preparation of soldiers for transition to civilian sector, 212; public spending on, 27, 28*f*, 236; strategies for improving, 236–38; for technology and innovation, 231–32, 236

Egypt, 144–48, 149

Eisenhower administration, 17, 18, 35–36, 53–54, 55–56, 58, 87, 105, 106, 219

Entitlement programs, 29

Environmental issues, 191

Ethiopia, 181

Europe: Cold War military capability and policy, 2–3, 135; current strategic significance of, 143, 177; defense spending, 29; economic challenges, 217; future prospects, 200; health care spending, 29–30; military research and development, 36–37, 137; Mutual Weapons Development Program, 36; neutron

bomb deployment proposal, 9; U.S. nuclear missiles in, 129, 139–41. *See also* North Atlantic Treaty Organization (NATO)

Evren, Kenan, 180

Executive branch: advisers on national security, 8; cabinet and staff relationship, 42; cabinet secretaries, 14; cabinet secretary disagreement with administration policies, 173; conflicts among advisers, 44–45; coordination of foreign and economic policy, 194–95; in Defense Department budgeting, 20; expressions of disagreement with policies of, from military, 174–75; power of, 35–36; recommendations for cabinet appointments, 196–97; Secretaries of defense and, 9, 14–15. *See also specific administration*

Executive Order 13491 on military interrogations, 235

F-4 aircraft, 143

F-5 tactical aircraft, 101

F-16 fighter aircraft, 32–33, 137

F-35 Lightning II fighter aircraft, 33

F-117 stealth aircraft, 113–14, 224

Fahd, Crown Prince, 144

Fannie Mae, 229–30

Fay, Paul, 92

Feisal, King, 106

Fisher, Adrian, 122

Five-year plans for defense policy, 19, 192

Force structure, 11

Ford, Gerald, 21

Ford administration, 4, 22, 116

Foreign aid, 28, 185

Foreign policy: aid spending, 28, 185; alignment of values and interests in foreign intervention, 186–89; coordination of economic policy with,

194–95; defense spending decisions, 25–26, 191–93; domestic political conflict and, 197; future of U.S.-China relations, 159–65; future U.S. strategic interests, 190–91; geopolitical future, 201–05; global status of U.S., 181, 189–90; lessons of Iran hostage crisis, 82–83; lessons of U.S.-South Korea relationship, 174; nation building, 184–85; Secretary of defense's role in, 8–9, 17, 43; significance of foreign opinion in U.S. policy formulation, 174; strategic significance of European countries, 177; U.S. global obligations, 178–79, 183–84; U.S. Middle East interests, 143–49

Forrestal, James, 104
Fortas, Abe, 248
Fowler, Tillie, 234
France, 27, 61, 105, 127, 143, 180–81, 217, 221
Frank, Barney, 211
Freddie Mac, 229–30
Fubini, Gene, 48, 64
Fubini, Guido, 64

Gaddafi, Moammar, 185, 187
Gates, Robert, 33, 164, 165, 185, 206
Gates, Thomas, 104
Geithner, Tim, 229
General electric, 32, 33, 222
Geneva Conventions, 235, 236
Geng Biao, 152
Germany, 127, 141, 142; NATO nuclear missile placement, 139–40; post–World War II, 135–36, 188
Gerstner, Lou, 245
Giaimo, Robert, 34
Gilpatric, Ros, 92–93
Gingrich, Newt, 237
Global positioning system, 31, 48, 110

Global warming, 191
Goldwater, Barry, 59
Goldwater-Nichols Act, 59–60
Gorbachev, Mikhail, 125, 140–41
Government-sponsored enterprises, 229–30
Great Depression, 193–94
Greece, 217
Green, Wallace, 95
Gromyko, Andrei, 97, 125
Gulf War, 114, 187, 205

Habib, Philip, 41
Haig, Alexander, 44, 55
Halleck, Charles, 248
Hamas, 204
Hamre, John, 244
Hanna, Richard T., 168
Hanson, Thor, 53
Hassan Ali, Kamel, 147
Hayden, Carl, 248
Hayward, Tom, 81
Health care spending: defense budget, 27–28, 234; future challenges for U.S. economy, 215–17, 246–47; international comparison, 29–30; as percent of national economy, 29–30; public spending, 27, 28f, 29
Hitch, Charles, 19
Holbrooke, Richard, 152
Holcomb, Staser, 53
Hollande, François, 217
Holloway, James L., III, 80–81
Holm, Jeanne, 213
Homosexuality, 210–11
Horner, Charles A., 234
Hua Guofeng, 152
Huang Hua, 152
Human rights, 181–82
Hungary, 205
Hussein, King, 144, 147
Huyser, Robert, 76

Idealism, 186–89
Immigration, 232
In-air refueling, 60–61
India, 126, 128, 129, 132, 156, 159–60, 177, 200
INF treaty, 141
Inman, Bobby Ray, 79–80
In-Q-Tel, 231
Institute of U.S. and Canada Studies, 117
Institute on Global Conflict and Cooperation, 63
Internet, 31
Interrogation of terrorist suspects, 234–36
Iran, 3, 128, 129, 131, 188, 196; future challenges, 19, 83–85, 132, 199
Iran hostage crisis, 3, 77; end of, 82; events leading to, 74–77, 84–85; initial U.S. responses, 77–78; lessons of, 81–83, 84–85; rescue mission, 60, 78–82
Iraq, 10, 26, 106, 184, 186–87, 189, 205, 206, 234–35
Israel: Carter administration policies, 144–46, 148; events leading to Camp David Peace Accords, 144, 145–47; future security issues, 203–04; Iran and, 84, 129, 199; military capability, 143–44; nuclear capability, 126, 127, 128, 129, 132; U.S. military and financial commitments to, 143, 146

Japan, 127, 156, 159–60, 166, 168–69, 188
JDAM, 110
Jobs, Steve, 245
Johns Hopkins University School of International Studies, 243
Johnson administration, 14, 25, 40, 65, 66, 95–98, 100, 102–03, 122

Joint Chiefs of Staff: Iran rescue mission investigation, 80–81; office of vice chairman, 15–16; in resource allocation decisions, 13; Secretary of defense's relationship with, 48–49, 51, 53. *See also* Chairman of the Joint Chiefs
Joint Cruise Missile Office, 58
Joint Forces Command, 60
Joint operability: definition, 54; efforts to establish and improve, 13, 53–59; Iran rescue mission and, 81, 82; in NATO, 137; outcomes of implementation, 59–61; procurement decisions and, 222; requirements for military career advancement, 54–55, 57–58, 59; resistance to, 57; superorganization for, 61–62; training, 58, 60; weapons development and, 57–58, 60–61
Joint Special Operations Command, 82
Joint Staff, 54, 58, 59, 80
Jones, David, 15, 55–57, 58, 76, 77–78, 80, 123
Jordan, 147
Jordan, Hamilton, 15, 77–78

Kazakhstan, 127
Kelly, P. X., 58
Kemp, Jack, 21
Kennedy, Joseph, 92, 94
Kennedy, Robert, 92
Kennedy, Ted, 32
Kennedy administration, 65, 86–95, 133
Kent, Glenn, 107
Kester, John, 41
Khomeini, Ayatollah, 75, 76, 77
Khruschev, Nikita, 86, 89
Kidd, Ike, 55–57
Kim Dae-Jung, 172–73

Kim Il-sung, 3
Kim Jae-kyu, 172
Kim Jong-un, 3
Kinsolving, Lester, 80
Kissinger, Henry, 98, 99, 120–23, 144, 186
Kohl, Helmut, 74, 140, 141
Komer, Bob, 48–49, 137, 152
Korean War, 105, 167
Kosygin, Alexei, 122
Kraft, Joe, 7
Kreps, Juanita, 149
Krugman, Paul, 216
Kuwait, 205

Laird, Melvin, 15, 21, 25, 38, 49, 99
Lance, Bert, 14–15
Latvia, 205
Lawrence, Ernest, 47, 69
Leber, Georg, 140
Lee Myung-Bak, 173
Legislative and Public Affairs meeting, 51
LeMay, Curtis, 55, 90, 239, 248
LeVan, C. J., 92
Libya, 27, 127, 143, 185–86, 187, 188–89
Lincoln, Franklin, 18–19
Livermore Laboratory, 3, 47, 62, 63, 69–72, 105, 219, 224
Lockheed Martin, 101, 224
Longworth, Alice, 248
Luns, Joseph, 141–42

M60 tanks, 24
MacArthur, Douglas, 174
Mackinder, Halford John, 201
Macmillan, Harold, 94
Madison, James, 41
Magnusson, Warren, 31
Mahon, George, 20
Management tools, 52–53
Marbury, William, 41

Marbury v. Madison, 41
Marine Corps, 12, 54, 58, 210–11, 233
Marshall, Andrew, 16
Marshall, F. Ray, 149
Marshall, George, 213
Martin, Joe, 174, 248
McCone, John, 66
McConnell, J. P., 100, 101, 103
McGiffert, David, 49, 139, 152
McIntyre, Jim, 14–15
McNamara, Robert, 14, 17, 19, 38, 39–40, 49, 55, 64–67, 87, 89, 92, 212
McNeil, Wilfred, 18
McRae, Jim, 63
McWethy, John, 176
Medicare, 215–16
Medvedev, Dmitri, 126
Meese, Edwin, 44
Memorial Day, 242
Merewether, Ray, 68
Meyer, Edward, 59
Middle East: Carter administration policies, 75–76, 144–49; future security issues, 203–04; Russian interests in, 160–61; Six-Day War, 143. See also specific country
Mideast, 3
Military capability: advisers to secretary of defense, 53; Cold War strategic concerns in Europe, 2–3, 135; compulsory service proposals, 207–09; current enlistment, 207–08; definition of readiness, 11–12; four measures of, 11–12; future of U.S.-China relations, 161–65; global obligations of U.S., 178–79; legacy of Carter administration, 182; long-range bomber, 202; national economic health and, 183; NATO forces, 138; quick response force, 206; recommendations for

planning, 191–99, 200, 201, 205–08; secretary of defense responsibilities, 11; South Korea's, 167; trends in China, 164–65, 201–02; U.S.-Soviet Union rivalry, 2–3, 90, 91, 123, 137, 176–77

Military departments of army, navy, and air force: chain of command, 10–11; competition among, for funding, 12–13. *See also specific department*

Military intervention: alignment of values and interests in, 186–89; chain of command, 10; definition of readiness, 11–12; future prospects, 200–01; lessons of modern experience, 205; prohibitions on torture during, 235–36. *See also* Military capability

Mills, Mark, 63

Minuteman missile program, 89, 90–91, 106–07, 111, 113

Mondale, Fritz, 77–78, 151

Monroe Doctrine, 179, 203

Mubarak, Hosni, 149

Mullin, Mike, 211

Multiple Independently Targetable Reentry Vehicle (MIRV) program, 109, 111

Murray, Russ, 49

Muskie, Edmund, 83

Mutually assured destruction (MAD), 104, 107, 128

Mutual Weapons Development Program, 36

MX missile program, 111–13

Myanmar, 159–60

National Command Authority, 133

National Economic Council, 194

National Military Command Center, 15

National security: alignment of values and interests in foreign intervention, 186–89; defense spending decisions, 25–26; foreign economic assistance and, 185; future challenges, 37, 190–91, 198–99, 214–15, 233–34, 240; future of Afghanistan and, 177–78; geopolitical threats, 199, 201–05; global climate change and, 191; legacy of Carter administration, 181–82; national economic health and, 183, 195; political environment of 1970s, 6–7; recommendations for structure of intelligence community, 197–98; reliance on allies, 180–81, 186; role of secretary of defense, 8–9; U.S. global presence and, 178–79, 183–84. *See also* Defense Department; Terrorism

National Security Act, 53–54

National security adviser, 8, 15

National Security Agency, 170, 171, 173

National Security Council, 8, 194–95

National War College, 54, 58

NATO. *See* North Atlantic Treaty Organization (NATO)

Navy, U.S., 55, 233; current fleet, 164, 205–06; future deployment, 202; significance of Panama Canal for, 179

Neutron bomb, 9

New Deal, 194

NEW START Treaty, 126

Nichols, William Flynt, 59

Nigeria, 203

Nike Zeus program, 91–93

Nitze, Paul, 40, 65, 150

Nixon administration, 4, 13, 34, 41, 55, 99, 115, 122, 150, 167

Nobel Peace Prize, 144, 191

North Atlantic Treaty Organization (NATO), 48, 52, 55, 56, 177;

Airborne Warning and Control System aircraft, 138–39; budget issues, 24, 136–37, 142; Carter administration accomplishments, 181; Cold War strategic concerns, 135; future prospects, 142–43, 199; goals of Carter administration, 135–36; interoperability issues, 137; Libya action, 185–86; membership, 136; nuclear strategy, 2, 136, 139–40; origins, 135; strategic mobility of forces, 138; strategic significance of, 177; Three Percent Solution to funding, 136–37; U.S. support, 136

North Korea, 127, 129; Carter administration policies, 3, 147; current policy, 84; future prospects, 19, 132, 200; South Korea and, 167, 168, 169–70; U.S. defenses against, 93, 128

Nuclear arms reduction: appointment of Joint Chiefs chairman and, 56; Carter administration policies and actions, 43; China-U.S. talks, 152; effects of U.S.-Soviet agreements, 120, 121t, 125; future reductions, 126, 132–33; intermediate-range missiles, 141; lessons from Cold War, 132; prospects for complete abolition, 131–32; Russia-U.S. agreement, 126; U.S.-Soviet negotiations, 3, 4. See also Strategic Arms Limitation Talks (SALT I, SALT II)

Nuclear Nonproliferation Treaty, 128

Nuclear weapons: Airborne Alert system, 107–08; anti-ballistic missile technology, 89–90, 91, 92–93; Cold War arms race, 2, 4, 24, 36, 37, 69, 70, 86–95, 104, 106–15, 142; command and control issues, 133–34; Cuban missile crisis, 107; deterrence rationale, 1–2, 3–4, 104, 128, 129; duck and cover

defense program, 92; future threats, 130–31, 199; global proliferation, 126–28; ground-launched cruise missiles, 24; intermediate-range, 107, 140, 141, 181; Iranian nuclear program, 83–85; missile siting strategies, 111–13; motives for acquiring, 128–29; NATO Cold War strategy, 136, 139–41; no first-use commitments, 129; penetration aids, 108–09; stockpiles, 2, 120, 121t, 125, 126; stockpile security, 130; Teller's work on, 69–72; test bans, 95, 105–06; tests, 1, 86–88, 89, 95; U.S. withdrawal from South Korea, 168–69. See also Nuclear arms reduction

Nunn, Sam, 20, 59

Nunn-Lugar Cooperative Threat Reduction program, 130

Nuri as-Said, 106

Obama administration, 8, 21, 33, 82, 126, 185–86, 194

Office of Management and Budget, 20, 48, 194

Office of Net Assessment, 16

Office of Program Analysis and Evaluation, 49

Office of the Secretary of Defense: bureaucratic structure, 50; lines of reporting and consultation, 49, 50, 51–52, 53; management tools, 52–53; policy alignment with executive branch, 50–51; Service Secretaries and, 103, 104. See also Secretary of defense, generally

Ogarkov, Nikolai, 123, 141, 182

Oil: China's reserves, 161; China's strategic vulnerability, 164; future U.S. strategic interests, 191, 199, 201, 203, 204; Russia's reserves, 204

Oksenberg, Mike, 152
O'Neill, Tip, 32, 34

Pakistan, 126, 128, 129, 132, 134, 176, 177, 190
Palestinian state, 203–04
Palmerston, Lord, 187
Panama Canal Treaties, 3, 9, 43, 180, 181
Panetta, Leon, 30, 178, 202–03
Park Chung Hee, 167, 169, 171, 172
Parkinson, C. Northcote, 72
Patman, Wright, 248
Pay rates, military, 210
Pension policy, 209–10
Perry, William, 47–48, 58, 64, 68, 113, 137, 139, 220
Pershing II missiles, 139–40
Philippines, 159–60, 189
Platt, Nick, 152
Ploumis, Eric, 68
Poland, 205
Polaris Steering Committee, 69–70, 219, 248
Political functioning: backgrounds of secretaries of defense, 13–14; cabinet appointment considerations, 197–98; cabinet secretary disagreement with administration policies, 173; in China, 157–58, 161, 165; in Defense Department budgeting, 10, 12–13, 20, 25, 32–33; effects on long-term strategic planning, 240; effects on secretary of defense, 38–39; military procurement and, 102–03; in MX missile basing, 111–12; obstacles to effective policymaking, 197; polarized environment, 214; problems of 1970s, 6–7; rationale for military draft, 207–08
Portugal, 217
Powell, Colin, 44, 45, 67, 69
Powell, Jody, 15

Power, Samantha, 185
Powers, Gary, 113
Pragmatic idealism, 186–87
Pratt & Whitney, 32
Precision-guided munitions, 48, 97, 109–10
President. *See* Executive branch; *specific administration*
President's Science Advisory Committee, 106
Price, Mel, 20
Prisoners of war, 236
Private sector: competition with government for human resources, 226; defense contracting procedures, 224–25; defense contractor and subcontractor base, 223; defense technology research and development in, 222–23; executive pay, 245–46; national security role, 37; recommendations for corporate governance, 244–46; recommendations for innovation corporation, 227–31
Procurement: contract award decisions, 224–25; contractor and subcontractor base, 223; dual-use technologies, 195–96; French system, 221; jointness considerations, 222; recommendations for improving, 192–94, 221–22, 224–25; skills for, 220–21; sources of high cost, 220; unified civilian-military service for, 61
Program control, 17, 18
Project Forecast, 109
Public relations, 49
Purple-suiters, 56–57, 60

Qian Xuesen, 153

Rabin, Yitzhak, 143, 144
Racial integration in armed services, 211

Radford, Arthur, 55
RAND Corporation, 19, 49, 210, 243
Rapid Deployment Joint Task Force, 58
Rayburn, Sam, 248
Reagan administration, 59, 114, 115, 181; ballistic missile early warning system, 21–22; Dense Pack missile deployment, 34, 141; national security advisers, 44–45; Star Wars program, 34, 71–72, 141
Reconstruction Finance Corporation, 230
Republican Party, 49
Resignation letters, 41
Resor, Stanley, 48, 96
Retirement benefits, military, 209–10
Reza Pahlavi, Mohammed, 74, 76–77
Rice, Condoleezza, 45
Rice, Susan, 185
Rickenbacker, Eddie, 248
Rockefeller, Nelson, 102
Rogers, Bernard, 55
ROLAND air defense missiles, 24, 137
Roman Empire, 189
Roosevelt (F. D.) administration, 194
Rosenberg, Anna, 213
Ross, Tom, 49
Rowe, Jim, 248
Rumsfeld, Donald, 13, 15, 38, 41, 45, 53, 68, 117, 206, 234, 236
Rusk, Dean, 94
Russell, Richard, 20, 25
Russia: Afghanistan and, 177; future prospects, 156, 160–61, 199, 200, 204–05; nuclear capability, 113, 126, 127, 129, 199

Sadat, Anwar El, 144–47, 149
Saltonstall, Leverett, 21
Sarkozy, Nicolas, 185, 217
Saudi Arabia, 75, 147, 204
Saville, Gordon, 109

Schacht, Henry, 245
Schlesinger, Jim, 16, 59, 68, 98, 149, 234
Schmidt, Helmut, 139–40, 142, 181
Schultz, George, 44–45
Schultze, Charles, 31
Scowcroft, Brent, 44, 244
Scowcroft Commission, 112
Scranton, Bill, 102
Seaborg, Glenn, 94
Secretary of defense, Brown's service as, 100, 124, 154; appointment and confirmation and swearing in, 39, 40–41, 99; appointment of Joint Chiefs chairman, 55–56; attention to short- and long-term issues, 16, 17, 51; in Camp David peace talks, 145–46; China relations during, 150–55; commitment to jointness, 54–62; foreign policy involvement, 8–9, 43; information flows during, 15; longevity in office, 38–39; Middle East relations, 75–76, 144–49; National Security Council meetings and actions, 8–9; in NATO policy and operations, 24, 135–43; number of Defense Department employees during, 5; opportunities for women in military during, 213; Panama Canal Treaty negotiations, 179–80; pension reform, 209–10; preparation for, 3–4, 39–40, 62–69; procurement systems during, 224; relationship with Congress, 49, 52–53; relationship with White House, 14–15, 45–46, 183, 239–40; relations with South Korea, 169–73; relations with Turkey, 180–81; resource allocation decisions, 13; SALT II process and, 116, 117–18, 120, 123–24; Shah of Iran and, 74–75; social obligations, 66–67; Soviet invasion of Afghanistan

during, 175–76; staff appointments, 46–50, 52, 53; subsequent careers of staff members, 68–69; technology development during, 48, 109–15. *See also* Iran hostage crisis
Secretary of defense, generally: attention to emerging and crisis situations, 16–17, 51; chain of command, 10–11, 235; decisionmaking challenges, 4, 11; disagreement with administration policies, 173; foreign policy involvement, 8, 17; information flows, 15–16; longevity in office, 38, 66; long-term planning requirements, 11, 16; main functions, 7–11; preparation for, 13–14; program management challenges, 17, 18; qualities for effective performance, 7; relationship with executive branch, 14; resource allocation decisions, 11–13, 18; scope of authority, 35; staff appointments, 46–47; transitions between administrations, 40–41. *See also* Office of the Secretary of Defense; Secretary of defense, Brown's tenure as
Secretary of state: national security adviser and, 15; structure and operations, 46; transition between administrations, 41. *See also* State Department
Seignious, George, 152
Sematech, 230
Sequestration, 193, 203, 214
Service Secretaries, 48, 49, 103–04
Seven Years War, 155–56
Shang Wenjin, 152
Shevardnadze, Eduard, 140
Shriever, Bernard, 109
Shuttle diplomacy, 144
Sidewinder missile, 137
Siemer, Deanne, 213
Singlaub, John, 174

Six-Day War, 143, 145
Skunk works, 224
Skybolt, 94
Slocombe, Walt, 41, 49
Smith, Carl, 53
Smith, Gerard, 120
Smith, Willie Y., 53
Social obligations of government officials, 66–67
Social Security, 31, 215–16
South America, 203
South Korea, 127, 159–60, 166–74, 200–01
Soviet Union: Brown's visit to, 117; causes of collapse of, 3, 140–41, 156; Cold War military capability and policy, 2–3; global nuclear proliferation and, 127; invasion of Afghanistan, 119, 152, 175–76; Middle East interests, 75; military presence in Cuba, 119, 173; military spending, 137; NATO and, 135, 139; nuclear arms limitation negotiations, 105, 165–66; nuclear capability, 2, 86–87, 89, 106–08, 139, 140–41, 142; U.S.-China relations and, 150, 151–52; Vietnam War and, 97. *See also* Cold War
Spanish-American War, 189
Special interest politics, 6–7
Sputnik, 70
SR-71 aircraft, 224
SS-20 missiles, 139
Staffing, secretary of defense office, 46–50
Star Wars program. *See* Strategic Defense Initiative
State Department, 194, 240–41. *See also* Secretary of state
Stealth technology, 113–14
Stein, Herb, 245
Stempler, Jack, 49
Stennis, John, 20

Stevenson, Adlai, 95

Strategic Arms Limitation Talks (SALT I): ballistic missile defense issues, 116; Brown's role in, 4, 115, 120; informal exchanges during, 118; Kissinger's role in, 122; missile range and design issues, 116; negotiating issues, 116; process, 120; significance of, 115

Strategic Arms Limitation Talks (SALT II): Brown's role in, 116; effectiveness, 125, 181; missile range issues, 117–18; ratification of, 43, 83, 118–20, 151; signing of treaty, 123–25

Strategic Arms Reduction Treaty (START I), 120, 125–26

Strategic Defense Initiative (Star Wars), 34, 71–72, 141

Sullivan, William, 76

Supreme Allied Commander, Atlantic, 56

Supreme Allied Commander, Europe, 55

Surveillance and reconnaissance, 37, 48, 173, 207

Sustainability of military engagement, 11, 12

Syria, 26, 160–61, 185, 186

Systems Analysis Office, 101–02

Szell, George, 68

Taiwan, 101, 127, 150–51

Taliban, 37, 83, 178, 190

Tax policy, 193, 215–16, 232

Taylor, Maxwell, 248

Technology, defense: China-U.S. talks, 153; conditions for efficient research and development, 219; contractor and subcontractor base for development in, 223; cost-benefit analysis, 93; development

under Brown's Defense Department, 48, 109–10; dual-use technologies, 195–96; education and training for, 231–32, 236; effects of revolving door rules on innovation in, 226; European system, 36–37; innovation in, as economic stimulus, 218–19; jointness considerations, 60–61; law of diminishing returns on investment in, 238–39; national security significance of, 37; private sector research and development, 222–23; recommendations for public-private innovation corporation, 227–31; sources of high acquisition costs, 220; structure of production lines, 192. *See also* Nuclear weapons; Precision-guided munitions

Teller, Edward, 63, 69–72, 238

Terrorists: current threat, 130, 134; interrogation and torture of, 235–36; jointness as defense against, 61; military justice and, 236; national security elements in fight against, 37; recommendations for defense against, 207

TFX Joint Air Force Strike and Navy Fleet Air Defense fighter, 55

Thailand, 159–60

Thatcher, Margaret, 74, 141

Thinking About National Security (Brown), 243

Thucydides, 163

Title 10 of U.S. Code, 54, 58, 103, 222

Tomb of the Unknown Soldier, 242

Tongsun Park, 167–68, 174

Torture, 234–36

Tower, John, 21

Toynbee, Arnold J., 179

Train, Harry D., III, 59

Training for post-military career, 212

Transport Security Administration, 134
TRICARE, 27–28, 234
Trident missile, 111
Truman, Harry, 35–36, 174, 211
Turkey, 180–81
Turner, Stan, 43, 77–78, 150

U-2 surveillance aircraft, 113, 224
Ukraine, 127, 204
Undersecretary for research and engineering, 47–48, 50
Undersecretary of defense for policy, 48
Unified Commands, 54
United Kingdom, 27, 94, 105, 127, 137, 141, 142, 155–56, 189
Unmanned aircraft, 206, 207
U.S. Atlantic Command, 56
Ustinov, Dimitri, 123–24

V-22 tilt-rotor aircraft, 12, 218–19, 227
Vance, Cyrus, 39, 65, 149, 151, 171, 182; Brown and, 14, 40, 43, 46; Brzezinski and, 15, 42, 43, 45–46; in Camp David negotiations, 144, 145, 146; Iran hostage rescue mission and resignation of, 80, 82, 149; qualities of, 42–43; in SALT negotiations, 116, 120, 123
Vessey, John, 170
Vietnam, 159–60
Vietnam War, 2, 19, 40, 66, 167, 189; air campaign, 4, 96–98, 100, 101, 206; evolution of U.S. policy, 95–96; failure of U.S. strategy,
97–98; lessons from U.S. experience in, 98–100, 186–87; supply surveillance and interdiction on Ho Chi Minh Trail, 66, 95, 96
Vinson, Carl, 20
Volcker, Paul, 31

Warner, John, 21
Waterboarding, 235–36
Weinberger, Caspar, 16, 38, 44–45
Weisner, Maurice, 170
Weizman, Ezer, 145, 148
West, Allen, 235
West, Togo, 69
Westmoreland, William, 96
Wheeler, Burton, 248
White, John, 49
White House Diary (Carter), 183
Wiesner, Jerry, 92, 95
Wilson, Charlie, 1, 38
Wisner, Frank, 41
Women in military, 213
Woolsey, James, 69
World Bank, 156
World Trade Organization, 156

Xi Jinping, 161
Xu Xiangqian, 152

Yazdi, Ebrahim, 77
Yemen, 190
Yom Kippur War, 145
York, Herb, 33–34, 47–48, 62–63, 65

Zero-based budgeting, 18–19
Zero CEP, 109
Zhang Aiping, 153

ENDNOTE

Over two years of interviews (and 700 pages of transcripts) Dr. Brown allowed me an insider's view into the decisions, weapons, international agreements, and national wrangling that have directly affected American lives for the past sixty years—and defined his.

A strong, practical, and formal man, he eventually revealed emotions he felt when he tested nuclear weapons at Livermore Lab; developed ballistic missiles as director of defense research and engineering; prepared airmen for bombing sorties in Vietnam as secretary of the air force; helped negotiate SALT I and II agreements (the Soviets asked him if the United States would join them in taking out China's nuclear facility); and grappled with the risks of various plans to rescue American hostages held in Iran near no airport or seaport and surrounded by millions of civilians.

Washington leaders told me that no matter the company, they usually considered Dr. Brown to be the smartest person in the room. Indeed, I soon realized that interviewing him was like sitting at Moses' knee hearing how both successes and mistakes, bravery, and humility enable a leader to reaffirm a nation's values and help sustain its security. There is information in this book I'd never read before in any news outlet, real wisdom, and specific advice—political, economic, and strategic— immediately applicable to America and its world role now. Some of his suggestions are downright surprising, like one to do away with Service Secretaries, and some deeply moving, like Dr. Brown's recommendations after formally reviewing behavior of some of our military personnel who tortured or humiliated prisoners at Abu Ghraib.

I believe the reader of this book, like the secretaries of defense Dr. Brown has advised for the last twenty years, will find his thinking clear, eloquent, and absolutely useful.

Joyce Winslow